The Mexican Novel Comes of Age

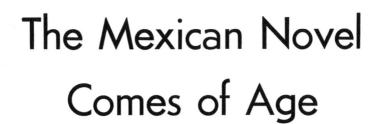

The Mexican Novel
Comes of Age

WALTER M. LANGFORD

UNIVERSITY OF NOTRE DAME PRESS
NOTRE DAME   LONDON

Library of Congress Catalog Card Number: 77-160486
Manufactured in the United States of America by
NAPCO Graphic Arts, Inc., Milwaukee, Wisconsin

CONTENTS

For Dit

PREFACE

ONE DAY, WHILE THE PREPARATION OF THIS BOOK WAS STILL IN THE early stages, I was stunned by a question from one of the most cultured persons it has been my good fortune to know. He said to me, "Walter, are there really enough Mexican novels to justify a study of them?" Coming from anyone else, this question would have been disturbing; as posed by this person, it was utterly distressing. Probably nothing else so thoroughly convinced me of the need for such a work as the present one.

Actually, the novel in Mexico and all of Hispanic America has for the past decade or more been in a so-called boom state. The boom refers primarily to the fact that throughout the world there has been a startling upsurge of interest in the novels and novelists of Hispanic America. The writers of Mexico have contributed at least as heavily to this boom as those of any other Hispanic-American country.

The fact that many novels from Mexico and other lands south of the border are attracting world attention is attributable in major part to the shifting of focus or approach in these novels over the past generation or so. The Hispanic-American novel began to achieve top currency when it ceased to be regional and *costumbrista*, when it shook off the trademark of social protest and turned its eyes away from the land and the jungle and the mountain, when in short, it began to "zero in" on man himself in his human condition and started probing the human spirit with all its complexities.

This new concern of the novel for man himself obviously did not originate with the Hispanic-American novelists. They are simply applying (sometimes with innovations and experimental aspects) a number of novelistic techniques already known in other literatures. It is easy to trace the influence upon them of such literary figures as James Joyce, John Dos Passos, William Faulkner, Malcolm

Lowry, Aldous Huxley, and Marcel Proust. Not that they have merely mimicked these outside influences. It is simply that they have studied the approach and devices of others and have adapted them to their own purposes. In so doing they have brought the reality that is Latin America before an international audience. It is for all of this that the Latin-American novel presently is in a state of boom. And, since the Mexican novel has remained in the forefront of this evolutionary process, it becomes more interesting and urgent for us to study the development of this genre in Mexico.

The decision to concentrate on the twentieth-century Mexican novel responds to the fact that during the current century the greatest changes and development have occurred. In any case, Ralph Warner and others have long since given us more-than-adequate studies on the Mexican novel in the nineteenth century, whereas I am aware of no study that treats the contemporary Mexican novel in the same manner. In view of the lack of familiarity in the U.S. with the Mexican novel (as evidenced by the question of my friend), an effort is made throughout this study to maintain a more popular level of discussion than is found in a strictly academic work of literary analysis.

The twentieth-century Mexican novel proceeds, inevitably, from the development witnessed in the century before. It had its beginning in 1816, when Fernández de Lizardi published the first Latin American novel, *El Periquillo Sarniento,* a picaresque effort concerned mostly with social criticism. Through the remainder of that century the novel in Mexico grew as any young child does—slowly, tentatively, and quick to imitate its elders. It assumed various forms and shapes, all cast in European molds. At times it essayed an historical stance, for a long while it was locked in the groove of romanticism. *Costumbrismo,* the cult of narrating social customs, exercised an uncommon attraction, and in the latter part of the century realism took over, never quite to loosen its grip thereafter as the basic novelistic approach. A few novelists staked a good claim to a high place in the literary history of Latin America, among them Fernández de Lizardi, Ignacio Manuel Altamirano, Rafael Delgado, and Federico Gamboa.

The twentieth century had hardly gained momentum before the

Mexican Revolution of 1910 changed many things in that land, including the novel. With Mariano Azuela the Mexican novel adopted a new posture, to become *puro mexicano* with characteristics all its own. The resulting "spinoff" gave rise to the Novel of the Mexican Revolution, which was to dominate almost until mid-century. In 1947 the novel took its sharpest turn when Agustín Yáñez brought forth *Al filo del agua,* which introduced into Mexican literature the novel of interiorization, the examining of human nature and the human psyche, and inescapable reader participation in the story. Since that date the new path blazed by Yáñez has been heavily and happily traveled, so that several additional names have merited hemispheric and international attention, Juan Rulfo and Carlos Fuentes prominent among them. These and other Mexican novelists now are read in translation around the world.

If the richness of the Mexican novel never has been more apparent than in the past two decades, it also is true that its promise for the future has perhaps never been brighter. Through an interesting series of circumstances, the "new wave" of Mexican novelists is larger in numbers, more skilled in techniques, and more professionally dedicated to a career of creative writing than any previous group in Mexico (and possibly in all of Latin America). Twentieth-century Mexican life, the raw material from which these novelists create their works, is in itself sufficiently varied, vital, and interesting to inspire and challenge the best that is in them. Definitely, they are rising to the challenge. This book tries to present and discuss these writers and their works in a manner that does justice to them.

It is my hope that perhaps many persons with limited knowledge of Mexico or of the novel in that land will find this study to be informative and revealing with regard to the aspects of Mexican life dealt with by her novelists. The decision to make the presentation of this material through the study of certain authors was carefully weighed and finally chosen as the approach which would be most meaningful to a large number of people. For the benefit of those readers who do not understand Spanish, the titles of almost all novels mentioned are translated to English. Also, I offer my own translations of all quotations excerpted from the novels under discussion or from critical works in Spanish. In addition to a general bibliography at the end of the book, each chapter is followed by a listing of the novels of the writer treated therein, along with selected studies on the novelist.

My reading in the Mexican novel began more than three decades ago and has continued steadily. Also, since 1933 I have visited Mexico some twenty times, in trips lasting from a few days to up to more than a year and ranging over most areas of that ever interesting land. This enduring association has given me, I hope, some insight into the Mexican temperament and the Mexican way of life, an insight I try to apply in the analyses of the books discussed.

Many persons have had a hand in making this book a reality, through encouragement, prodding, discussion, and ideas. The end product, however, whatever its values and faults, has to be accounted all mine. Appreciation, nevertheless, causes me to state that it might never have been ready for the press were it not for the assistance of Mrs. Marcie Webber, a typist *par excellence* and a generous friend always ready to type "just one more chapter." To her and all others who helped in any way I am indeed grateful.

The Mexican Novel
before Mariano Azuela

As THE SPANIARDS EXPLORED, CONQUERED, AND OCCUPIED ENORMOUS
expanses of territory in the Americas, they transplanted their culture, then in the full glory of its Golden Age, to even the far reaches
of their overseas colonies. As early as 1539 printing presses were set
up in Mexico, and by 1551 universities were chartered in Mexico
and Peru.

An epic poem of splendid stature, *La araucana* by the Spanish
warrior Alonso de Ercilla y Zúñiga, grew out of the long and difficult
conquest of Chile. Bernal Díaz del Castillo, one of the foot soldiers
of Cortez in the fantastic conquest of the Aztec empire, left us in
his *True History of the Conquest of Mexico* one of the great narrative documents in any literature. A little later the mestizo Inca
Garcilaso de la Vega (son of a Spanish father and a princess of
Inca royalty) produced in *Royal Commentaries of the Incas* a
charming picture of life among the Incas, perhaps the first *costumbrista* piece in Spanish-American literature.

During the seventeenth century Mexico contributed two notable
figures to literature. Juan Ruiz de Alarcón took his dramatic talent
to Spain and (along with Lope de Vega, Tirso de Molina, and
Calderón de la Barca) merited recognition as one of the Big Four in
the Spanish drama of the Golden Age. Back at home Sor Juana
Inés de la Cruz, a nun, was to compose the finest lyric poetry ever to
come out of the colonies. Had there been a Nobel Prize for Literature in her time, she would have been a shoo-in.

Numerous literary figures of enduring value emerged in the
course of the three centuries of Spanish rule in America—essayists,

poets, dramatists, religious writers, historians. What is striking, is that no one turned out a work which can properly be labeled a novel.[1] At first glance, this may seem baffling and illogical. Spain herself in those times had a proud tradition in the novel, although this was not yet a highly cultivated form in any literature. In the sixteenth century the picaresque novel flowered in Spain and to this day has a lingering influence in Spanish-speaking lands. Popular, too, were pastoral novels and novels of chivalry. And finally, in 1605 and 1615, Cervantes gave the world the immortal *Don Quijote de la Mancha*. Why, then, were there no novels in all of the vast Spanish colonies throughout those hundreds of years—at least, until 1816, at the very fag end of Spanish rule in Mexico?

A variety of reasons may be adduced, any one of which could be enough to explain the phenomenon, given all the circumstances of the colonial epoch. The physical or material problems facing a would-be novelist were in themselves discouraging: the scarcity of printing presses, the shortage of paper, and the costliness of the whole process. But, before any printing could be done on a substantial work like a novel, there was the matter of obtaining the approval of the royal censor. Had a censor been available in each of the larger colonial cities, this hurdle might have been taken in stride. Such, however, was not the case. Censors qualified to grant licenses for the printing of this sort of work were only in Spain. This meant that the novelist, after laboriously fashioning the manuscript by hand, would have had to send his only copy off to Spain by ship. With the British and other buccaneers, freebooters, and pirates harassing Spanish shipping from Cádiz to Maracaibo and all points in between, not every Spanish vessel reached its destination. But suppose it did and that the censors finally issued their approval for the work to be printed, and then suppose that the manuscript (which quite possibly wasn't worth any of this trouble in the first place) made it back across the seas intact. By this time, a year or two—or four or five—after it was dispatched, the author might not even be among the living, or if alive not affluent enough to afford the costs of underwriting the publication of his book.

These obstacles should have been enough to discourage any budding novelists in the colonies, but some bureaucrats in Madrid (either civil or religious, or both) were taking no chances. As early as 1531 there was an official prohibition against the printing or even circulation of novels in the Spanish colonies of the New World, a prohibition which continued right down to the end of colonial times. The ban was effective, however, only in regard to the *printing* of novels, for there is ample evidence that some novels from the Old World were circulated in the colonies. This kind of underground traffic is almost impossible to extinguish completely. However, it was no great trick to keep an eye on the few presses and make sure the prohibition against printing was not violated. So, then, how was it that the first New World novel made its appearance in Mexico in 1816, five years before Mexican independence was secured?

The answer is to be found in Spain and in the Mexican capital. When Napoleon invaded the Iberian Peninsula in 1807 and the next year placed his brother Joseph Bonaparte on the Spanish throne in place of Fernando VII, the legitimate Spanish Cortes, or parliament, went underground and continued operating in the southern port city of Cádiz. In 1810 this body voted freedom of the press for Spain and all her colonies. In that same year the *criollos* (full-blooded Spaniards born in the New World) turned the Napoleonic takeover of Spain to their own interests. Failure by the Spanish Crown to understand the *criollos* and duly appreciate them had through generations increasingly antagonized and alienated this group which was naturally growing in size and potential. The puppet Bonaparte in Madrid gave the *criollo* leaders the chance to make their play for freedom. Asserting that the colonies were the personal property of the Spanish Crown (which was legally true), they rose up all over Spanish America in 1810, claiming that they were taking over the colonies and would govern them in the name of Fernando VII until his return to the throne.

Starting with the May uprising in Buenos Aires, *criollo* control was established in nearly all the major colonies: Venezuela, Chile, Colombia, Ecuador, and Mexico. With the single exception of Buenos Aires, all of these patriot movements were soon temporarily suppressed, though by 1824 all of the colonies were lost to Spain except Cuba and Puerto Rico. In Mexico, the original movement led by Father Hidalgo was quickly blunted by his capture and execution, but the revolutionary movement was carried on by Father Morelos until he met the same fate in 1815. Independence was not to come until 1821, when a turnabout by royalist officer Agustín de Iturbide settled the issue almost overnight.

Although Mexico City was firmly in Spanish hands when the first Spanish-American novel was published in 1816, it was a period of confusion and transition. There had been a change of viceroys, the Cádiz decree of 1810 was finally made public in Mexico, despite the fact that this was largely neutralized by a viceregal edict decreeing the death penalty for any author of incendiary pamphlets or other writings. Amid all this uncertainty a most unusual person named José Joaquín Fernández de Lizardi (1776–1827), who thrived on confusion and spent a lifetime creating more and more of it, seized upon the idea of producing a novel as a means of sneaking past the censors many of his reform notions about social conditions, education, and political evils. He persuaded a printer to risk printing it, and thus was born the first real Spanish-American novel, *El Periquillo Sarniento* (*The Itching Parrot*).

While the purist might profess disappointment that the novel came into being in those countries in such a back-handed manner, playing second fiddle to the reform intentions of a social critic, it seems to me fortunate that the novel was propelled on stage by such a lively figure as Lizardi, who knew the social reality around him as few others did and who had devoted his life to writing about it. As a result, we have a work which is steeped in the reality of the Mexican populace of its time.

It was probably Fernández de Lizardi's social instinct which urged him to tell his story in the form of a picaresque novel, a near-perfect vehicle for the purposes he had in mind. A major characteristic of the picaresque works, always founded in satire, is that they contrast the social mores of the affluent class with the oppressed existence of the lower class. The *pícaro* or rogue, who in his poverty must attach himself to one upper-class master after another, discovers and exposes the sham, the shallowness, the insensitivity and crassness, the selfishness and arrogance and false values of the masters he serves.

The sprightly *El Periquillo Sarniento* commands attention and respect both for what it says and how it says it. The one trouble with the book is that Lizardi didn't really want to write a novel. He simply wanted to get before the reading public his biting attacks on the system and his ideas for reforming it. Interlarded throughout the narrative are nearly all the pamphlets he had written over the course of some years, many of which he had failed to get past the baleful eye of the censor. The result is a work of approximately a thousand pages, first published in four volumes. The fourth volume was indeed stopped by the censor and not published until after Independence. Since American readers lack the patience for all this extraneous material, the English translation made by Katherine Anne Porter sifted it down to 290 pages and an edition prepared for classroom use in this country offers just 160 pages.[2]

But if American readers won't sit still for several hundred extra pages of moralizing and pamphleteering, the readers in Spanish lands seem to welcome it, for new editions continue to appear up to our day, usually embodying the whole long text. Until the outbreak of the Spanish Civil War in 1939, it is said, one Barcelona pub- lishing house reprinted it over and over at the rate of more than a million copies a year.[3] In any case, this is probably one of the all- time best sellers in the Spanish language.

Fernández de Lizardi, who often used the pen name of "The Mexican Thinker," reserved much of his choicest satire for doctors, hospitals, funeral customs, politicians, and religious. In one chapter the *pícaro* Perico serves for a time a pedantic old medico called Doctor Purgative. After observing closely his manner and his prac- tices and reading all the medical and anatomical books in his library, Perico departs one night with the doctor's mule, books, money, medical diploma, and assorted other items, with the intention of passing himself off as a doctor in other parts. This sort of gambit is commonplace in the Spanish picaresque novels.

Having established himself in Tula (with an assistant, no less), Perico is called to the home of a tax collector who seems on the brink of death. The scene develops in the following manner:

> Affecting a great serenity of spirit and with the confidence of a prophet, I told them: "Calm yourselves, ladies, why should he

die? This is only the effervescence of sanguinary humor which, oppressing the ventricles of his heart, stifle his cerebrum, because it presses with all the *pondus* or weight of the blood upon the medular and the trachea; but all of this will be ended at once, for if *evaquatio fit, recedet pletora,* that is, by evacuation we will free ourselves of the plethora."

The ladies listened to me astonished and the priest kept looking me up and down, no doubt scoffing at my nonsense, which he interrupted by saying:

"Ladies, spiritual remedies never do harm, nor are they opposed to temporal aid. It will be well to absolve my friend and anoint him, and let God's will be done."

After this has been accomplished, Perico takes over:

At once I approached the bed, took his pulse, and gazed at the beams of the ceiling for some time; then I took his pulse again, all the time putting on an act by arching my eyebrows, wrinkling my nose, staring at the floor, biting my lips, moving my head from side to side, and going through every pantomime I could think of to stupefy those poor people who, never taking their eyes off me, remained in deep silence, taking me for a second Hippocrates; at least, that was my intention. . . .

Finally the point is reached when he can stall no longer, and so he addresses his assistant, Andrés:

"You, as a good phlebotomist, will give him without delay a pair of bleedings of the cava vein."

Andrés, although frightened and knowing as little as I about cava veins, tied his arms and gave him two slashes that looked like dagger wounds. After he had bled enough to shock all those present, the sick man opened his eyes and began to recognize and speak to the people surrounding him.

This success and another "cure" shortly after make Perico's fame as a doctor, so that he and Andrés prosper mightily for a time.

In spite of my ignorance, some sick people were cured by accident, although the ones who perished from my mortal remedies were much more numerous. Despite this, my fame did not diminish, for three reasons: first, most of the ones who died were poor, and neither their life nor their death was much noticed;

second, I had already gained renown and so I could sleep without worry, even if I killed more Toltecs than the Cid did with the Saracens; third, and this is what most favors the doctors, because those who were cured lauded my skill and those who died couldn't complain about my ignorance. . . .[4]

Some time later a plague puts an end to Perico's medical career, and he returns to the life of a *pícaro*. One significant difference to be noted between the Spanish *pícaro* and Lizardi's rogue is that in the end the latter repents of his misdeeds and settles down to a normal and decent existence, something no self-respecting *pícaro* of the Spanish breed would be caught dead at.

Having created Spanish America's first novel, Fernández de Lizardi went on to write a couple of others. *La Quijotita y su prima* (1818) is too pedantic and moralizing and does not convince. But *Don Catrín de la Fachenda* (published posthumously in 1832), another picaresque effort, has some of the same qualities found in *El Periquillo Sarniento*. Thus, the first novelist gave us not just one novel but three, an output which not many nineteenth-century Spanish-American novelists would surpass.

Yet the significance of José Joaquín Fernández de Lizardi rests not merely on his role as the first to use the novel form in the New World. The enduring popularity of *El Periquillo Sarniento* over more than a century and a half is but one evidence that this work possesses extraordinary qualities. This outsized picaresque effort ranks well up among the leaders of all the novels of its century. In fact, some critics regard it definitely as the foremost novel of the 1800s.[5] And it has still other distinctions. Always ahead of his time, Lizardi gave us in this work a novel of social protest and a novel expressed in the language of the people. These two characteristics are hardly to appear again in Mexico until the second decade of the present century in the works of Mariano Azuela.

The publication of *El Periquillo Sarniento* and the achieving of independence shortly thereafter, with the consequent relaxation of censorship, did not have the effect of opening the gates of a dam behind which pressuring waters were just waiting to rush through. The truth is that there was no immediate response at all. An anonymous historical novel, *Jicoténcal,* dealing with the Indian warrior of the same name who opposed Cortez in the latter's conquest of Mexico, appeared in 1826, but it was printed in Philadelphia and the probability is that the author was not Mexican. There is almost no other example of a full-bodied novel in Mexico until the mid-1840s.

Manuel Payno's *El fistol del diablo,* published in two volumes in 1845–46, was the first important novel in Mexico since Lizardi. It launched the romantic novel in that country and signaled the beginning of a steadily growing novelistic output. Many years later (1889–91) Payno was to produce a much superior work, *Los bandidos de Río Frío,* which many feel is Mexico's premier romantic effort; it is equally important for its *costumbrismo* and even shows some tinges of realism.

To summarize the history of the Mexican novel prior to the work of Mariano Azuela, it is sufficient to review a few more names and indicate certain tendencies. From the literary and artistic point of view, perhaps the most important figure in the whole nineteenth century is Ignacio Manuel Altamirano (1834–93). His most admired work is *Clemencia,* published in 1869. The story takes place in Guadalajara during the French Intervention of the 1860s. Patriotic fervor in *Clemencia* is overshadowed by tragedy and suffering, almost invariable ingredients of true romanticism. Ralph Warner said of this novel that "through its simple style and the unity of its form and its characters—in spite of the inevitable romanticism—*Clemencia* is the first modern novel in Mexico."[6] It is also worth noting that Altamirano was the first novelist in his country to exert visible literary influence on a number of other writers.

Romanticism was a bit tardy in catching on in Hispanic America, and one reason may be found in the chaos and confusion of the 1810–25 period, in which independence was being won, and of the following years when the problems of self-government beset the new nations. As if compensating for its slow start, romanticism was to perdure in all areas of Hispanic America almost to the end of the century. Even in its heyday, however, romanticism often had to share top billing with that hardy perennial, *costumbrismo.* And as the last half of the century wore on, realism emerged as the new movement of greatest vitality.

Rafael Delgado (1853–1914) combined judiciously all three of these literary tendencies. More than that, he is the best stylist of the nineteenth-century novelists and better at developing plot than practically any of them. Mariano Azuela says of two of Delgado's works, *La calandria* and *Los parientes ricos,* that "they are the most important impulses in the Mexican novel and the efforts of Rafael Delgado are the most legitimate success in this literary genre up to our day."[7]

As the century rolled on toward its close, naturalism gradually filtered into the Mexican literary picture. The naturalism of the French masters never was fully accepted by novelists in Mexico, who indeed seem to have made but slight distinction between realism and naturalism.[8] While several writers show naturalistic traits, Federico Gamboa is commonly cited as the most loyal follower of Zola. Gamboa deserves mention, however, not because of his naturalistic tendencies but simply as one of the three or four best novelists in Mexico prior to the time of Mariano Azuela. Some regard him as "the best novelist Mexico had produced up to his time."[9]

There is little doubt that Gamboa is most widely known for his *Santa* (1903), the story of young prostitute (not quite so saintly as her name). Santa is, nevertheless, basically decent and is pushed into the oldest trade by her family's lack of understanding, support, and love after she has been victimized. Gamboa's descriptions of the lower depths and the brothels of Mexico City would be difficult to surpass. He applies the clinical attitude typical of naturalism to most scenes, particularly those involving sex. Santa goes to the top of her profession and later descends to the bottom, from which fate she is finally salvaged by the love of Hipólito, a poor blind pianist.

Of Gamboa's several other novels, the best surely is *Suprema ley,* 1896. For Gamboa, at least in this work, love is the "supreme law" in this life; even if it is extramarital love that ruins a family, it is still apt to be an overpowering and irresistible force. In *Suprema ley* a court clerk named Julio Ortegal feels compassion for a woman who is on trial for killing her lover. When she is acquitted and has nowhere to go, Ortegal takes her into his own home where, it is to be admitted, things haven't been going too well anyway. The presence of Clothilde is not calculated to make the wife, Carmen, click her heels with joy, although for a time the arrangement does seem to work out well. But later, as the reader suspected all along, Julio and Clothilde become lovers and everything and everybody is ruined, even though Clothilde is eventually forgiven and received back into her own family. Not an original plot, it is convincingly handled by Gamboa, who presents us with many authentic scenes of urban existence in Mexico City at the close of the past century.

In his literary career Federico Gamboa bridges the nineteenth and the twentieth centuries. By the time his last novel appeared (*La llaga* in 1910), Mariano Azuela had already published the first three of the many he was to produce. Thus it can be said that Gamboa, in many ways as fine a representative of Mexican letters as the past century has to offer, made way for Azuela, who was to take the Mexican novel in a direction it had never before known.

NOTES TO CHAPTER 1

1. While there are a few scattered narrative works with novelistic elements, there is none that fully merits being called a novel in the modern sense of the term. The Spanish-born Bernardo de Balbuena, long resident in Mexico, wrote while there a pastoral novel, *El siglo de oro en las selvas de Erífile* (1607), but he published it in Spain. In 1620 Francisco Bramón published in Mexico a kind of pastoral novel, *Los sirgueros de la Virgen,* but this really was just an effort to sugarcoat a strongly didactic work about the Immaculate Conception. And Carlos de Sigüenza y Góngora, a contemporary and close friend of Sor Juana Inés de la Cruz, wrote *Los infortunios de Alonso Ramírez* (1690), which perhaps was allowed to be printed in Mexico because it is a biographical account of the wanderings and doings of Alonso Ramírez.

2. *The Itching Parrot,* translated from the Spanish by Katherine Anne Porter (Garden City: Doubleday, Doran and Co., Inc., 1942) and *El Periquillo Sarniento,* edited by Erwin K. Mapes and Frances M. López-Morillas (New York: Appleton-Century-Crofts, Inc., 1952).

3. This statement is offered by Katherine Anne Porter in her Introduction (p. xxxvi) to the English translation detailed in the previous note.

4. *El Periquillo Sarniento* (Mexico City: Editorial Porrúa, 1949), II, pp. 128–131, 142.

5. Introduction to the English edition, p. xxxv.

6. Ralph E. Warner, *Historia de la novela mexicana en el siglo XIX* (Mexico City, 1953), p. 53.

7. Mariano Azuela, *Obras completas*, III (Mexico City: Fondo de Cultura Económica, 1960), 629.

8. John S. Brushwood, *Mexico in Its Novel* (Austin, 1966), p. 128.

9. Ibid., p. 150.

SELECTED NINETEENTH-CENTURY MEXICAN NOVELS

Altamirano, Ignacio Manuel (1834–93)
Clemencia, 1869
La Navidad en las montañas, 1871 (Translated into English as *Christmas in the Mountains*. Gainesville: University of Florida Press, 1961.)
El Zarco, 1901 (Translated into English as *El Zarco the Bandit*. London: Folio Society, 1957.)

Campo, Angel de (1868–1908)
La rumba, 1890

Castera, Pedro (1838–1906)
Carmen, 1882

Cuéllar, José Tomás de (1830–94)
El pecado del siglo, 1869
La linterna mágica, 1871–72; 1889–92

Delgado, Rafael (1853–1914)
La calandria, 1890
Angelina, 1893
Los parientes ricos, 1902

Díaz Covarrubias, Juan (1837–59)
Gil Gómez el insurgente, 1858
La clase media, 1858
El diablo en México, 1859

Fernández de Lizardi, José Joaquín (1776–1827)
El Periquillo Sarniento, 1816 (Translated into English as *The Itching Parrot*. Garden City: Doubleday, Doran, 1942.)
La Quijotita y su prima, 1818
Don Catrín de la Fachenda, 1832

Frías, Heriberto (1870–1925)   *Tomochic,* 1894
                                     Naufragio, 1895
                                     El último duelo, 1896
Gamboa, Federico (1864–1939)   *Suprema ley,* 1895
                                     Metamorfosis, 1899
                                     Santa, 1903
Inclán, Luis Gonzaga (1816–75)   *Astucia,* 1865
López Portillo y Rojas, José   *La parcela,* 1898
  (1850–1923)
Mateos, Juan Antonio (1831–1913)   *El cerro de las campanas,* 1868
                                     El sol de mayo, 1868
                                     Memorias de un guerrillero, 1897
Payno, Manuel (1810–94)   *El fistol del diablo,* 1845–46
                                     Los bandidos de Río Frío,
                                     1889–91
Paz, Ireneo (1836–1924)   *La piedra del sacrificio,* 1871
                                     Amor y suplicio, 1873
Pizarro Suárez, Nicolás (d. 1891)   *El monedero,* 1861
                                     La coqueta, 1861
Rabasa, Emilio (1856-1930)   *La bola,* 1887
                                     La gran ciencia, 1887
                                     El cuarto poder, 1888
                                     Moneda falsa, 1888
Riva Palacio, Vicente (1832–96)   *Martín Garatuza,* 1868
                                     Calvario y tabor, 1868
Roa Barcena, José María (1827–1908) *Novelas,* 1870
Rodríguez Galván, Ignacio (1816–42) *La hija del oidor,* 1836

SELECTED STUDIES ON THE NINETEENTH-CENTURY MEXICAN NOVEL

Azuela, Mariano. *Cien años de novela mexicana.*
Brushwood, John S. *Mexico in Its Novel.*
————. *The Romantic Novel in Mexico.*
———— and Rojas Garciadueñas, José. *Breve historia de la novela mexicana.*
González, Manuel Pedro. *Trayectoria de la novela en México.*
González Peña, Carlos. *History of Mexican Literature.*

Grass, Roland. "Cómo se hace una revolución según Emilio Rabasa," *Cuadernos Americanos,* año 24, no. 5 (1965), 276–281.

Jiménez Rueda, Julio. *Historia de la literatura mexicana.*

———. *Letras mexicanas en el siglo XIX.*

Martínez, José Luis. "Las letras patrias. De la época de la independencia a nuestros días." *México y la cultura,* pp. 387–472.

Meléndez, Concha. *La novela indianista en Hispanoamérica.*

Moore, Ernest, "Una bibliografía descriptiva: *El Periquillo Sarniento.*" *Revista Iberoamericana,* X (1946), 383–403.

———. "Heriberto Frías and the Novel of the Mexican Revolution." *Modern Language Forum,* XXVII (1942), 12–27.

——— and Bickley, James. "Bibliografía, Rafael Delgado, Notas bibliográficas y críticas." *Revista Iberoamericana,* VI (1943), 155–202.

———. "Bibliografía de obras y crítica de Federico Gamboa." *Revista Iberoamericana,* II (1940), 271–279.

Ocampo de Gómez, A.M., and Prado Velázquez, E., eds. *Diccionario de escritores mexicanos.*

Navarro, Joaquina. *La novela realista mexicana.*

Read, J. Lloyd. *The Mexican Historical Novel, 1826–1910.*

Sánchez, Luis Alberto. *Proceso y contenido de la novela hispanoamericana.*

Seymour, Arthur R. "The Mexican 'novela de costumbres.'" *Hispania,* VIII (1925), 283–289.

Spell, Jefferson Rea. *The Life and Works of José Fernández de Lizardi.*

———. "The Costumbrista Movement in Mexico." PMLA, L (1935), 290–315.

———. "The Literary Works of Manuel Payno." *Hispania,* XII (1929), 347–356.

———. "Mexican Society as Seen by Fernández de Lizardi," *Hispania,* VIII (1925), 145–165.

———. "The Genesis of the First Mexican Novel." *Hispania,* XIV (1931), 53–58.

———. "New Light on Fernández de Lizardi and His *Periquillo Sarniento.*" *Hispania,* XLVI (1963), 753–754.

Torres Manzo, C. "Perfil y esencia de Rafael Delgado." *Cuadernos Americanos,* año XII, no. 4 (1953), 247–261.

Urbina, Luis C. *La vida literaria en México* and *La literatura mexicana durante la guerra de la independencia.*

Warner, Ralph E. *Historia de la novela mexicana en el siglo XIX.*

2

Mariano Azuela:
A Break with the Past

AT THE DAWNING OF THE TWENTIETH CENTURY MEXICO WAS IN A RUT. The nation responded as if mesmerized to the orders and decrees of the old dictator Porfirio Díaz, whose seemingly endless control—dating from 1876—still had ten years to run before disintegrating with the onslaught of the 1910 Revolution. Any liberal instincts within the regime had long been forgotten as more and more it exemplified the classical concern of an aging dictatorship for perpetuating its power and preserving existing conditions. The boast of Díaz and his ruling group was that they had brought to Mexico the heretofore rather unknown blessings of peace and prosperity.

What was obvious to any observer was that the peace was artificial and tenuous, achieved and maintained solely through the armed power of the dictator. Prosperity was certainly a reality, but only for those of a select group. Fortunes were being made and the nation's credit before the world was excellent, yet a *peón* was scarcely more valued than a steer on any of the great Mexican haciendas. As is frequently said today of the world's nations, the chasm dividing the rich and the poor was constantly widening. In all political, economic, and social matters Mexico found itself in 1900 effectively throttled by Díaz and his cohorts.

The state of the Mexican novel was virtually stagnant. Although the Spanish-American literary world at the time was in the midst of the Modernist period, commonly regarded as Spanish America's only authentic literary movement, the effect on the Mexican novel was minimal. This was so because Modernism manifested itself preeminently in poetry and because its influence, in any event, was less evident in the literature of Mexico than in that of various other Spanish-American countries. The novels which appeared in Mexico in the first years of this century were from the same old mold that had been in use for decades. The paramount trait of these works was their imitation of European models. Whether examples of romanticism, realism, or regional *costumbrismo*, they tended to be lengthy, rhetorical to the point of becoming florid, and moralizing. Being imitations, they were in a sense false and artificial.

This state of affairs was to end suddenly, dramatically, and violently. The Díaz machine was destroyed quickly and with surprising ease by the Revolution of 1910, Latin America's first great social upheaval. With various modifications imposed by changing times and needs, this revolutionary movement has retained political control of Mexico from that day to this. Reduced to dangerously simple terms, the program of the Revolution can be said to have opposed the old ruling oligarchy, the Church, and foreign imperialism and to have promoted distribution of land among the poor, increased power for organized labor, and the growth of a nationalistic spirit. This last item gave rise to the expropriation of various foreign-owned properties (including the vast oil holdings of American, British, and Dutch interests) and to the glorification of everything Indian in Mexican life.

What interests us for the moment, however, is the fighting phase of the Revolution. Although the Díaz government was soon disposed of and the leader of the revolt, Francisco Madero, became president in 1911 in Mexico's first free elections, the Revolution was to suffer further convulsions and internal bloodshed until 1920. Indeed, peace and stability did not really come until 1930. Reactionary forces under General Victoriano Huerta overthrew and then assassinated Madero in February, 1913. The Revolution came to life again and succeeded in ousting Huerta seventeen months after he seized power. Then the leaders of the Revolution fell to fighting among themselves, and in the bloodiest battles of the 1910–20 period the forces of Pancho Villa, Emiliano Zapata, Venustiano Carranza, and Alvaro Obregón struggled for ascendancy. Carranza became the recognized president in 1917 but was forced out in 1920 before finishing his term. While fleeing toward the Gulf coast he was hunted down and shot like a wild beast. Obregón was elected to the presidency later in the same year.

Whatever else the Mexican Revolution might be called, it was the one compelling reality throughout that ten-year fighting span, and surely had cataclysmic effects on nearly all aspects of existence for practically all Mexicans. Anything with such total impact as the Revolution had to be the one great issue in the life and thought of that decade. It is entirely natural to assume, therefore, that it would provoke an immediate repercussion in every form of human expression. One would expect the novelists in particular to seize upon the dramatic—and tragic—national phenomenon of the Revolution as inspiration for their works. If an immediate reaction was not forthcoming, certainly it seems reasonable to look for a good number of novels based on the revolution prior to 1920. Surprisingly, this was not the case. The startling truth is that only one novelist, Mariano Azuela, recognized the Revolution for what it was during those years and wrote about it. It seems that all others were too stunned by the violence and brutality of the fighting to reflect it in their writing. Between 1911 and 1918 Azuela published no fewer than six novels about the Revolution, including *Los de abajo* (*The Underdogs*), almost uniformly recognized as the most outstanding work among the many score of novels eventually to be written on this theme.

Not only was Mariano Azuela the first to write about the Revolution and its effects, but in doing so he broke with the novelistic tradition so long in vogue in his country and initiated a new treatment of the novel. In *Los de abajo*, Azuela etches an approach and a style that will characterize the cascade of works comprising the Novel of the Mexican Revolution, an output which rather completely dominated the novel from 1925 until about 1945. Attuned in remarkable degree to the military struggle and the social upheaval it attempts to mirror and interpret, *Los de abajo* is of course set in the historical reality of the Revolution and is narrated in terse, simple, colloquial language.

Uncomplicated both as to style and to plot, this novel truly reflects the Revolution as it was. And all of the novelists of the Revolution who came after Azuela have continued to tell it the same way.

Action takes precedence over description and characterization, conciseness and directness replace the verbosity and sermonizing of the past. As a result, the twentieth-century Mexican novel emerges with legitimacy and is able to stand on its own feet.

Not often does one man and one work exert such influence on the literature of a country. While Azuela was to produce more than twenty novels, it is safe to affirm that his influence on other novelists of the Revolution would have been much the same had he written only *Los de abajo*. And this is not at all intended to downgrade the value and importance of some of his other works. It is simply that *Los de abajo* stands forth from the outset as the bellwether of the novel of the Mexican Revolution.

Mariano Azuela, born on January 1, 1873, in the town of Lagos de Moreno in the state of Jalisco, began to manifest his true vocation as a writer even before receiving his medical degree in 1899. His first novel appeared in 1907 and another the next year, but his first work of any importance was *Mala yerba* [Bad weed], 1909. This is a fairly powerful story which exposes the corruption of wealthy landholders and politicians. It is a sort of preview of Azuela's novels on the Revolution but even more a keynote work in that it tackles one of the social ills, inveighing against the exploitation of the little man by the more powerful.

With the triumph of the Madero movement in 1911, Dr. Azuela was appointed the political chief of Lagos de Moreno. It wasn't long, however, before he became disenchanted with the political situation prevailing in the first takeover of the Revolution. His feelings are exposed quite plainly in *Andrés Pérez, maderista,* 1911, at once the first novel of the Revolution and a remarkable document but in no sense a great novel. It seems to have been hastily constructed, the minimal development of an outline. The style is simple, almost journalistic, and the few important characters do not come to life as real individuals but personify types.

The action line of *Andrés Pérez, maderista* is not complicated and the novel covers little more than one hundred pages in any of its editions. Andrés Pérez, a young newspaperman in Mexico City, receives an invitation from his former classmate Toño Reyes to visit him and his wife, María, at their hacienda. On an impulse Andrés quits his job and goes. Toño shows immense interest in the rumors of a possible revolution and queries Andrés, who describes the restless spirit in the country and ends by saying, "One has the presumption that something serious is going to happen."[1] Thereafter he indicates clearly his lack of interest in revolutionary talk and activity.

Shortly thereafter the Revolution breaks out. Toño is disillusioned with the attitude of Andrés, who decides to return to the capital. But before he can leave an order comes from the district political leader for his arrest as a "revolutionary agent of Francisco I. Madero who has gone to the hacienda to arouse the people." Despite the denials by Pérez, Toño—and soon everyone in the area—comes to believe that he really is an undercover agent for the Madero uprising. They even gather money to aid the cause and hand over to Andrés a thousand pesos. A sleepless night brings him to the decision to skip town with this windfall and go to the U.S. for a few months.

Picked up by the police on his way to the train station, Pérez in jail becomes an ever larger hero. Toño Reyes leads a successful local uprising but is killed in the skirmish. Andrés Pérez is of course released when the rebels take control of the area. He is almost alone in recognizing the cynicism and opportunism of various figures who embrace the revolutionary cause only to save their own hides and their fortunes. The last lines are the final cynical touch. Once more on his way to the train, Pérez passes the doorway of Toño's widow, María, who has clearly been attracted to Andrés from the beginning. He pauses, thinks a moment, and then turns into the doorway.

The most interesting thing about *Andrés Pérez, maderista* is the stance Azuela takes toward the Revolution. He is asserting that some of the most committed and idealistic revolutionaries are either killed off in the fighting or are so lacking in the practical realm that opportunists and revolutionaries in name only are able to gain control of the operation (especially on the local level), with the result that there is really no revolution but only a change in bosses. Actually, this disenchanted view is not at all unique. It is an attitude quite common throughout the literature on the Revolution. The amazing part is that Azuela, in the very first months of the Revolution and in the full flush of victory, perceives clearly what was to become evident to many others only with the passage of time, namely, that the Revolution from the outset was infiltrated, adulterated, and undermined by large numbers of antirevolutionaries who shrewdly protected their power position merely by proclaiming loudly and insistently their adherence to the cause.

Because Azuela in most of his subsequent novels keeps hammering at this same Achilles heel of the Revolution, he has often been accused of being too critical of the movement and of writing antirevolutionary novels. The charge is untrue and unfair. Azuela's own life and actions between 1910 and 1920 reveal him to be a convinced proponent of the Revolution and an active fighter for it, both in administrative posts and on the field of battle. Without doubt Azuela is wholeheartedly *for* the Revolution. Precisely because he is so dedicated intellectually and practically to its aims he reacts strongly to the threat posed by the pseudorevolutionaries. It galls the sincere, forthright Azuela to see the Revolution betrayed by cynical, selfish opportunists of that breed.

With the murder of Madero and the return to power of the old guard, Azuela was forced to flee Lagos de Moreno and to go to the north of the country where revolutionary elements were still in control. Once Huerta was overthrown, Azuela accepted the invitation of General Julián Medina to serve as Director of Education in Jalisco. Only a few months later open warfare erupted between the several revolutionary chieftains, and Azuela became a lieutenant colonel in charge of medical services for the troops of Medina, who allied himself with the army of Pancho Villa.

After Villa suffered crushing defeats in successive battles with the forces of General Alvaro Obregón in April and May of 1915, Azuela took refuge for a time in El Paso, Texas. Here he finished and first published his most famous work, *Los de abajo.* As he said later, he had started writing the novel while in the field with Medina's army,[2] and Medina himself serves as the genesis of the novel's protagonist, Demetrio Macías.

Completely without funds on arriving in El Paso, Azuela worked out a deal with the editor of the newspaper *El Paso del Norte* whereby he was allowed to sleep in the printing shop and received a few dollars weeky in exchange for the publication of *Los de abajo* in serial form in the newspaper. And so between October and

December, 1915, one of the landmarks of Mexican literature made its first appearance, an event which at the time escaped the attention of practically everyone. Early in 1916 the El Paso printer brought it out as a book, still with no popular reaction.

Los de abajo breaks sharply and abruptly with the Mexican novelistic tradition. True, it is strongly anchored to historical fact, but in this it is not innovative, since the historical novel had previously been cultivated in Mexico. Also, it is decidedly realistic and again this is nothing new, for realism was already established as a strong current in all of Spanish-American literature. What is new about *Los de abajo* may be summarized as follows:

1) It plants the Revolution firmly in center stage as the overriding theme. In fact, one can correctly say that the Revolution itself is the true protagonist of *Los de abajo*. In this respect it goes much farther than *Andrés Pérez, maderista,* which, though it was the first novel of the Mexican Revolution, still revolved on the outer periphery of the Revolution itself.

2) In style *Los de abajo* abandons the former cult of verbiage. Instead, Azuela rides the pendulum almost to the other extreme and initiates a new tendency toward brevity, terseness, and suggestion. Sentences usually are short, sometimes piling upon one another in staccato manner. A few words, through the device of suggestion and projection, do the work of many. Description is sublimated; dialogue assumes a prime role.

3) The speech of the Mexican peon is highlighted. Nothing on this same scale had been attempted in earlier Mexican novels. For the uninitiated, the use of the highly colloquial language of the common man may pose a slight problem in comprehension, but undeniably it imparts a distinct and genuine flavor to the conversation and the work as a whole.

4) Plot gives way in considerable degree to episode and incident. There is progression from start to finish, and the loosely linked episodes do lead to change and eventual resolution, but of greater concern seems to be the creation of the *ambiente* (atmosphere), of a mood keenly attuned not so much to the specific incident as to the whole Revolution itself. *Los de abajo* is an admirable example of how style, speech, action, attitude, and thought create a pervasive

atmosphere that reflects faithfully the spirit of the moment, the spirit of the Mexican Revolution as it was.

It is a tribute to Azuela that each of these features became characteristic of the flood of novels about the Revolution, an outpouring triggered by Azuela and later to become the most widely cultivated cycle in the history of the Mexican novel. If imitation is the highest form of flattery, then Mariano Azuela is a most flattered person.

As already mentioned, *Los de abajo* is a direct outgrowth of Azuela's own participation in the Revolution. Written partly in the very heat of battle and finished as soon as the author reached safety in El Paso, this work understandably carries the trademark of authenticity. It would be difficult to imagine a set of circumstances more favorable for capturing the intimate mood of a given time.

The story of *Los de abajo* is built around the revolutionary activities of Demetrio Macías and his followers. Demetrio, modeled somewhat on General Julián Medina, finds himself in the Revolution not through any conviction whatever but through personal differences he has had with the *patrón*, don Mónico. Demetrio is a simple peasant, unable to read and not intellectual enough ever to understand the political ideals, nuances, and aspirations of the revolutionary movement. Demetrio leaves his wife and small son and, with his little band of twenty-five men, all of the same background as himself, ambushes a larger federal force in a canyon close to his home, inflicting heavy damage on them but being rather seriously wounded himself.

He and his men find shelter and a warm welcome in a "rancho" or tiny village in the mountains. Here Demetrio recuperates for two or three weeks, treated by one of his principal followers, Venancio, who has been a barber and is easily the best educated and most intelligent of the group. A girl of the village, Camila, serves as nurse for Demetrio, who comes to look upon her with fond eyes. But Camila has fallen completely for Luis Cervantes, a sort of dandy who has been picked up and brought in by one of the sentries.

Cervantes is intelligent and educated (he has studied a bit of medicine and has been a journalist), but the reader quickly tags him as an opportunist. Drafted by the federals, he has deserted and when caught by Demetrio's men insists that his one ambition is to serve the Revolution. His colors begin to show when he keeps hands off the willing Camila because he senses that Demetrio will want her. But Cervantes is a good one with words and articulates all the right phrases about the Revolution, its aims, ideals, and principles. Thus, he entrenches himself as Demetrio's "brain truster" and idea man.

Although Demetrio's forces continue to grow and to win a few skirmishes with the federals, Cervantes convinces him that he must align himself with one of the important generals if he is really to amount to anything and contribute much to the cause of the Revolution. The decision is taken to join up with General Pánfilo Natera, who in turn forms part of the army of Pancho Villa. As the townsfolk express their fond good wishes, they depart from Camila's village, leaving her behind to pine for Luis.

After winning along the way a fierce encounter with the federals, Demetrio with a hundred men meets Natera in Fresnillo. Cervantes and Captain Solís of Natera's command recognize each other from former days and engage in a most interesting dialogue about the Revolution. Solís, once imbued with the fire and enthusiasm which Luis now has (or pretends), admits to much disillusionment: "There are deeds and there are men who are nothing but pure gall. And that gall keeps falling drop by drop into the spirit, and it embitters everything, it poisons everything. Enthusiasm, hopes, ideals, joys . . . nothing! Then one has nothing left but to become a bandit like the others or to disappear from the scene, hiding himself behind the walls of a fierce and impenetrable egotism." And a little later: "I ask myself why I keep on fighting. The Revolution is a hurricane, and the man who goes into it is no longer a man, but just a miserable dry leaf driven by the wind." Some time later, during the course of a battle, Solís exclaims: "How beautiful the Revolution is, even in its very barbarity!" Then he adds: "What a disappointment, my friend, if those of us who offered all our enthusiasm and our very life to overthrow a miserable assassin should turn out to be the builders of an enormous pedestal on which a hundred or two hundred thousand monsters of the same species might place themselves. . . . What a waste of blood!"[3] A moment later Antonio Solís is hit and adds his own to all that other wasted blood. Azuela almost certainly is speaking his own thoughts and feelings through the words of Solís.

When Demetrio is made a colonel in Natera's forces the tempo picks up, though what is revealed is the gradual demoralization of Demetrio and his followers. He decides he wants Camila with him and Cervantes goes back for her, letting her think he has come to take her for himself. Later Camila is stabbed to death by la Pintada, a gross and brassy camp follower. There is a lot of drinking between battles, much boastful talk, some seducing of young girls, and a few fatal arguments. The taking of any town triggers unrestrained looting and pillaging.

Inexorably, the fortunes of Demetrio and his men follow the fate of Pancho Villa's army. A high point is reached and then the tide turns. As they give ground and move back toward the north, morale falls and desertions increase. They meet stony aloofness in villages which a year before had embraced them warmly. Among the deserters is Luis Cervantes, who has made off with a good bit of plundered loot to El Paso, from where he writes to Venancio to relate how he is prospering. By now Demetrio is a general, but he commands few more than the small band with which he started.

They return for the first time to where Demetrio had lived. His wife is beside herself with joy. His little son, terrified, doesn't know him. The woman begs him not to leave again and asks why they must keep on fighting. Tossing a stone down the side of the canyon, Demetrio answers, "See that stone, how it can't stop. . . ." As he departs with his few men, they are ambushed in the same spot where he had won his first victory. Though hopelessly trapped, Demetrio is possessed for a moment with the wild joy of battle, of his own fabulous marksmanship ("where he puts his eye, he puts the bullet"). "And at the foot of a crevice as enormous and sumptuous as the portico of an old cathedral, Demetrio Macías, with his eyes fixed forever, keeps aiming with the barrel of his rifle."[4]

Although new editions of *Los de abajo* appeared in Tampico in 1917 and in Mexico City in 1920, this work which was later to receive world acclaim and to become most influential in Mexican letters remained virtually unknown until the end of 1925.

In 1916 Azuela was able to return to Mexico. He established

himself in the capital, where he built up a medical practice and continued writing. Soon he had produced several more works with revolutionary themes: *Los caciques* (*The Bosses*), published in 1917, and *Las moscas* (*The Flies*), *Domitilo quiere ser diputado* [Domitilo wants to be a congressman], and *Las tribulaciones de una familia decente* (*The Trials of a Respectable Family*), all published in 1918. Except for *Las tribulaciones de una familia decente*, these works are so short they can barely be called novels. In each of them Azuela continues his mordant analyses of the Revolution and its effects and with sarcasm and irony restates and reinforces his deep disappointment with the venality and unprincipled actions of many self-proclaimed leaders and supporters of the Revolution. *Las Tribulaciones*, the longest of these works, is also the strongest.

As the title indicates, this novel is the story of the hardships suffered by a formerly well-to-do provincial family after the Porfirian regime gave way to the Revolution. Moving to the capital from Zacatecas, the Vázquez Prado family hopes somehow to cling to its accustomed social and economic position. At least this is the driving motive of Agustinita, the mother, who until now has ruled the family by virtue of having been the source of its wealth. The father, Procopio, at the outset appears henpecked and somewhat insecure. Of the two daughters, Lulú comes through a bit colorless, while Berta is headstrong and ambitious. One son, Francisco José, has no great part in the novel, whereas his brother César, having set himself the task of writing the family history, narrates the first half of the story.

Known to be opponents of Carranza, the Vázquez Prado family sees its fragile hopes of rehabilitation disintegrate with the triumph of the Carranza forces. Berta provides a momentary ray of hope by marrying Pascual, a thoroughgoing opportunist and hypocrite whose complete lack of principles allows him to insinuate himself into high office in the new regime. But before long Pascual provokes his own downfall, and this time the social and economic ruin of the family seems complete.

Procopio, no longer in the shadow of Agustinita's money, now moves into command. He takes an ordinary position with a business firm, something which, back in Zacatecas, custom and the "right thing" would not have permitted him to do. Procopio's genuine and

Christian qualities emerge as he organizes the life of the family around its new and humble yet honest and decent orientation, and furthermore he claims the respect—even from Agustinita—which is his due as head of the household. He then sends for Archibaldo, erstwhile suitor of Lulú, who has been scorned for his humble origins, and invites him to come to claim the hand of the daughter.

In *Las tribulaciones de una familia decente* Azuela is again displaying his revulsion toward hypocrisy and opportunism, and he leaves us with the moral that money brings no assurance of happiness. He likewise says to the rich that plain, honest work—even manual labor—is dignifying and can bring true peace of mind.

The influence of Emile Zola is perhaps more noticeable in this novel than in any other of Azuela's works. The naturalistic tendencies in *Las tribulaciones* drew these comments from one observer: "The concept of the novel as a laboratory, of the 'experimental novel,' on which Zola's theory rests, is here employed with a fidelity and a mastery never achieved by Federico Gamboa, the most loyal and tenacious disciple which the French master was to have in the Spanish tongue. The changing fortunes of the Revolution and economic misery serve here as reagents or tests to 'experiment' with the characters and observe their reactions, through which they come to define themselves."[5]

Furthermore, the characters as a group are as fully delineated in this novel as in any other Azuela work. Procopio in particular, and also Agustinita, Berta, and Señora de Tabardillo (a family friend) emerge as truly human and individual personalities. Agustinita can claim the added distinction, in the opinion of one critic, of being the first well-drawn female in any Mexican novel who plays a prime role in the plot.[6]

One thing which weakens the overall effect of *Las tribulaciones* and puzzles all observers is that in the middle of the story Azuela shifts the vantage point from which the action is related. The first part of the book is narrated by César, who then is permitted to die. Thereafter the author himself takes over in the guise of the omniscient observer. The reader finds no reason for this unusual technique, which, if nothing else, is disconcerting at the time it occurs.

Nevertheless, the novel is one of the three or four best among the score or more which Azuela published.

Following the appearance of *Las tribulaciones de una familia decente* in 1918, Azuela gave us no new novel until 1923. Looking back over his literary career, one must conclude that this was a truly difficult period for Mariano Azuela, perhaps even a crucial one. It is my own conviction that during this time he was frustrated and disheartened, and that the underlying cause for this state of mind was the poor reception given his works by both readers and critics. It may be a bit unfair to blame the readers in this matter, for in those days comments and reviews by critics in the public press constituted the principal means of publicity for any newly printed work. And the critics remained almost 100 percent silent in the face of the ten novels and novelettes which Azuela had published by the end of 1918.

Manuel Pedro González has documented the nearly complete refusal, or at least failure, of the Mexican literary critics to discuss Azuela's works between 1907 and 1923.[7] Indeed, González sees the whole thing as almost a conspiracy on the part of the critics to keep his books from becoming known. While it may be overreacting to see such a conspiracy, the attitude of the critics does seem fairly transparent. In their eyes his revolutionary theme and style represented a disturbing departure from the comfortable norm they had known and cultivated. They felt threatened by this new novelist and since they did not have Azuela's vision, nor had they shared his involvement in the epochal events of the Revolution, they completely ignored him.

In any case, when Azuela began writing again things had changed. The Revolution as such was no longer his theme, nor did he employ the sincere, straightforward style which had helped break the spell of the nineteenth-century novel. Deciding, as one critic puts it, to see if he too couldn't "dar gato por liebre" (pass off a cat as a rabbit), Azuela began experimenting generously with cubist techniques and published three novels which he later admitted were written with tongue in cheek.[8]

These three novels are *La Malhora* [Evil woman], *El desquite* [The retaliation], and *La luciérnaga* [The firefly], published respectively in 1923, 1925, and 1932 (though apparently this last work was written in 1926). These are often called hermetic novels, in contrast to the open and easily understood wo:ks which Azuela produced earlier. They are avant-garde, tinged with surrealism, at times difficult to comprehend.

La Malhora misses—though not by too much—being a fine novel. Certain things about it make it both interesting and important. It is one of the earliest of the Mexican novels to depict with stark realism and shattering pessimism the subhuman existence of degraded individuals in the poorest parts of Mexico City. When the protagonist, la Malhora, has sunk about as low as humans can, she is regenerated by an unstable doctor and is taken in by three overly pious women, until one day her past suddenly confronts her again and she reverts to type. Environment has played a determining and disastrous role in her life.

It is in the narrative techniques employed by Azuela that *La Malhora* holds the most interest for us. Here there is generous use of confused and unexpected images, elliptical sentences, tricky metaphors, single words expected to do the work of many. Yet the author's most significant innovation lies in his entering the subconscious thoughts of one of his characters. When the demented doctor indulges in an interior monologue, Azuela is anticipating by two decades the utilization of this and other techniques by Agustín Yáñez in his *Al filo del agua,* which (as we shall see later) is to take the Mexican novel around a sharp turn into new paths. Azuela's role as a precursor of the trend which now dominates the novel in Mexico, and elsewhere, is generally overlooked because it was but a momentary experiment on his part, one which found no echo in the style and technique of his fellow novelists until Yáñez came along.

Another unusual feature of *La Malhora* is that almost no one really understood its conclusion. On the final page la Malhora goes looking for her two mortal enemies, la Tapatía and Marcelo, who have been the cause of most of her grief, with the intent of killing them. When it appears that she is about to carry out her purpose, we come to the closing words of the story: "La Malhora talló dos cristales que corrigieran su astigmatismo mental."[9] This says that la Malhora ground two lenses to correct her mental astigmatism.

This puzzling finish confounded even the best critics for some time. Those who commented on it interpreted it as saying that she had indeed killed la Tapatía and Marcelo. After nearly twenty years of this guesswork, Azuela himself gave this clarification: La Malhora "saw clearly the true situation of her enemies, now old and beaten down by life, and she forgave them with the most profound contempt. She didn't kill either la Tapatía or Marcelo. Her vengeance was in scorning them."[10]

While *El desquite* is of small consequence, the last of these "untypical" Azuela novels, *La luciérnaga,* ranks high among his total output. In fact, it probably stands, along with *Los de abajo* and *Las tribulaciones de una familia decente,* as one of Azuela's three best works. *La luciérnaga* is a psychological study in some depth of three characters who, while they come through quite clearly as individuals, at the same time represent three rather common types in Mexican society.

José María personifies the miserliness and narrowness of one so self-centered and self-righteous in his provincial existence that he sees nothing of value in big-city life. His brother, Dionisio, is one tabbed by destiny for a lifetime of failure. He is a middle-class provincial who rushes to the metropolis completely confident of conquering, only to suffer unrelieved disaster. The lesson nevertheless is lost upon him. Conchita is the exemplification of the best in Mexican motherhood. Long-suffering, compassionate, and understanding, her strength and integrity serve to redeem the shortcomings of her husband, Dionisio, and her brother-in-law, José María. She is the strongest female figure in all the Azuela novels. Indeed, these three are among the most clearly depicted characters of the hundreds created by Mariano Azuela.

La luciérnaga is also a study in contrasts between the urban capital and the provincial town. In this it has a close kinship with *Las tribulaciones,* though the contrast here is more effective because it is in evidence from start to finish.

The story narrated in *La luciérnaga* is not complicated. On the death of their father the two brothers inherit a modest fortune. Despite the opposition of José María, Dionisio takes his wife and children to Mexico City, with the announced intention of giving his family a better education and of multiplying his fortune. But he proves a soft touch for the city slickers, who fleece him at every turn. As everything goes wrong, the reader is witness to the gradual degeneration of Dionisio—physically, economically, and morally. With the last of his money he buys an old bus and then, while under the influence of drugs, drives it into the side of a streetcar, killing some passengers and demolishing the bus.

It is this scene which opens the story, and Dionisio's subconscious thoughts and recollections as he lies stupefied fill in for us much of the background. Desperate now for means of feeding his family, Dionisio writes to José María for help. The story turns then to the stingy brother back in the little town of Cieneguilla. José María, a most complex personality, is dying of tuberculosis. He is withdrawn, and through his inner thoughts we see the aridness of his heart and his soul. He justifies his refusal to send any money by saying he can not contribute to Dionisio's sinful existence.

Things continue to go downhill for Dionisio's family in Mexico City. The oldest of the children, the teen-aged María Cristina, gets a job to help out—and also gets in with the wrong sort of people. During a wild night of orgy, María Cristina is killed. Dionisio too is becoming involved with a variety of highly questionable characters who turn him more and more toward the underworld. There seems to be an upturn in his fortunes when he lays hands on the hoard left by José María and opens a store, but again he fails. He invests heavily in a cheap tavern called La Noche Buena as a partner of la Generala, an overpowering sort of woman.

While this venture makes money, it also contributes to Dionisio's degeneracy, for he is soon a confirmed alcoholic and marijuana addict. At this point Sebastián, one of the children, becomes seriously ill. Conchita is distraught, but Dionisio is too wrapped up in La Noche Buena and too far down the ladder to be concerned. When the boy dies, Conchita, driven beyond the point of endurance, makes good her threat to take the remaining two children back to Cieneguilla.

The story now swings to her life in the provincial town, where her integrity, dignity, and self-sufficiency win the respect of all. One day the message reaches her that Dionisio (now fallen to depths not known before), has been stabbed and is near death. To the dismay of the townspeople, Conchita sells her things to buy tickets back to Mexico City ("I'm fulfilling my duty"). She and the children reach the hospital as Dionisio is being released. On seeing them, he smiles "without surprise, without emotion, without expression," and the story ends as he says "I had a hunch you would have to come back."[11]

The message of *La luciérnaga* has already been revealed in these lines referring to Conchita: "She is not just a mother; a mother can be a she-wolf, a hyena, a snake. She is the Christian wife who follows her companion, even if he is beset by sickness, by misery, by vice, or by crime itself. If the mission of the firefly is to make the night blacker with its tiny light, the firefly, by twinkling, fulfills its mission."[12]

La luciérnaga brings to a peak the obscure, hermetic style first attempted by Azuela in *La Malhora*. Here he has refined it and has it better under control. Actually, the probing of the subconscious and the use of interior monologue play a much larger role in this work than in *La Malhora*, further confirming Azuela as a precursor of Yáñez and the many who followed him. While Azuela later belittled his three experimental novels, the critics now are largely agreed that in writing them he achieved more than he realized.

It is perhaps most unfortunate that in the years between 1919 and 1937 the only novels which Mariano Azuela published were the three experimental works just mentioned, for these could have been some of his best productive years. If the five-year lapse between *Las tribulaciones* and *La Malhora* is attributable to his very human disappointment over the critics' failure to respond to his earlier works, it is more difficult to account for his silence in the latter years of this period. There is a seven-year lapse between the appearance of *El desquite* in 1925 and the publication of *La luciérnaga* in 1932 (even though Luis Leal and others assure us that this work was written around 1926),[13] and his next novel didn't come out until 1937. The nonproductive years after 1925 can't be a manifestation of the same disappointment, for the critics' silence was finally broken in that year.

Julio Jiménez Rueda, highly respected in Mexican letters and criticism in that day, published an article in the newspaper *El Universal* on December 20, 1924, entitled "Effeminacy in Mexican Literature." He bemoaned the absence of any vigorous national spirit in the Mexican literary efforts of that time. Five days later in the same newspaper Francisco Monterde, a colleague of Jiménez Rueda and equally respected, replied to the earlier article. Taking strong issue with it, Monterde insisted that virile Mexican literature was being written. The only problem, he said, was that the critics didn't recognize it and do justice to it. As an example, he cited Mariano Azuela, the novelist of the Revolution, as a powerful writer who never had received any attention. From that point the debate gained momentum and continued—with other literary figures joining in the discussion—until April 1925.[14]

By that time *El Universal*, gauging correctly the surge of interest generated by the debate, printed *Los de abajo* serially in its pages. There was instantaneous acceptance of Azuela's works. Thus Mariano Azuela was finally "discovered" by the literary public of Mexico and shortly thereafter in many other countries. Recognition and even fame came to *Los de abajo* and Azuela when the novel was almost ten years old and the author had already passed fifty-two.

By the time *La luciérnaga* appeared in 1932, Azuela was near the peak of his popularity and influence. Widely acclaimed as one of his very best efforts, this novel was his greatest literary and critical success. While Azuela continued to write, almost to his last day, none of his later works quite measures up to the best of his earlier production. All of these novels are interesting and a few (*El camarada Pantoja* and *Nueva burguesía*, particularly) approach the level of his finest work, but for the most part he was not quite the novelist he had been. After *La luciérnaga* he returned to his former style, in in which (as he himself tells us) he felt much more honest and comfortable.[15]

Mariano Azuela devoted nearly half a century to writing. In 1949 he was awarded the Premio Nacional de Literatura at the age of seventy-six, after many lesser writers had been so honored in previous years. He averaged just about one published work every two years, including the two novels published posthumously in 1955 and 1956 following the author's death in 1952 at the age of seventy-nine.

One is impressed by the fact that, despite a somewhat late start and a long dry spell (1919–37), Azuela remained the most prolific novelist of any consequence in twentieth-century Mexico.

Perhaps Azuela's outstanding trait as a novelist is his unswerving support of the little man, the common person, the underdog where-ever found, and his unceasing and scornful attack on venality, corruption, opportunism, and misused bureaucracy. His heroes practically without exception are the uprooted, the downtrodden, the maladjusted, the exploited, the well-intentioned turned sour or evil by environment. The fact that hardly any of these protagonists wind up on top was undoubtedly intended by Azuela as a searing indictment of the morals, motives, values, and practices of those who had benefitted by the Revolution and, like a tossed kitten, knew how to land on their feet in any situation, however ruthless their means.

From the publication of *Andrés Pérez, maderista* onward, Azuela carried on an implacable and running battle against the nonrevolutionaries and the counterrevolutionaries who infiltrated the Revolution and emasculated its principles and ideals. As the years rolled on, his contempt for these *sinvergüenzas* (shameless ones) grew and his assaults acquired a tone of bitterness which stained somewhat the superb satire and sarcasm he heaped upon these enemies of society almost from his earliest works. Azuela may have wearied of the battle but he never called a truce.

While it may be proper to contend that Mexico has seen better novelists (technically and stylistically, for example) in recent decades, it would seem that only Agustín Yáñez is in a position to challenge Azuela in terms of his influence in shaping the course of the Mexican novel. Both literally and figuratively Mariano Azuela brought the Mexican novel into the twentieth century. He gave it a new direction, new characteristics, a new life. The road he opened is traveled by so many followers that the old one is abandoned forever. It is probably true that if some of Azuela's best works were published today for the first time they would not create too much of a stir. He would be outflanked by the army of young writers who are devotees of the new type of novel featuring a variety of techniques and experimentation. But any writer must to be judged by the circumstances of his times and by the impact he exerts upon his contemporaries. By this yardstick Mariano Azuela remains one of the few and true beacons of Mexican literature.

NOTES TO CHAPTER 2

1. Mariano Azuela, *Obras completas* (Mexico City: Fondo de Cultura Económica, vols. I and II, 1958; vol. III, 1960), II, 769.

2. F. Rand Morton, *Los novelistas de la Revolución mexicana* (Mexico City, 1949), pp. 44–45.

3. *Obras completas*, I, 361–362, 368.

4. Ibid., pp. 416, 418.

5. Manuel Pedro González, *Trayectoria de la novela en México* (Mexico City, 1951), p. 163.

6. Morton, p. 52.

7. González, pp. 164–168.

8. Morton, pp. 52–53.

9. *Obras completas*, II, 977.

10. Quoted in Bernard M. Dulsey, "Azuela Revisited," *Hispania*, XXXV (1952), 332.

11. *Obras completas*, I, 667.

12. Ibid., p. 663.

13. Luis Leal, *Mariano Azuela, vida y obra* (Mexico City, 1961), p. 57.

14. John E. Englekirk, "The 'Discovery' of *Los de abajo*," *Hispania*, XVIII (1935), 53–62.

15. *Obras completas*, III, 1118.

THE NOVELS OF MARIANO AZUELA

María Luisa, 1907

Los fracasados, 1908

Mala yerba, 1909 (Translated into English as *Marcela: A Mexican Love Story*. New York: Farrar and Rinehart, 1932.)

Andrés Peréz, maderista, 1911

Sin amor, 1912

Los de abajo, 1915 (Translated into English as *The Underdogs*. New York: Brentano's, 1929; New American Library, 1963.)

Los caciques, 1917 (Translated into English as *The Bosses*. Berkeley: University of California Press, 1956.)
Las Moscas, 1918 (Translated into English as *The Flies,* Berkeley: University of California Press, 1956.)
Domitilo quiere ser diputado, 1918
Las tribulaciones de una familia decente, 1918 (Translated into English as *The Trials of a Respectable Family.* San Antonio: Principia Press of Trinity University, 1963.)
La Malhora, 1923
El desquite, 1925
La luciérnaga, 1932
El camarada Pantoja, 1937
San Gabriel de Valdivias, comunidad indígena, 1938
Regina Landa, 1939
Avanzada, 1940
Nueva burguesía, 1941
La marchanta, 1944
La mujer domada, 1946
Sendas perdidas, 1949
La maldición, 1955
Esa sangre, 1956

SELECTED STUDIES ON MARIANO AZUELA

Alegría, Fernando. *Breve historia de la novela hispanoamericana,* pp. 146–153.

Berler, Beatrice. "The Mexican Revolution as Reflected in the Novel." *Hispania,* XLVII (1964), 41–46.

Brushwood, John S. *Mexico in Its Novel,* pp. 166–172, 178–184, 218–220, 224–225.

———— and Rojas Garcidueñas, José. *Breve historia de la novela mexicana,* pp. 92–98.

Carter, Boyd G. "The Mexican Novel at Mid-Century." *Prairie Schooner,* XXVIII (1954), 143–156.

Dulsey, Bernard M. "The Mexican Revolution as Mirrored in the Novels of Mariano Azuela." *Modern Language Journal,* XXXV (1951), 382–386.

Englekirk, John E. "The 'Discovery' of *Los de abajo*." *Hispania,* XVIII (1935), 53–62.

González, Manuel Pedro. *Trayectoria de la novela en México,* pp. 108–199.

González de Mendoza, José María. "Mariano Azuela y lo mexicano." *Cuadernos Americanos,* año 11 (1952), no. 3, pp. 282–285.

Henricks, Frances Kellam, ed. & trans. "Introduction" to *Two Novels of the Mexican Revolution* (San Antonio, 1963), pp. xxi-xxvii.

Kercheville, Francis M. "El liberalismo en Azuela." *Revista Iberoamericana,* III (May 1941), 381–398.

Leal, Luis. *Mariano Azuela, vida y obra.*

Menton, Seymour. "La estructura épica de *Los de abajo* y un prólogo especulativo." *Hispania,* L (1967), 1001–1011.

Monterde, Francisco. "Mariano Azuela y su obra." Prologue to vol. I of *Obras completas* of Azuela, pp. vii-xxi.

Moore, Ernest R. "Novelists of the Mexican Revolution: Mariano Azuela." *Mexican Life,* August, 1940, pp. 21–28, 81–87.

Morton, F. Rand. *Los novelistas de la Revolución mexicana,* pp. 21–69.

Ocampo de Gómez, A.M., and Prado Velázquez, E., eds. *Diccionario de escritores mexicanos,* pp. 29–31.

Sánchez, Luis Alberto. *Proceso y contenido de la novela hispano-americana,* pp. 517–520.

Spell, Jefferson Rea. *Contemporary Spanish-American Fiction,* pp. 64–100.

Torres-Ríoseco, Arturo. *Grandes novelistas de la América Hispana,* vol. 1, 3–40.

Woolsey, A. W. "Los protagonistas de algunas novelas de Mariano Azuela." *Hispania,* XXIII (1940), 341–348.

Zum Felde, Alberto. *Indice crítico de la literatura hispanoamericana.* Vol. II: *La narrativa,* pp. 294–300.

The Novel of
the Mexican Revolution

DESPITE THE EXAMPLE SET BY MARIANO AZUELA FROM 1911 ONWARD, Mexico's writers were decidedly slow to embrace the theme of the Revolution. Not until the late twenties was there an upsurge in works about this shattering experience which shook Mexican life more than anything since the protracted struggle between Liberals and Conservatives in the middle of the nineteenth century. If this tardy flowering of the novel of the Mexican Revolution is surprising, it is equally a source of awe to observe the extent to which it dominates the literary scene in that country until around the mid-forties. Indeed, it has not yet disappeared entirely, for each year finds a few more titles added to the lengthy list. One indication of the importance of this outpouring is the fact that no history of Latin American literature fails to devote a section to the novel of the Mexican Revolution.

Some novelists go back to probe the conditions existing in Mexican society prior to the outbreak of the Revolution. A most notable example of this is *Al filo del agua* (*The Edge of the Storm*) by Agustín Yáñez, which may properly be classified as a novel of the Revolution but is also something very much more. But many—perhaps most—of these works represent the personal involvement of the authors in the revolutionary struggle. And many others have to do with the aftermath of the Revolution in its political, social, and economic implications and influences.

It is impossible to overlook a peculiar phenomenon with regard to the literature of the Mexican Revolution. I refer to the fact that almost every narrative account dealing with that upheaval, if it is not indisputably a short story, has been labeled a novel. It matters little that the work in question may be only fifty pages (or less) in length, or that it may be a book of personal memoirs or an auto-biographical account, or just a loosely connected series of episodes in a narrative pattern. Critics early began speaking of these efforts as "novels of the Revolution," and nearly all subsequent observers have accepted this designation.

To the question, "When is a novel not a novel?" the purist might be tempted to reply, "When it's a novel of the Mexican Revolution." This obviously is an exaggeration, for many of the works are legiti-mate novels, yet it is undeniable that many efforts have been classi-fied as novels which in another place and another time would scarcely have attained this designation. It is hard to understand while reading José Vasconcelos's brilliant memoirs how they can be considered novels. Yet the Peruvian critic Luis Alberto Sánchez assured us some years ago that the first two of these four volumes, *Ulíses criollo* [A Creole Ulysses], published in 1935, and *La tor-menta* [The storm], 1936, together constitute the greatest contem-porary Mexican novel.[1] And Mariano Azuela feels the same way: "However much it may be that Vasconcelos has not written novels, I regard him as the best novelist in Mexico. I judge his famous memoirs in four volumes to be novels and—may I be permitted the audacity—I regard as a novel his *Breve Historia de Mexico*."[2]

Some observers have also suggested that every novel written on Mexican life since 1910 deserves to be considered a novel of the Revolution, arguing that the Revolutionary Party has never loosed its grip on the seat of power since that year and so the aspects of Mexican life which these works treat are the direct product of the Revolution. While this clearly carries the point too far, it does give rise to the question of when the novel of the Revolution got its start and when it ended—if it has ended.

Chronologically speaking, the first novel about the Revolution, as we have already remarked, was Azuela's *Andrés Pérez, maderista*, published in 1911. Almost no other writer produced books on the Revolution until the late 1920s. When Martín Luis Guzmán brought forth in 1928 his two volumes of somewhat novelized personal memoirs titled *El águila y la serpiente* (*The Eagle and the Serpent*),

it was like the breaking of a dike. Works of all sorts about the Revolution began to appear in rapid-fire order, and until the mid-1940s
or thereabouts there was no cessation. In these two decades a host
of Mexican writers made their contribution to the growing collection
of novels of the Revolution. The list is long even when restricted to
the more prominent figures in this literary phenomenon: Gregorio
López y Fuentes, Rafael F. Muñoz, José Rubén Romero, José Vasconcelos, Nellie Campobello, José Mancisidor, Jorge Ferretis, Francisco L. Urquizo, Francisco Rojas González, Miguel N. Lira, Jesús
Goytortúa Santos, Mauricio Magdaleno, José Revueltas, and Agustín Yáñez. It could be extended, but to no purpose.

In my opinion the Revolutionary cycle can be regarded as having
come to a close with the publication in 1947 of *Al filo del agua* by
Agustín Yáñez. Definitely there are Revolutionary novels which
appeared a good deal later—for example, Juan Rulfo's *Pedro Páramo*
in 1955, and Carlos Fuentes's *La muerte de Artemio Cruz* (*The
Death of Artemio Cruz*) in 1962 (both of which along with Yáñez's
Al filo del agua will receive attention in upcoming chapters)—but
the Mexican novel takes such a clear turn after this epochal work
by Yáñez that the focus thereafter is rarely on the Revolution itself.

The most common characteristics of the novel of the Revolution
were pretty well established by Azuela and remained rather constant. The theme was the Revolution itself or its effects on the Mexican people in one way or another. The focus was semihistorical,
documentary, often personal. As a result, little imagination is found
in these works, to the extreme that their sameness of theme becomes
almost monotonous and surely constitutes a limitation if not an
outright defect.

Experimentation in the approach to the theme was even more
rare. Three distinct exceptions are Fuentes's *La muerte de Artemio
Cruz*, Yáñez's *Al filo del agua*, and José Rubén Romero's *La vida
inútil de Pito Pérez* (*The Futile Life of Pito Pérez*). Those knowl-
edgeable about Mexican literature may be surprised that I cast this
latter work as a novel of the Revolution. It is customary to speak of
it as a picaresque novel, which it certainly is. A close analysis of the
work, however, seems to me to reveal more reasons for calling it a
novel of the Revolution than can be adduced for many books com-

monly put in that category. In any case *Pito Pérez* is beyond argument a novel, and its protagonist most surely is launching a call to revolution.

La vida inútil de Pito Pérez, first published in 1938, is built around an actual flesh-and-blood village character who clearly fascinated Romero. The tempo and the orientation of life in his village of Santa Clara del Cobre can be likened to that created by Yáñez in *Al filo del agua*. Both towns are hermetic, ultraconservative, and religion-dominated. In each work the intent is to demonstrate the rigid, exceedingly pious outlook of the people and to spotlight the crying need for change. Yáñez adopts a lugubrious tone about it all and heightens his effect by repetiiton and lengthy probing into the inner conscience of many characters; Romero achieves somewhat the same effect by malicious humor, by a happy-go-lucky irreverence, and by contrasting his "rebel," Pito Pérez, with the rest of the townspeople. It should be noted at this point that José Rubén Romero is one of the most humorous of all Mexican novelists. Yáñez placed his novel in the last moments of the prerevolutionary days, while Romero has Pito's biography straddle the period of the Revolution as a military reality. Thus, in the final parts of Romero's novel when we see Pito Pérez embittered by the futility of his continuing one-man campaign against dehumanizing forces, we have to interpret it as Romero's backhanded slap at the Revolution, which has largely failed to change life in the rural villages.

As to style, structuring, and techniques, the Revolutionary novels are not too revolutionary. Following the example of Azuela, they tend to be terse, relatively brief, frequently colloquial in moments of conversation. Practically always they are lineal accounts which carry the story straight through from start to finish. The content or message takes precedence over all else to the detriment of the artistic ideal. The techniques which are to dominate the Mexican novel after the appearance of *Al filo del agua* are almost completely absent. Plot, as stated before, is usually subordinated to a narration of events, episodes, anecdotes, often revolving around the personal participation of the author in what is related.

In the works dealing with the Revolution itself, there is a visible—given the Mexican temperament, perhaps unavoidable—tendency toward "machismo," the he-man cult admired all over Latin America and particularly in Mexico. The principal historical figure in these narratives is Pancho Villa—no surprise at all since he much more than any other leader personifies the "machismo" type and is also the one with whom the masses can most easily relate. Villa absolutely dominates the Revolutionary output of both Martín Luis Guzmán and Rafael F. Muñoz, and he is at least a background figure whose presence is frequently felt in numerous works of various other authors.

Few people came to know Pancho Villa better than Martín Luis Guzmán. Honored now as the grand old man of Mexican letters (he was born in 1887) and always respected as one of the finest minds to espouse the Revolutionary cause, Guzmán also was endowed with more writing talent than many other novelists of the Revolution. At once an idealist and an activist, he attached himself to the Villa faction in the apparent conviction that the Villa campaign was the most viable and the least committed politically—thus, the most pliable too. Guzmán spent much time at Villa's side, eventually to become his adviser. He has left us numerous descriptions of Pancho Villa's appearance and actions, but none more penetrating, and devastating, than this symbolic interpretation of his personality:

> This man would not exist if the pistol didn't exist. The pistol is not only his tool of action: it is his fundamental instrument; the center of his work and his play; the constant expression of his intimate personality; his soul made substance. Between the fleshy concavity of which his index finger is capable and the rigid concavity of the trigger there is a relation which establishes the contact of being to being. On firing it will not be the pistol that fires, but he himself; the bullet will be coming from his own entrails when it leaves the sinister barrel. He and his pistol are one single thing. Whoever can count on one can count on the other, and vice versa. From his pistol have come, and will continue to come, his friends and his enemies.[3]

The fascination which Villa holds for Muñoz appears to rest on an emotional base and perhaps is best illustrated by the following lines from "El repatriado," one of Muñoz's numerous short stories of the Revolution. The *jefe* or leader in the story clearly is Villa, and the boy, Andrés, who falls under his hypnotic power could well be Muñoz himself.

His voice was indelible; what he said was never erased later. His gesture was like a compass: he pointed a route, forever. His look was like a mountain that falls upon and crushes one's will. Everything about him was an order: "You're going with me, for me you'll die."[4]

The one work by Martín Luis Guzmán which is undeniably a novel is *La sombra del caudillo* [The shadow of the dictator], published in Spain in 1929 during an extended period of exile there. This work, commonly thought of as one of the strongest novels against dictatorship yet to appear in Latin American literature, combines two critical moments in Mexican political history under the Revolution: the unsuccessful revolt of Adolfo de la Huerta against Obregón's government in 1923 and the ruthless extermination by the dictator Calles of a serious opposition threat in the persons of Generals Gómez and Serrano in 1928. All of the principal characters in the book represent prominent Mexican politicians of the day, so that anyone familiar with the Mexican scene of that time would have little difficulty in identifying most of them.[5] Later Guzmán himself divulged the model for each major character.[6] One observer shrewdly points out that the only unidentifiable character is also the only really honest man in the book, adding that "it is quite a commentary on the Calles regime that, when Guzmán needed an honest man, he had to invent him."[7]

Written in the heat of righteous anger and in frustration over what Guzmán believed to be the betrayal of the ideals of the Revolution (a situation which already had led him off to exile in Spain), *La sombra del caudillo* is a powerful and fast-moving account of a tragic effort to insist on democratic procedures aimed at unseating the dictator. Its defects are that it was written in much haste, with its theme eclipsing the artistic aim, and that it is too literally bound by the historical facts it interprets. The plot lacks creative imagination, a defect which indeed is visible in all of the works of Guzmán, who is superb as an observer, journalist, and analyst but lacks some of the primary instincts of a novelist.

Gregorio López y Fuentes, like Guzmán and Muñoz a long-time journalist, was considerably more prolific as a novelist than either of the other two. Of his dozen novels, several are specifically about the Revolution and at least one of them, *Tierra* [Land], published in 1932, merits enduring fame. Here he focuses on the agrarian aim of the Revolution and traces the course of the struggle for land through the 1910–20 fighting period. Because of its theme and historical setting, Emiliano Zapata (the prime figure in the agrarian movement) assumes a role of consequence in the story, yet neither Zapata nor anyone else emerges as a central character. López y Fuentes of course wanted it this way, so that the Revolution itself might be seen as the true protagonist. Aside from Zapata, the only prominent character is Antonio Hernández, who symbolizes both the plight of the Indian and the spirit of the Revolution. *Tierra* is a sombre, pessimistic work. Like so many other novels of its time, it expresses disillusionment with the Revolution by showing, as Azuela's novels did earlier, that the big landowners (the *patrones*) thwarted the aims of the movement by quickly changing sides and thus gaining control again on the local scene. Before the end of the novel Zapata has disappeared, murdered treacherously in 1919, and Antonio Hernández has been killed in the fighting.

A strong work which is primarily an *indigenista* novel and (almost automatically) a novel of social protest, *El resplandor* (*Sunburst*) by Mauricio Magdaleno, is also rightly called a novel of the Revolution. Magdaleno, recently Undersecretary of Education in the government of President Díaz Ordaz, has several other creditable works in his bibliography, but *El resplandor*, published in 1937, is generally considered his principal contribution to Mexican letters. In fact, it has been called "the best Mexican novel of the 1930s."[8] Though this is strong praise, it is rather well merited. Another observer declares it to be, regarded from the point of view of literary form, the best novel of the Revolution.[9] This may seem to be going too far, yet perhaps it is justified inasmuch as the qualifying phrase about its literary form and artistry tends to disqualify a considerable number of the entries right from the start.

El resplandor tells the usual story of a group of Indians who endure a dehumanized existence comprised of indignities, discrimination, deceit, exploitation, false hopes, broken promises, disillusionment, and the like. In this case it is the Otomí Indians (considered to be direct descendants of the Aztecs) whose village is San Andrés de la Cal, less than a hundred miles to the north of Mexico City. The failure of the Revolution to help these Indians is presented in direct fashion: the leader Cavazos makes big promises to them about better things and fails to deliver. Then he offers to take one of their young boys off to be educated, so that he can come back and give them effective leadership. This hope is cruelly dashed when the young man (a *mestizo,* or of mixed blood) simply merges into the white world, enters politics, and returns to San Andrés only to offer them the customary hollow promises of the politician.

The novel penetrates the Indian mind and temperament. Magdaleno is sensitive to the Indian past and realistic in finding the present just as unlikely to bring justice to the large and long-oppressed Indian segment of the Mexican population. This reality, almost uniformly presented in the *indigenista* novels, is a serious indictment of the Revolution from a different direction than that taken by Azuela and other novelists. The failure of the Revolution to improve effectively the lot of the Indian, at the same time that it purports to glorify the Indian's role in Mexico's past, is a serious business which the ruling party can scarcely blink away.

Magdaleno makes good use of flashbacks and stream-of-consciousness narration in *El resplandor.* The time gradually is approaching when Agustín Yáñez will pick up these two devices and, adding various others to his repertory, will turn the Mexican novel inside out with *Al filo del agua.*

An interesting offshoot of the novel of the Revolution is the so-called *cristero* novel, given this name because it refers to the revolt of Catholic elements who fought under the banner of Christ the King in the 1926–28 period. The regime of Plutarco Elías Calles (president from 1924 to 1928 and dictator until 1934) not only implemented all of the anticlerical provisions of the radical Mexican Constitution of 1917 but by decree made even more onerous the position of all religions and all religious groups. While theoretically indiscriminate in its attitude against organized religion, this campaign in reality was aimed directly at the power and influence of the Catholic Church.

The Catholic hierarchy and faithful were seriously divided as to the best means of confronting the situation, which they regarded as outright persecution of religion. Many felt that the only effective response was to take up arms, but the proponents of less-violent action prevailed for a time and declared the Church in Mexico to be on strike, suspending all public services in the churches around the nation. This did not, however, prevent the activists from initiating military response, which soon built into large-scale revolt, continuing with marked violence and bitterness until a truce was arranged in 1928.

The Cristero revolt quite naturally gave rise to a number of novels, though none of them achieved high literary status. Some were far too polemical or emotional to be good literature. Among the examples of this kind of writing we find *Héctor,* 1930, and *Jahel,* 1935, by Jorge Gram (pseudonym of a militant priest). Some think that *Los cristeros,* 1937, by José Guadalupe de Anda is the best of the lot, though others might prefer *Pensativa,* 1944, by Jesús Goytortúa Santos for its compelling plot and swift-moving narrative. And Fernando Robles' *La virgen de los cristeros,* 1934, is above the ordinary. Reminiscent of the earlier memoirs of the Revolution in novelized form is *Entre las patas de los caballos* [Under the horses' hooves], 1953, by Luis Rivero del Val, in which he builds the story around his own experiences as one of the top echelon of the Cristero movement. Other novels, some of distinctly higher quality, use the Cristero revolt more as a backdrop. Examples of this are *Nayar,* 1941, by Miguel Angel Menéndez and *Los recuerdos del porvenir* (*Recollections of Things to Come*), 1963, by Elena Garro.

The novel of the Mexican Revolution, for all its accumulation of titles, authors, and approaches, may not have produced many truly outstanding works until 1947 and later, yet its importance in the evolution of the novel in that country is undeniable and indeed crucial. It gave a special identity to the Mexican novel, it turned the literary lens upon the national life, made a clean break with the form, content, and inspiration of the nineteenth-century novel, and fomented a climate of openness which made possible the later advances that have brought the present-day novel into the mainstream of world literature.[10]

NOTES TO CHAPTER 3

1. Luis Alberto Sánchez, *Proceso y contenido de la novela hispanoamericana* (Madrid, 1953), p. 521.

2. Mariano Azuela, *Cien años de novela mexicana*, in *Obras completas*, III (Mexico City, 1960), 702.

3. Martín Luis Guzmán, *El águila y la serpiente* (Madrid, 1932), II, 53.

4. Rafael F. Muñoz, *Si me han de matar mañana* (Mexico City, 1934), p. 185.

5. Luis Leal, "*La sombra del caudillo*, roman a clef," *Modern Language Journal*, XXXVI (1952), 16–21.

6. Emmanuel Carballo, *Diecinueve protagonistas de la literatura mexicana del siglo XX* (Mexico City, 1965), p. 74.

7. John S. Brushwood, *Mexico in Its Novel* (Austin, 1966), p. 202.

8. Ibid., p. 218.

9. F. Rand Morton, *Los novelistas de la Revolución mexicana* (Mexico City, 1949), p. 212.

10. In 1967 the Chilean critic Luis Harss and Barbara Dohmann published a study of the entry of the Latin American novel into the main channel of world literature, giving the English version of their work the title *Into the Mainstream* (New York: Harper & Row).

A SELECTION OF NOVELS OF THE MEXICAN REVOLUTION

(Excluding the Works of Mariano Azuela)

Almanza, Héctor Raúl (1912)   *Detrás del espejo*, 1962
Anda, José Guadalupe de (1880–1950) *Los cristeros*, 1937
                                       Los bragados, 1942
Campobello, Nellie (1909–69)   *Cartucho*, 1931

Dávila, José María (1897) — *Yo también fui revolucionario,* 1945

Ferretis, Jorge (1902–62) — *Tierra caliente,* 1935
Cuando engorda el Quijote, 1937

Garro, Elena (1920) — *Los recuerdos del porvenir,* 1963 (Translated into English as *Recollections of Things to Come.* Austin: University of Texas Press, 1969.)

Goytortúa Santos, Jesús (1910) — *Pensativa,* 1945
Lluvia roja, 1947

Gram, Jorge (1889–1950) — *Héctor,* 1930
Jahel, 1935

Guzmán, Martín Luis (1887) — *El águila y la serpiente,* 1928 (Translated into English as *The Eagle and the Serpent.* New York: Knopf, 1930; Garden City: Dolphin Books, 1965.)
La sombra del caudillo, 1929
Memorias de Pancho Villa, 4 vol., 1938–40 (Translated into English as *Memoirs of Pancho Villa.* Austin: University of Texas Press, 1965.)

Lira, Miguel N. (1905–61) — *La escondida,* 1948
Mientras la muerte llega, 1958

López y Fuentes, Gregorio (1897–1966) — *Campamento,* 1931
Tierra, 1932
Mi general, 1934

Magdaleno, Mauricio (1906) — *El resplandor,* 1937 (Translated into English as *Sunburst.* New York: Viking Press, 1944.)
La tierra grande, 1949

Mancisidor, José (1894–1956) — *La asonada,* 1931

Menéndez, Miguel Angel (1905) — *Nayar,* 1940 (Translated into English with the same title. New York: Farrar & Rinehart, 1942.)

Muñoz, Rafael F. (1899) — *¡Vámonos con Pancho Villa!,* 1931
Se llevaron el cañón para Bachimba, 1941

Ocampo, María Luisa (1905) — *Bajo el fuego,* 1947

Quirozz, Alberto (1907)	*Cristo Rey o la persecución*, 1952
	Lupe Fusiles, 1957
Revueltas, José (1914)	*El luto humano*, 1943 (Translated into English as *The Stone Knife*. New York: Reynal & Hitchcock, 1947.)
Rivero del Val, Luis (1909)	*Entre las patas de los caballos*, 1953
Robles, Fernando (1897)	*La virgen de los cristeros*, 1934
Rojas González, Francisco (1904–51)	*La negra Angustias*, 1944
Romero, José Rubén (1890–1952)	*Desbandada*, 1934
	Mi caballo, mi perro y mi rifle, 1936
	La vida inútil de Pito Pérez, 1938 (Translated into English as *The Futile Life of Pito Perez*. Englewood Cliffs, N.J.: Prentice-Hall, 1967.)
Spota, Luis (1925)	*La pequeña edad*, 1964
Traven, B. (1890–1969)	*La rebelión de los colgados*, 1938 (Translated into English as *The Rebellion of the Hanged*. New York: Knopf, 1952.)
	El General: Tierra y libertad, 1967
Urquizo, Francisco L. (1891–1969)	*Tropa vieja*, 1943
	Fui soldado de levita de esos de caballería, 1967
Vera, Agustín (1889–1946)	*La revancha*, 1930

SELECTED GENERAL STUDIES ON THE NOVEL OF THE MEXICAN REVOLUTION

Alegría, Fernando. *Breve historia de la novela hispanoamericana.*
———. *Historia de la novela hispanoamericana.*
Anderson Imbert, Enrique. *Historia de la literatura hispanoamericana.* Vol. II.
Aub, Max. *Guía de narradores de la Revolución Mexicana.*

Azuela, Mariano. *Cien años de novela mexicana.*

Berler, Beatrice. "The Mexican Revolution as Reflected in the Novel." *Hispania,* XLVII (March, 1964), 41-46.

Brushwood, John S. *Mexico in Its Novel.*

———— and Rojas Garcidueñas, José. *Breve historia de la novela mexicana.*

Carballo, Emmanuel. *Diecinueve protagonistas de la literatura mexicana del siglo XX.*

Carter, Boyd G. "The Mexican Novel at Mid-Century." *Prairie Schooner,* XXXVIII (1954), 143–156.

Castro Leal, Antonio, ed. General introduction, chronology, history, and prologues to *La novela de la Revolución,* 2 vols.

Gamboa de Camino, Berta. "The Novel of the Mexican Revolution," in *Renascent Mexico* (New York: Covici-Friede, 1935).

Gómez-Gil, Orlando. *Historia crítica de la literatura hispanoamericana.*

González, Manuel Pedro. *Trayectoria de la novela en México.*

Henry, Elizabeth M. "Revolution as Mexican Novelists See It." *Hispania,* XV (1932), 423–436.

McManus, Beryl J.M. "La técnica del nuevo realismo en la novela mexicana de la Revolución," in *Memoria del IV Congreso del Instituto Internacional de Literatura Iberoamericana* (Havana, 1949).

Martínez, José Luis. *Literatura mexicana, siglo XX, 1910–1949.*

Moore, Ernest R. *Bibliografía de novelistas de la Revolución Mexicana.*

Morton, F. Rand. *Los novelistas de la Revolución Mexicana.*

Ocampo de Gómez, Aurora Maura, and Prado Velázquez, Ernesto, eds. *Diccionario de escritores mexicanos.*

Sánchez, Luis Alberto. *Proceso y contenido de la novela hispano-americana.*

Uslar Pietri, Arturo. *Breve historia de la novela hispanoamericana.*

Valadés, Edmundo and Leal, Luis. *La Revolución y las letras.*

Zum Felde, Alberto. *Indice crítico de la literatura hispanoamericana: La narrativa.*

SELECTED STUDIES ON PRINCIPAL NOVELISTS OF THE MEXICAN REVOLUTION

(Excluding Mariano Azuela)

Martín Luis Guzmán (1887)

Abreu Gómez, Ermilo. "Martín Luis Guzmán, crítica y bibliografía," *Hispania,* XXXV (1952), 70–73.

————. "Martin Luis Guzmán." *Revista Interamericana de Bibliografía,* IX (1959), 119–143.

————. *Martín Luis Guzmán: Un mexicano y su obra.*

————. *El pensamiento político de Martín Luis Guzmán.*

Alegría, Fernando. *Breve historia de la novela hispanoamericana,* pp. 153–157.

Aub, Max. *Guía de narradores de la Revolución Mexicana,* pp. 39–43.

Brushwood, John S. *Mexico in Its Novel,* pp. 200–203.

Carballo, Emmanuel. *Diecinueve protagonistas de la literatura mexicana del siglo XX,* pp. 63–99.

Castro Leal, Antonio, ed. *La novela de la Revolución,* I, 159–161.

González, Manuel Pedro. *Trayectoria de la novela en México,* pp. 200–214.

Houck, Helen Phipps. "Las obras novelescas de Martín Luis Guzmán," *Revista Iberomericana,* III (1941), 139–158.

Moore, Ernest. "Novelists of the Mexican Revolution: Martín Luis Guzmán," *Mexican Life,* September, 1940, pp. 23–25.

Morton, F. Rand. *Los novelistas de la Revolución mexicana,* pp. 115–140.

Ocampo de Gómez, Aurora Maura, and Prado Velázquez, Ernesto, eds. *Diccionario de escritores mexicanos,* pp. 166–168.

Stanton, Ruth. "Martín Luis Guzmán's Place in Modern Mexican Literature." *Hispania,* XXVI (1943), 136–138.

Gregorio López y Fuentes (1897–1966)

Alegría, Fernando. *Breve historia de la novela hispanoamericana,* pp. 163–170.

Brushwood, John S. *Mexico in Its Novel,* pp. 209–211, 215–217, 231–232.

Castro Leal, Antonio, ed. *La novela de la Revolución,* II, 137–139.

González, Manuel Pedro. *Trayectoria de la novela en México,* pp. 249–267.

Holmes, Henry A. and Bara, Walter A. Introduction to López y Fuentes's *Tierra* (Boston: Ginn and Co., 1949), pp. ix–xxx.

Mate, Hubert. "Social Aspects of Novels by López y Fuentes and Ciro Alegría." *Hispania,* XXXIX (1956), 287–292.

Moore, Ernest. "Novelists of the Mexican Revolution: Gregorio López y Fuentes." *Mexican Life,* November, 1940, pp. 23–25, 52–60.

Morton, F. Rand. *Los novelistas de la Revolución mexicana,* pp. 95–114.

Ocampo de Gómez, Aurora Maura, and Prado Velázquez, Ernesto, eds. *Diccionario de escritores mexicanos,* pp. 203–204.

Rafael F. Muñoz (1899)

Aub, Max. *Guía de narradores de la Revolución Mexicana,* pp. 43–44.

Brushwood, John S. *Mexico in Its Novel,* pp. 206–207, 225.

Carballo, Emmanuel. *El cuento mexicano del siglo XX,* pp. 39–40.

———. *Diecinueve protagonistas de la literatura mexicana del siglo XX,* pp. 265–279.

González, Manuel Pedro. *Trayectoria de la novela en México,* pp. 278–282.

Langford, Walter M. "The Short Story in Mexico." *Kentucky Foreign Language Quarterly,* I (1954), 52–59.

Martínez, José Luis. *Literatura mexicana siglo XX, 1910–1949,* I, 45–46.

Morton, F. Rand. *Los novelistas de la Revolución mexicana,* pp. 141–160.

Ocampo de Gómez, Aurora Maura and Prado Velázquez, Ernesto, eds. *Diccionario de escritores mexicanos,* pp. 245–246.

José Rubén Romero (1890–1952)

Alegría, Fernando. *Breve historia de la novela hispanoamericana,* pp. 156–163.

Arce, David N. *José Rubén Romero: Conflicto y logro de un romanticismo.*

Arreola Cortés, Raúl. "José Rubén Romero: vida y obra." *Revista Hispánica Moderna,* XII (1946), 7–34.

Aub, Max. *Guía de narradores de la Revolución Mexicana,* pp. 47–48.

Brushwood, John S. *Mexico in Its Novel,* pp. 211–213, 222–224.

Castagnaro, R. Anthony. "Rubén Romero and the Novel of the Mexican Revolution." *Hispania,* XXXVI (1953), 300–304.

González, Manuel Pedro. *Trayectoria de la novela en México,* pp. 223–248.

Iduarte, Andrés. "José Rubén Romero, retrato." *Revista Hispánica Moderna,* XII (1946), 1–6.

Koons, John F. *Garbo y donaire de Rubén Romero.*

Moore, Ernest. "José Romero: Bibliography." *Revista Hispánica Moderna,* XII (1946), 35–40.

———. "Novelists of the Mexican Revolution: José Rubén Romero." *Mexican Life,* October, 1940, pp. 21–25, 43.

Morton, F. Rand. *Los novelistas de la Revolución mexicana,* pp. 71–94.

Ocampo de Gómez, Aurora Maura, and Prado Velázquez, Ernesto, eds. *Diccionario de escritores mexicanos,* pp. 336–338.

Phillips, Ewart E. "The Genesis of Pito Pérez." *Hispania,* XLVII (1964), 698–702.

Stanton, Ruth. "José Rubén Romero, costumbrista of Michoacán." *Hispania,* XXIV (1941), 423–428.

Woodbridge, Hensley C. and Dulsey, Bernard. "José Rubén Romero (1890–1952)." *Modern Language Journal,* XXXVI (1952), 335–338.

4

B. Traven, Mystery Man

ON WEDNESDAY EVENING, MARCH 26, 1969, THE NEWS MEDIA BROAD-
cast word of the death in Mexico City of B. Traven, who for nearly
half a century had been the mystery man of Mexican letters. My
first thought on hearing the news was that Traven had remained
faithful to himself, that is, he did indeed finish his life without
divulging his true identity, which surely is one of the best kept
literary secrets of all time.

Only four months before, I stood on the sidewalk across the street
from his modest home just a couple of blocks off Mexico City's great
boulevard, the Paseo de la Reforma, pondering the life, achievements, and attitudes of this foreigner who became more Mexican
than most Mexicans and who simply wanted to be left alone. Known
to literally millions of readers in more than thirty languages, he
shunned publicity to the end and insisted that he was someone else
rather than the novelist himself.

As I stood there, perhaps hoping subconsciously that this famed
enigmatic figure would emerge so that I might at least have the
chance to see him in person, there ran quickly through my mind a
melange of what I knew about him and his strange but fascinating
career in literature. I would have welcomed a chance to chat with
him, but the thought of trying to reach him was not seriously enter-
tained. After all, the persons who had managed to interview him
through the years numbered hardly a handful, and in no case had
he acknowledged his identity as B. Traven but doggedly insisted
that he was merely a close friend named Hal Croves, a cover-up he
began using apparently in the 1940s. Now nearing eighty years of

age and quite hard of hearing, he still showed no willingness to remove his mask and talk, as was discovered in 1966 by a person who perhaps got as close to him as anyone could.[1]

It all began back in June, 1925, when a Berlin newspaper started publishing in serial form a short novel called *The Cotton-Pickers* by an unknown author with the name of B. Traven. The setting was in Mexico, and the author's realistic approach to the subject aroused the interest of an editor of a socialist publishing house, Buchergilde Gutenberg (Gutenberg Book Guild), said to be the world's first successful book club. He managed to contact Traven by letter in Mexico, asking for the right to print *The Cotton-Pickers* in book form. Traven was then engaged in preparing a longer version of this work and replied that it would be better for them to publish another novel which he already had in finished form, *The Death Ship*. Traven said it was in English but that he would have it translated into German in thirty days. This book, which appeared in 1926, is one of his two novels without a Mexican setting and is considered by some Traven's finest work.

The Death Ship is a strongly realistic and convincing story, widely regarded as a classic novel of the sea. An American seaman named Gales (who also narrates other Traven stories) misses his ship in Antwerp and is left without any papers. Since he can't prove his identity, he becomes a sort of man without a country. He moves about Europe, pushed from one country to another, for no nation will allow him to stay. Finally, in Spain, he lands a job on the S.S. *Yorikke*, a so-called "death ship." His sufferings, along with the rest of the crew, are vivid and depressing, relieved only by Traven's frequent digressions on a wide variety of subjects: the causes of war, customs officers, nationalism, etc. The *Yorikke* is hijacked by another death ship and the wretched struggle goes on until death itself intervenes.

In 1927 appeared *The Treasure of the Sierra Madre*, (from which one of Hollywood's great movies was to be made two decades later), and the next year saw the publication of a book of short stories. Also in 1928 Traven brought out a travel book about Mexico. The following year witnessed the appearance of no fewer than three of his novels: *The Bridge in the Jungle*, *The White Rose*, and the final

version of *The Cotton-Pickers. The Carreta* came out in 1930 and
Government in 1931.

All of these works had a prompt and wide acceptance among the
German reading public. *The Death Ship* alone quickly sold over
200,000 copies. But with the advent of the Hitler regime the circulation of Traven's books in Nazi Germany halted. He refused to let
his books be printed under the Nazi rule and the Nazis banned all
of Traven's works. Editions were then hurried into print in most
other European countries. One source reports that *The Death Ship*
sold 1,650,000 copies by April, 1935, in the Soviet Union alone.[2]

It is worth pausing a moment to remind ourselves what type of
book we are talking about that had such splendid success in the
book stalls—regardless of whether the Russian sales were 50,000
copies or the stated 1,650,000. Traven's works are not light reading,
nor pleasant. There is almost no love interest in any of his stories
and practically no sex. They are largely devoid of humor, except
sometimes of a biting, satirical type. Besides, Traven believes in
frequent digressions wherein he strikes out at one or another of a
long list of pet peeves. His style is harsh, often disjointed, yet
remarkably effective.

Traven is a novelist with a cause, the cause of the common man.
He writes always of what he knows, and it is obvious that he feels
deeply the daily problems and the fate of his characters. In fact, we
can say he achieves a rather perfect spiritual empathy with the
persons whose lives he manipulates realistically and convincingly in
his novels, whether he is dealing with farm laborers (*The Cotton-
Pickers*), workers in the oil fields (*The White Rose*), sailors (*The
Death Ship*), or Indian woodcutters in the forests of Chiapas (*The
Rebellion of the Hanged*). In every case Traven shares in their
sufferings and usually compels the reader to embrace a strongly
partisan stance in favor of the downtrodden.

A striking authenticity and tremendous respect for human dignity
(especially when it's being trampled) mark the Traven novels but
that isn't all. They are also slanted novels, truly revolutionary and
heavy with political implications. They seem to come from the pen
of a convinced socialist who espouses Marxist—though not communist—doctrine. Surely part of Traven's early success in Germany can

be ascribed to the popularity in that epoch of proletarian novels. In comparison with the German efforts Traven's works are more sophisticated and reach a higher level of art and of appeal by virtue of his talent for introducing effective variations on the old theme of the class struggle.

Interestingly none of the Traven novels were published in either the United States or—ironically—even in Mexico prior to 1933, despite their considerable success for nearly a decade in Europe. In fact, a few of his works have not yet appeared in Mexican or American editions, even though there have been several hundred editions of his books all told.[3] The generally poor acceptance U.S. readers have customarily given to proletarian novels is a partial explanation for this. However, as Charles Henry Miller, a dedicated student of the Traven case, has pointed out, "few living authors can equal Traven's record of four decades of sustained popularity and critical acceptance with so many readers in so many languages and nations."[4]

In 1932 Alfred A. Knopf, the New York publisher, heard about B. Traven for the first time while in Berlin on business. Asking the editors of Buchergilde Gutenberg for information about this best-selling author, Knopf was told that they knew little more than his name and that he sent his manuscripts from Mexico. Traven declined to give them data for publicity purposes. Indeed, once when they asked for a photo, he sent them a picture of several hundred people and said that he was somewhere in the crowd! It was a typical flash of sardonic Traven humor.

After some time Knopf succeeded in contacting Traven by mail and asked for the right to bring out American editions of some of his books. Traven replied that he didn't want his books to be published in the United States. That seemed to end the matter, but a little over a year later Traven wrote to Knopf saying that he had changed his mind. Putting two and two together, we can reasonably assume (in the Traven case you must remember that we are assuming a good part of the time) that the cause for this change of heart was the loss of the German market resulting from his differences with the Nazis. All at once our reluctant author discovered that he could not afford to spurn new editors.

Even so, the agreement drawn up between Traven and Knopf

specified that there be no blurbs on the book jackets, no publicity about Traven, and a true minimum of advertising. In one of his letters to Knopf, Traven said that "an author should have no other biography than his books."[5] He is also quoted as having said, "If a writer, who he is and what he is, can not be recognized by his works, either his books are worthless, or he himself is."[6]

The American market did not respond to Traven's books in the same manner as the Germans and other European readers. A Knopf representative revealed that up to 1938 only 3,288 copies had been sold of *The Death Ship* and just 2,692 copies of *The Treasure of the Sierra Madre*.[7] However, after the latter story attracted Hollywood's attention and in 1948 was made into a successful film (although Traven was given only $5000 for the movie rights), a new paperback edition of *Treasure* was published and quickly sold over 400,000 copies.[8] Traven's widow, the charming Rosa Elena Luján, assures me that the sales of the U.S. editions of this work eventually reached a million and a half copies.

When Hitler took over in Germany the Buchergilde Gutenberg moved to Zurich, Switzerland, and there continued bringing out new works by Traven: *The March to Caobaland*, 1933; *The Rebellion of the Hanged* and *Die Troza*, 1936; *The Creation of the Sun and the Moon* (a Tzeltal Indian myth), also in 1936; *General from the Jungle*, 1937. After a long silence, Traven published *Macario* in 1949 and eleven years later brought out *Aslan Norval*.

Although Traven wrote, or at least published, almost nothing from the beginning of World War II until 1960, except for a number of movie scripts, critical interest and attempts to penetrate his mystery continued at a lively clip. Occasionally would come word of someone who had managed to enter into correspondence with him, and from the reports of these contacts emerged bits of information, albeit at times confusing and puzzling if not downright contradictory.

In one letter to H. W. Schwartz, a book dealer in Milwaukee, Traven protested that his first name was not Bruno.[9] This denial was provoked by the fact that he was commonly referred to as Bruno Traven, apparently because Bruno Dressler, director of the Buchergilde Gutenberg, once commented that the *B* of B. Traven probably stood for Bruno.

Throughout the years Traven himself insisted that his identity was of little consequence and that his works were really all that mattered. While no one can argue very strongly against this attitude, given human nature it is not surprising that the mystery became a challenge picked up by countless curious persons around the world. The matter was kept alive for forty years by a ceaseless stream of articles and reports in which conjecture and guesswork usually played the major part. And yet, just as there is nearly always some wheat to be found with the chaff, certain bits of information about the elusive figure of Traven did emerge from the efforts of all the amateur sleuths.

The attempts to unmask Traven turned in two directions, one concerned with establishing the physical identity of the person in Mexico who wrote under the name of Traven and the other determined to find out who Traven had been before he came to Mexico in 1922. While we know now that a few of the "detectives" did occasionally uncover some facts out of Traven's past and were able to make some correct guesses, Traven himself never acknowledged that they might be close to the mark. He endeavored to the last to preserve his anonymity and to insist on his right to privacy. As far as I know, his case is unparalleled in modern literary annals.

The physical identity of Traven was effectively settled in 1948, though some doubt always remained because Traven admitted nothing. This success was achieved by Luis Spota, then a very young reporter for the magazine *Mañana,* who since has become one of Mexico's most prominent novelists. It grew out of the filming of *The Treasure of the Sierra Madre.* The director John Huston contacted Traven by letter and arranged to meet him in Mexico City to discuss the proposed movie. A "tiny, thin man with gray hair" kept the appointment, giving the name of Hal Croves and saying that he was secretary and translator for Traven, who would not be able to meet with Huston. Croves was hired by Huston as a technical advisor and was on hand during most of the ten weeks of shooting location scenes in Mexico in 1947. Several things combined to convince Huston that Hal Croves in fact was the author B. Traven.

During this time Croves refused to be photographed, but someone snapped a picture of him without his realizing it. This photo, when compared with a known picture of Traven (taken in Chiapas in 1926) indicated strongly that Croves and Traven were one and the same person. Humphrey Bogart (who starred in the film with Tim Holt and Huston's father, Walter) was shown the 1926 photo of Traven and at once identified him as Hal Croves. Both *Life* and *Time,* in reviewing the film version of *Treasure* on February 2, 1948, mentioned that Croves apparently was Traven. A few weeks later (on March 15) each of these magazines printed a letter to the editor from Hal Croves in which he heatedly denied he was Traven.

The editor of *Mañana* told Spota he would be a great reporter if he found out who Traven really was. Spota undertook the assignment with zest, determination, and ingenuity. For weeks he tracked down leads, made shrewd guesses, persuaded—even bribed—various persons to make available to him records and materials of a confidential sort (bank statements, personal mail, etc.). The pursuit finally paid off. Learning that Croves had repaid a $100 loan with a personal check, and that Traven was supposed to be living somewhere around Acapulco, Spota bribed persons in Acapulco banks to check the accounts of all Americans in search of the $100 check.

When the check was uncovered, Spota found it had been written by Berick Torsvan, identified as being connected with a second-rate garden restaurant. Checking with Mexican immigration authorities, Spota got copies of the vital records of Torsvan, including Form 14 for Registry of Foreigners, dated July 12, 1930, which said that his true name was Berick Traven Torsvan and that he was born in Chicago of Swedish parents on May 3, 1890. Next, Spota bribed a servant to let him read some of Torsvan's mail. After that he had no doubt that Torsvan was Croves and Croves was Traven.

Spota then went to the restaurant El Parque Cachú to talk with the person who was known locally as "el gringo." For five hours he conversed with the unwilling and confused Torsvan, who never directly admitted his identity but did let slip a few revealing items. Spota's sensational "exposé" of B. Traven (seventeen pages long) appeared in *Mañana* on August 7, 1948. Though for twenty years more Torsvan would admit only that he was Croves and not Traven, Spota's article did reveal substantial information relative to the background and identity of the mysterious B. Traven.

But there were persons who, while perhaps content to accept the fact that Traven was masquerading under the name of Hal Croves, did not believe at all that in earlier years he was simply an unknown named Berick Torsvan from Chicago. These persons, searching in another direction, were convinced that Traven had lived in Germany during and just after World War I under the name of Ret Marut. It was known that Marut started a socialist newspaper, *Der Zeigelbrenner* [The brickmaker], which regularly printed violent polemics against militarism, nationalism, and reactionary tendencies in German politics. He was deeply involved in the short-lived Bavarian Socialist Republic, and on its overthrow in May, 1919, he was arrested. Under sentence to be shot, Ret Marut escaped at the last moment and was never seen thereafter. Prominent among the researchers who identified Traven with Marut are Leopold Spitzegger, Manfred George, Rolf Recknagel, and Judy Stone. For the most part, they maintained that he was born in 1882, and they tended to bypass the Torsvan connection.

Through the gracious cooperation of Rosa Elena Luján, we now know that Berick Torsvan, Ret Marut, B. Traven, and Hal Croves were all the same person. Born in Chicago in 1890, Traven was quite young when he moved with his parents to England and later to Germany. Here he became an actor for a time. Subsequently, he founded *Der Zeigelbrenner* and was deeply involved in the Bavarian Socialist Republic. On escaping his death sentence, he wandered across several European countries, without papers, until he finally signed on as a crewman of a "death ship" out of Spain. As already stated, he reached Mexico in 1922. The publication in Berlin in 1925 of *The Cotton-Pickers* launched his amazing and significant literary career.

The circumstances just summarized answer the question of why Traven was so determined to shield his identity and his background. After all, when his books began appearing in Germany, Ret Marut was still a hunted man and so he couldn't comply with the Book Guild's request for "just a little biography." Having entered Mexico illegally, neither did he want to be identified as Berick Traven Torsvan. In fact, he didn't want to be identified at all. And so he devised the rather logical pen name of B. Traven.

The above reasons alone would not account for Traven's enduring determination to avoid publicity and identification. After a time, when the worry over his one-time death sentence was gone and he had become a naturalized Mexican citizen, he could easily have owned up to his true identity. But Traven by nature truly wanted to be left alone. This desire was completely genuine rather than a pose, and it was not a manifestation of extreme shyness, as was claimed by John Huston following his contact with Traven during the filming of *The Treasure of the Sierra Madre:*

> Traven is a proud man who has retired from active participation in human affairs. In contact with people he disintegrates and becomes ridiculous. Knowing this, his desire to keep the name of Traven free from scorn leads him to disguise himself as somebody else.[10]

Added to the long-time mystery over Traven's identity is another question which likewise finds the experts divided. This is the matter of whether B. Traven has a proper claim to a place in Mexican literature. A number of critics of Mexican literature pass him over without a word, apparently because he was not born in Mexico and because all his works were published originally in German. These would seem to be valid reasons, but the case on the other side is even stronger. Traven lived nearly half a century in Mexico; he held Mexican citizenship from 1951 onward; practically everything he wrote had its setting in Mexico; and no writer, Mexicans included, has better understood the *campesino* of that country or defended his cause in more fiery manner.

The editors of the *Diccionario de escritores mexicanos* acknowledge Traven's position in Mexican letters by saying that "his books . . . give him the right to take a place as a Mexican author through the depth with which he has treated and dramatized a most important aspect of the social reality of the country."[11] The noted Peruvian critic, Luis Alberto Sánchez, says that for him Traven is *the* novelist of the Mexican Revolution, even though he was not Mexican by birth or tongue. Sánchez adds that Traven is the most complete, profound, broad, tense, and keen novelist of the Revolution.[12] And the colorful Cuban, Manuel Pedro González, states flatly that

"Traven is an authentic Mexican novelist and Mexico ought to feel honored and proud to proclaim him as such."[13] I would only add that B. Traven is, indeed, as much Mexican as the vast majority of the Mexican-born novelists and that to deny him his place in the history and development of the Mexican novel in the twentieth century is unjustified.

It is time, then, to turn our attention away from Traven the man and give consideration to Traven the writer. It is interesting to note that his first published novel, *The Death Ship*, is not about Mexico at all and that the next one, *The Treasure of the Sierra Madre*, is set in Mexico but tells the story of three American adventurers. Thereafter, when Traven had adjusted to Mexican life and had found in the plight of the simple *campesino* the cause to which he would devote the rest of his writings, he poured out a series of works which have no exact counterpart in Mexican literature in terms of interpreting with understanding and compassion the hardships and injustices which fill the lives of the *campesinos*.

The Treasure of the Sierra Madre is just the timeless story of partners who strike it rich and then fall to quarreling among themselves, with violent results. Dobbs and Curtin, two American wanderers down on their luck, meet up in Tampico with an old prospector named Howard. The latter convinces them he knows the whereabouts of a fabulous mine, and the three pool their scanty resources and set forth. They find the mine and have a load worth a fortune ready to bring out when complications arise in the form of unfriendly Indians, another American who stumbles in and demands a cut, and finally bandits. The partnership founders on the shoals of avarice and distrust, with Dobbs finally cornering all the gold only to fall victim to bandits in search of hides. They kill Dobbs but scatter the gold on the ground thinking that it is merely dirt. The surviving partners on discovering this can only sit and laugh ironically. What we have in *Treasure* is a sort of sardonic fable, an engrossing study of three characters who change drastically under the sinister influence of gold. It is an interesting adventure story, yet it does not have the depth, nor does it carry the impact, of *The Death Ship*.

The Cotton-Pickers is essentially the story of Traven's activities and reactions in his early days in Mexico, around the area of Tampico. The German title of this work, *Der Wobbly*, refers to Traven's sympathy with and promotion of the I.W.W. during his first years in Mexico. Once again, as in *The Death Ship*, the story is related by Gales, who is Traven himself. After laboring for some time as a cotton-picker for an American farmer named Shine, Gales moves on to other jobs—oil driller, baker, cowhand. The value of *The Cotton-Pickers* lies mostly in what it reveals about Traven's first experiences after reaching Mexico. While not necessarily autobiographical, it at least gives some of his first impressions on life in that country which was to become his permanent home.

A simple, revealing, and even haunting story is told in *The Bridge in the Jungle*, regarded by many as Traven's best work. Gales once more is narrator but the plot is almost nonexistent. A young boy disappears and is presumed to have fallen from a bridge which an American oil firm has built across the river. After a considerable search his body is found, and Gales movingly relates the pathos and grief of the all-night wake and the funeral. The incongruities which can result from the mixing of two cultures are suggested in the fact that the song chosen by the people as they march to the cemetery is none other than "Taintgonnarainnomo." Indeed, the whole story hinges on a kind of parable of cultural differentiation: the reason Carlitos slips off the bridge (built, you will recall, by an American oil company) is that he is wearing shoes for the first time —shoes brought him from the U.S. by his older brother. In other words, what is accepted and automatic in one culture can be dangerous and even tragic if imposed on another. Traven's empathy with these simple Indians is obvious, and he adjusts his pace to the tempo of their uncomplicated existence. The result is a low-key, detached rendition which definitely suits the circumstances but which might not be sufficiently fast-moving for some readers.

Two underlying concerns run through all of Traven's writings. One is that the "little man" is the forgotten man, consistently buffeted and victimized and exploited by the more powerful elements of society. The other concern is that as the forces of industrial civilization advance inexorably, they callously destroy most of what is simple and good in the primitive societies which they engulf. These two preoccupations (or convictions) are notable both in *The Bridge in the Jungle* and in Traven's next novel, *The White Rose*.

The White Rose takes its name from a hacienda in the Huasteca region of Veracruz which becomes the target of American oil interests. Traven gives a powerful and emotional account of the ruthlessness of these foreign interests, in this case the Condor Oil Company, headed by C. C. Collins, who typifies everything bad in the capitalistic system. Showing no human decency whatsoever, he takes by force and deceit and lawbreaking what he cannot get legally. The plot revolves around the fact that Collins wants to buy "The White Rose" land and its owner, don Jacinto, doesn't want to sell. To Collins it is a financial problem; to don Jacinto, a spiritual one. Inevitably, the power and inhumanity of the impresarios of "economic progress" bring the struggle to a brutal climax in which they finally obtain the hacienda at the price of human blood. Whereas in *The Bridge in the Jungle* Traven presented cultural differences in a quiet, detached way with lyrical tinges, here he creates a cultural confrontation of emotional, noisy, and violent proportions. The only English version of *The White Rose* appeared recently in London, but this does not justify the charge of Charles Henry Miller that the novel has been "suppressed" in the United States for almost forty years.[14] While none of us should be proud of the type of imperialism practiced by C. C. Collins and his cohorts, certainly our reading public could take *The White Rose* as well as it has the criticisms hurled by Jack London (with whom Traven is sometimes compared) and C. Wright Mills, to cite a couple of quick examples.

The setting of Traven's novels changes at this point in his career, shifting from the Gulf coast region to the jungle area of Chiapas. We know that Traven spent some time in this extreme southeastern part of Mexico in the later 1920s. Between 1930 and 1939 Traven published (in Germany, Switzerland, and Holland) six novels about the Indians of the Chiapas region. These novels share a close relationship in theme (a fierce protest against the subhuman and inhuman conditions imposed upon the Indians of the southern jungles), and they have also a unity of time (the period just prior to and at the beginning of the Mexican Revolution.) They are further related in that several characters appear in two or more of the novels. For our purposes, it seems that a discussion of two of these works will suffice.

The Rebellion of the Hanged was the fifth in this series of six jungle novels. It is also perhaps the most powerful. It can be said that the most common theme in Traven's writings is the struggle for land and liberty. In *The White Rose* it was the fight to retain land against imperialistic domination, while in *Rebellion* it is the desperate bid for the most elemental liberty. In the mahogany forests the three Montellano brothers hire Indian loggers and require each of them to cut a certain quota every day. As an incentive they whip the ones who don't—or, more accurately, can't—meet the quota and then hang them from tree limbs by their hands and feet, with honey smeared on their bodies to attract the innumerable insects. After so much of this the protagonist, Cándido Castro, and the others rebel, murder the bosses, and take over. Hence the title of the book. Some critics feel that in *Rebellion* Traven sometimes descends to the level of a "doctrinaire hack" and that the book shows us a lot of the worst of Traven's manner, along with some of the best.[15] My own reaction to this is that the critic perhaps is culturally unprepared to receive and assimilate fully the stunning blast of reality which Traven delivers.

The last of his jungle novels is *The General from the Jungle*, a direct sequel to *Rebellion*. After the successful uprising against the overseers and masters, a schoolteacher named Martín Trinidad convinces the Indians they won't be safe until all the loggers in all the surrounding camps are likewise freed from their oppressors. So, an "army" is formed under the leadership of Méndez, an ex-sergeant in the army of the dictator Díaz, and Méndez becomes the "general from the jungle." Their battle cry is "tierra y libertad"—land and liberty—the slogan also of agrarian leader Emiliano Zapata during the Mexican Revolution. The revolt of the illiterate rebels under General Méndez is a symbolic cry for freedom by all the Indians of Mexico. The general is a shrewd tactician, so that they win battles against superior forces and go on to divide the estates and mutilate their enemies. After their triumphs they learn that the Díaz dictatorship has fallen, and the location of their last camp becomes the site of a new village which, idealistically, they name "Solipaz"—Sun and Peace.

Macario, called a novelette, can just as properly be labeled a long short story. As a matter of fact, it isn't as long as "The Night Visitor," which customarily is considered a short story. Regardless of what it is in that sense, *Macario* is in fact a Mexican folk tale and a real gem. Macario, a woodchopper, is a simple good man with an understanding wife and eleven children. The family exists precariously on the few pennies he earns daily by cutting wood in the forest. His one ambition in life is to have—just once—a whole roast turkey to eat all by himself. After years of wishing, his faithful wife scrapes together enough to buy the turkey, and he goes off into the woods to eat it alone. Promptly the Devil appears, dressed in a *charro* outfit, and tries to get part of the turkey by offering several bribes, all of which Macario parries ingeniously. Then the Lord appears in the guise of a kindly, weary traveler and asks for a portion of the turkey, but again Macario protects his treasure with arguments which our Lord understands and respects. Finally comes Death, bony and hungry. Realizing he can't outwit the Bone Man, Macario offers to split the turkey fifty-fifty, figuring he will at least be granted enough time to eat as long as his guest is also eating.

In appreciation of Macario's gift and shrewdness, the Bone Man gives him the power to heal through using just one drop of a bottle of medicine he leaves with Macario, who will always know if he can cure a patient by observing whether Death is standing at the foot of the patient (affirmative) or at the head (negative). So, Macario becomes a great and famous and wealthy doctor and uses his power well and wisely for many years. He is called with his last two drops of medicine to treat the dying son of the viceroy, who says Macario will be burned at the stake if he fails. This would mean disgrace for his family and loss of all their earthly possessions. And of course the Bone Man shows up at the head of the patient. Desperate, Macario whirls the bed around and around trying to make Death stand at the foot of the bed, but the effort results only in his breaking the flask with the two precious drops. He pleads with the Bone Man, who sympathizes but is powerless to hold off the death of the boy. He observes, however, that he can keep Macario from being burned at the stake and publicly defamed, and so saying he takes up his position beside Macario's head.

Traven's short stories, starting with "The Night Visitor" and a dozen or so more, are for the most part admirable in their conception and delightful in their execution. In contrast with the loose-jointedness and digressions of some of his novels, they have a conciseness and an incisiveness which make the reader wish that he could trade perhaps a couple of the jungle novels for a couple of dozen more stories like these.

Besides the film version of *The Treasure of the Sierra Madre*, movies have been made from several other Traven works: *The Bridge in the Jungle, The Rebellion of the Hanged, Macario, The Death Ship* (produced in Germany), and *The White Rose*. This last case is an interesting one. Made in Mexico in 1962 and reputed to be one of the finest Mexican movies ever produced, the film has never been released. This is by decision of the Mexican government, which apparently feels that it is very strong anti-imperialist fare and that it could perceptibly damage the amicable Mexican-American relations and lead to a dropoff in the essential flow of tourist dollars. Even Traven himself (who was technical adviser on most films made from his novels and always wrote the original scripts) is said to have admitted that release of the movie of *The White Rose* would be contrary to good international relations.[16]

As a writer, Traven is no great stylist and he worries little about the structure of his novel. The style is careless, at times slipshod, and we have the impression he puts his thoughts rapidly on paper, with little concern about revision or refinement. He lets his own strong feelings, his proletarian instincts, intervene in his works at every turn. Some of these digressions are palatable and even lyrical, but for the most part they are didactic, too clearly interposed, too lengthy, and too frequent. At times his manner is brash, even brutal, yet in other moments he exhibits a tenderness toward some intimate aspect of the simple Indian life, to which he is perfectly attuned psychologically and emotionally.

With Traven, plot is something quite casual. In several works there really is no plot in the classic definition of the term, but rather a series of incidents which have relation to one another only because one character is involved in each of them. Traven's interest is more in people and in what happens to them (especially to their basic rights) than in carefully structuring a complex plot which builds up from initial problem into climax and final resolution. Readers who expect to find a plot and subplots with a generous dose of conflict and suspense would be disappointed.

Although Traven's concern is for the underdog, he rarely paints an individual character in strong, clear colors. Mostly they remain as types, while the emphasis is largely on the cruelty and ruthlessness of those who exercise power. Against the latter he wields biting satire, bulwarked by cold cynicism and frequent invective. It is, then, a group cause he espouses and his characters are symbols of their group. Preoccupied with the dignity of man, he fulminates against anything which degrades the human spirit.

Another word or two may be added about the poor reception accorded by the American reading public to nearly all of Traven's works. As we know, proletarian literature has never had much appeal in this country. On top of this, Traven usually is lashing out at the brutalizing effects of machine-age civilization upon the poor and defenseless in underdeveloped cultures, and there is a segment of our society which doesn't care to face up to such criticism. It also is to be admitted that some of the English translations are not the best. Seymour Krim, a reviewer of some Traven novels, has a criticism which may have some validity. He sees Traven as a writer limited in his interests, dealing always with relatively primitive people and a world strong in biology but not in psychology, so that a a good half of existence is left out entirely. Krim views this as a deficiency of the novelist himself. He goes on to say that the "serious-minded reader can hardly retreat into Traven's literary simple-mindedness." "We can appreciate," he concludes, "what he does, but what he leaves out makes us call for something that really *involves* us."[17]

I can agree with Krim's analysis to a point, yet I feel that only a reader who had fed himself a steady diet of one Traven work after another would react so. Constant reading about any segment of society may tend to pall through excessive exposure. But a Traven work interspersed in one's reading every so often will be for most people a stimulating experience. I find interesting these lines of Charles Henry Miller:

> The United States will catch up with Traven, though tardily, and recognize his neglected body of work as a major contribution to philosophical-proletarian literature. It is ironical that Traven has been neglected so long in the United States, for he is very much the American individualist.[18]

Miller may be right. I hope he is. The American public has a tradition of sympathizing with the underdog in almost everything, and no better champion of the little man can be found than B. Traven. It was quite typical of him to request that after his death his ashes be taken back to the southern jungle state of Chiapas—scene of so many of his works—where they are to rest permanently.

NOTES TO CHAPTER 4

1. Judy Stone, "Conversations with B. Traven," *Ramparts*, VI, October, 1967, p. 57.

2. A. Calder-Marshall, "The Novels of B. Traven," *Horizon*, I (July, 1940), 523.

3. Charles Henry Miller, Introduction to B. Traven, *The Night Visitor and Other Stories* (New York: Hill and Wang, 1966), p. ix.

4. Ibid.

5. "On the Trail of B. Traven," *Publishers' Weekly*, CXXXIV, July 9, 1938, p. 106.

6. W. W. Johnson, "Who Is Bruno Traven?" *Life*, XXII, March 10, 1947, p. 16.

7. "On the Trail of B. Traven," p. 106.

8. E. R. Hagemann, "¡Huye! A Conjectural Biography of B. Traven," *Inter-American Review of Bibliography*, X (October-December, 1960), 379.

9. Quoted in Miller, p. x.

10. *Life*, XXIV, February 2, 1948, p. 66.

11. A. M. Ocampo de Gómez and E. Prado Velázquez, eds., *Diccionario de escritores mexicanos* (Mexico City, 1967), p. 386.

12. Luis Alberto Sánchez, *Proceso y contenido de la novela hispanoamericana* (Madrid, 1953), p. 527.

13. Manuel Pedro González, *Trayectoria de la novela en México* (Mexico City, 1951), p. 321.

14. Charles Henry Miller, "B. Traven y el 'Problema Petrolero,' " *Cuadernos Americanos*, año 26, no. 4 (July-August, 1967), p. 227.

15. "Cándido and the Capitalists," *Time*, LIX, April 21, 1952, p. 114.

16. Charles Henry Miller, "B. Traven y el 'Problema Petrolero,' " p. 229.

17. Seymour Krim, "The Passion of the Peons," *Commonweal*, LVI (June 13, 1952), 250.

18. Charles Henry Miller, Introduction to *The Night Visitor and Other Stories*, p. xiii.

THE WORKS OF B. TRAVEN

In German, Spanish, and English Editions

Das Totenschiff (Berlin, 1926). *El barco de la muerte* (Mexico City, 1951). *The Death Ship* (New York: Knopf, 1934; Collier Books, 1962).

Der Wobbly (Berlin, 1926). Appeared in its final German form as *Die Baumwollpflucker* (Berlin, 1929). *Salario amargo* (Mexico City, 1969). *The Cotton-Pickers* (New York: Hill and Wang, 1969).

Der Schatz der Sierra Madre (Berlin, 1927). *El tesoro de la Sierra Madre* (Mexico City, 1946). *The Treasure of the Sierra Madre* (New York: Knopf, 1935; Pocket Books, 1961; Hill and Wang, 1967; Modern Library, 1969).

Land des Frühlings (Berlin, 1927). A general study of Mexico (especially the state of Chiapas) along anthropological lines. Not yet available in Spanish or English, although scheduled for publication soon by Hill and Wang.

Der Busch (Berlin, 1928). *Canasta de cuentos mexicanos* (Mexico City, 1946). A collection of short stories, some of which have been translated individually into English.

Die Brücke im Dschungel (Berlin, 1929). *Puente en la selva* (Mexico City, 1936). *The Bridge in the Jungle* (New York: Knopf, 1938; Hill and Wang, 1967).

Die Weisse Rose (Berlin, 1929). *La rosa blanca* (Mexico City, 1940). *The White Rose* (London: R. Hale, 1965).

Der Karren (Berlin, 1930). *La carreta* (Mexico City, 1950). *The Carreta* (New York: Hill and Wang, 1970).

Regierung (Berlin, 1931). *Gobierno* (Mexico City, 1951). *Government* (New York: Hill and Wang, 1971).

Der Marsch ins Reich der Caoba (Zurich, 1933). *March to the Monteria* (New York: Dell, 1964). *The March to Caobaland* (London: R. Hale, 1960). Not yet in Spanish.

Die Rebellion der Gehenkten (Berlin, 1936). *La rebelión de los colgados* (Mexico City, 1938). *The Rebellion of the Hanged* (New York: Knopf, 1952).

Die Troza (Zurich, 1936). Not yet available in Spanish or U.S. editions.

Sonnensschöpfung (Zurich, 1936). *The Creation of the Sun and the Moon* (New York: Hill and Wang, 1968). This Tzeltal Indian legend is to be found as "La creación de los soles" in the volume of stories titled *Cuentos de B. Traven*.

Ein General kommt aus dem Dschungel (Amsterdam, 1939). *El general. Tierra y libertad* (Mexico City, 1966). *The General from the Jungle* (London: R. Hale, 1954).

Macario (Zurich, 1949). *Macario* (Mexico City, 1960). This Mexican folk tale appears in *The Night Visitor and Other Stories*, as well as in *Best American Short Stories, 1954* (Boston: Houghton Mifflin, 1954).

Aslan Norval (Munich, 1960). Not yet published in Spanish or in English.

Cuentos de B. Traven (Mexico City, 1963). *Stories by the Man Nobody Knows* (Evanston, Ill.: Regency Books, 1961).

El visitante nocturno y otros cuentos (Mexico City, 1967). *The Night Visitor and Other Stories* (New York: Hill and Wang, 1966; Pocket Books, 1968).

SELECTED STUDIES ON B. TRAVEN

Calder-Marshall, A. "The Novels of B. Traven." *Horizon,* I (July, 1940), 522–528.

"Cándido and the Capitalists." *Time,* LIX, April 21, 1952, p. 114.

García Cantú, Gastón. "Traven, páginas inéditas." *Revista de la Universidad de México,* XXII (September, 1967), 1–7.

George, Manfred. "B. Traven's Identity." *New Republic,* CXVI, March 24, 1947, p. 35.

González, Manuel Pedro. *Trayectoria de la novela en México,* pp. 316–321.

Hagemann, E. R. "¡Huye! A Conjectural Biography of B. Traven." *Inter-American Review of Bibliography,* X (October-December, 1960), 370–386.

Hays, H. R. "The Importance of B. Traven." *Chimera*, IV (Summer, 1946), 44–54.

Jannach, Hubert. "The B. Traven Mystery." *Books Abroad*, XXXV (Winter, 1961), 28–29.

———. "B. Traven—An American or German Author?" *German Quarterly*, XXXVI (November, 1963), 459–468.

Johnson, William W. "Who Is Bruno Traven?" *Life*, XXII, March 10, 1947, pp. 13–16.

Krim, Seymour. "The Passion of the Peons." *Commonweal*, LVI (June 13, 1952), 250.

McAlpine, William Reid. "B. Traven: The Man and His Work." *Tomorrow*, VII (August, 1948), pp. 43–46.

Miller, Charles Henry. "B. Traven y el 'Problema Petrolero.'" *Cuadernos Americanos*, año 26, no. 4 (July-August, 1967), pp. 225–229.

———. "Introduction" to B. Traven's *The Night Visitor and Other Stories* (New York: Hill & Wang, 1966), pp. vii–xiii.

———. "Traven no es un misterio." *Siempre!*, no. 565 (April 22, 1964), pp. 44–45.

———. "¿Cuál misterio? Dejen en paz a Traven." *Siempre!*, no. 701 (November 30, 1966), pp. 14, 70.

———. "B. Traven in the Americas." *Texas Quarterly*, VI (Winter, 1963), 208–211.

———. "B. Traven, American Author." *Texas Quarterly*, VI (Winter, 1963), 162–168.

Ocampo de Gómez, A.M., and Prado Velázquez, E., eds. *Diccionario de escritores mexicanos*, p. 386.

"On the Trail of B. Traven." *Publishers' Weekly*, CXXXIV, July 9, 1938, pp. 105–106.

Restrepo Fernández, Iván. "Lo que pasa en México." *Mundo Nuevo*, no. 41 (November, 1969), pp. 90–91.

Sánchez, Luis Alberto. *Proceso y contenido de la novela hispano-americana*, pp. 527–529.

Sommers, Joseph, "Changing View of the Indian in Mexican Literature." *Hispania*, XLVII (March, 1964), 47–55.

Stone, Judy. "The Mystery of B. Traven," *Ramparts*, VI, September, 1967, pp. 31–49.

———. "Conversations with B. Traven," *Ramparts*, VI, October, 1967, pp. 55–71, 74–75.

Suárez, Luis. "*Siempre!* revela al fin, el misterio literario más apasionante del siglo y presenta al mundo a B. Traven." *Siempre!*, no. 695 (October 19, 1966), pp. 4–9, 70.

———. "Traven y *Siempre!*, una polémica en Europa." *Siempre!*, no. 699 (November 16, 1966), p. 4.

Agustín Yáñez: A Quantum Jump for the Mexican Novel

THE YEAR 1947 MARKED THE PUBLICATION OF THE SINGLE MOST important work in the history of the Mexican novel. With Agustín Yáñez's *Al filo del agua,* called a "landmark" effort,[1] the novel in Mexico took a quantum jump into a respected place in the main channel of modern world literature.

Thirty-two years before *Al filo del agua,* Mariano Azuela produced in *Los de abajo* another milestone of Mexican literature, one which also gave a change in direction to the novel both there and in other parts of Spanish America. But if Azuela provoked a 90-degree change in the direction to be followed by the novel, Yáñez imposes a full 180-degree turn. In the three decades separating these two works, the Spanish-American novel probed insistently and searchingly into certain themes: the Mexican Revolution and its aftermath; many common evils and injustices, which inspired endless works of social protest; the powerful and sometimes overwhelming challenges faced by man in his struggle with some of nature's more flamboyant manifestations: the jungle, the plains, the desert, the mountains. There also are regional works, *costumbrismo* efforts, *indigenista* novels concerned with the fate of the Indians.

The outgrowth of all this was a considerable yield of novels, mostly oriented somehow toward the land, with a not infrequent tendency toward the mass protagonist. We have already noted that the Revolution can be called the protagonist in *Los de abajo* and other Revolutionary novels. In *Tierra* it is the land and the question of who will control it which overshadows all else. Gregorio López y Fuentes does not give a specific name to any character in *El indio* because he intends that the Indians as a people emerge as the clear-cut protagonist. Although Mauricio Magdaleno uses names in *El res-plandor,* his purpose is not dissimilar. Elsewhere, the Colombian José Rivera's *La vorágine* (*The Vortex*), published in 1924, casts the Amazon jungle as the dominant figure in the story; Ricardo Güiraldes's *Don Segundo Sombra* (1926), masterful idealization of the *gaucho,* shows how the vast pampa region of Argentina forces men to bend to its will and its way; and *Doña Bárbara* (1929), by the notable Venezuelan novelist Rómulo Gallegos, depicts the battle between civilization and barbarity on the plains of Venezuela. Even in the novels of outright social protest the land plays a primary role, for the social injustices usually exist because landowners are greedy to extract more and more wealth from the land itself.

Al filo del agua changes all of this. Yáñez turns the camera away from wide-angle views of the land and the forces of nature to focus on man himself. The protagonist from now on is distinctly human rather than geographic, or social, or abstract. And it is to be largely the inner man that matters as the novelists begin to enter into the mind and psychology of their characters and to plumb the human spirit. This "interiorization" penetrates the conscious and subconscious thoughts, the motivations, the problems, and the complex pressures that force the decisions and deeds of the people who populate these works. It is the individual person and his troubled existence within our society that matters today, and the novelists invite and, in fact, force the reader to become deeply involved in the segment of life under discussion.

It isn't that Yáñez discovered or invented a whole new technique or a completely new approach. In *Al filo del agua,* he merely brought together certain techniques and devices that other novelists in different literatures had used well before him. In fact, he wasn't the first in Latin America or even in Mexico to use some of these methods. It is just that in the Spanish language no one prior to Yáñez utilized so many of these elements and allowed them to dominate. This approach caught on quickly and now, little more than two decades later, many novelists have carried the "new look" much further.

Al filo del agua is innovative chiefly in its use of inner monologue, psychological probing of the subconscious, flashbacks, and certain stylistic devices (such as highly effective and skilled repetition of words, phrases, and images). To a considerable degree, the reader is drawn into active participation in the lives of the characters. In subsequent works by an ever growing circle of novelists, all of these elements are carried to greater lengths and additional techniques are explored. A significant new element found in Yáñez's works and now highly popular is that of narration on two planes. This simultaneity may be relatively simple, like the alternation of present and past almost indiscriminately, or it may become quite complex through a blending of the real and the unreal, truth and imagination, the natural and the supernatural, realism and "magical realism." Thus, the traditional unities of time, place, and action are freely ignored. In fact, time is sometimes suspended if not eliminated as a factor, so that (as in Rulfo's *Pedro Páramo*) the reader is hard put to distinguish the living from the dead. Indeed, the novelist sometimes shifts from one plane to another with so little warning or so negligible a clue that the reader is kept guessing and off-balance and struggling to hang on to some understanding and appreciation of the total story. This is all a part of the determination to coerce the reader into full and active participation in the story.

Another device utilized by Yáñez and common in the modern novel is that of insuring that the work has "density," which we may define as the piling of detail upon detail, thought upon thought. Naturally, this tends to slow the narrative pace. The fast-moving action story, once the popular thing nearly everywhere, is now nearly as extinct as the dodo bird. These techniques have become so refined that it is impossible to read many of the new (and sometimes the best) novels without total involvement in the action and intimate identification with the characters of the story.

Before examining *Al filo del agua* and the other novels of Yáñez, it might be well to look at the author himself and his literary career up to 1947.

Born in 1904 in Guadalajara, Yáñez received his law degree in 1929 and later took his M.A. in philosophy at the Universidad Nacional de México. During a twenty-year period prior to 1953 he held teaching posts in such places as Guadalajara, the National Preparatory School, the National University, and El Colegio de México; he was briefly head of the radio division of the Ministry of Public Education and coordinator of humanities at the National University; in 1946 he was an ambassador in South America; he was president of the editorial commission of the university and several times a member of the University Council.

Between 1940 and 1953 Yáñez also published more than fifteen works, including short stories, novels, biographies, essays, and studies. Among them were such diverse items as studies on indigenous myths, Fernández de Lizardi, the social content of Ibero-American literature, a biography of Fray Bartolomé de las Casas, and *Al filo del agua.*

In 1953 Yáñez was elected governor of his home state of Jalisco, one of the most populous and important in the country, and he served in this position with obvious credit until 1959. He then spent five years as a full-time professor at the National University. In 1960 he was accorded one of the highest honors to which a writer in Mexico can aspire, namely, acceptance into the ultraselect Academia Mexicana de la Lengua. When Gustavo Díaz Ordaz took over as Mexico's president in 1964 he called on Agustín Yáñez to be his Secretary of Public Education, a post he filled with distinction for six years.

During his time as governor of Jalisco, Yáñez published almost nothing, but from 1959 to the present he has given us more than fifteen published works, including four novels and studies on Dante, the Revolution, and Diego Rivera. Although he has now passed the age of sixty-seven, we can confidently expect to see further works from the pen of this remarkably active and capable figure in Mexican national life.

Imposing in appearance, Yáñez is a serious—one might say sombre—man. In his writing and in his public utterances he shows little humor. And he obviously takes himself seriously as a novelist. Certainly, beginning with *Al filo del agua*, he has structured each novel with extreme care and with specific objectives in mind. Therefore, we are not the least surprised to find that he (like Azuela) was in his mid-thirties before he began any consistent literary production. This stands in sharp contrast with the youngest generation of Mexican novelists, nearly all of whom are bringing forth novels in their early twenties.

Although he rejects the idea with some vehemence, Agustín Yáñez is really at his best when re-creating the people and the scenes of his own provincial background, that is to say, of Jalisco.[2] Most of his fictional output has its setting in the province. The two works laid in metropolitan Mexico City (*La creación*, 1959, and *Ojerosa y pintada*, 1960) have not been too kindly received by the critics. If the works of Yáñez possessed no other virtue than his genuine and affectionate interpretation of provincial life, he no doubt would be entitled to a firm place in Mexican literature, albeit primarily in the category of a superb *costumbrista*, a consummate *regionalista*, rather than in the role of innovator and pioneer he claims mainly on the strength of *Al filo del agua*.

We know from Yáñez himself that his prime inspiration in attempting this novel was John Dos Passos's *Manhattan Transfer*. His own straightforward words are: "I proposed to apply to a small town the technique which Dos Passos employs in *Manhattan Transfer* to describe the great city."[3] There are, nevertheless, some differences. For instance, *Al filo del agua* covers chronologically a period of about two years, whereas the work by Dos Passos ranges over many years. One feels safe, too, in associating in some ways this novel by Yáñez with Aldous Huxley's *Point Counter Point*.

The title, *Al filo del agua* or "the edge of the storm," is a common rural expression, as the author tells us on the page prior to the opening of the story. He says that it is used by the campesinos to indicate the very moment when it starts to rain and quite frequently is extended in the figurative sense to refer to the imminence or the beginning of some happening.[4] Its use as the title of the novel has reference to the approach and outbreak of the Revolution. The action of the story embraces a period of nearly two years prior to the eruption of the Madero revolt in 1910.

The novel opens with a twelve-page "Acto preparatorio" (presented in italics) which is nothing less than masterful. Without naming a single citizen, it describes and dissects the town physically and spiritually. More than that, it creates the atmosphere which is to prevail to the end. The ambience is one of fear, repression, morbidity, secret desires, guilt feelings, and of waiting—waiting for the feared and yet anticipated blowup. Without the "Acto preparatorio" the rest of the novel would unfold in a semivacuum, lacking much of its punch and impact.

Yáñez's technique is almost poetic: truncated syntax, that is, short phrases that convey a picture but are not complete sentences; image stacked upon image, page after page; rhythmical repetition of images, phrases, and words, either in the same or in varying patterns. The eye of the author is like the eye of a TV camera. The opening shots are panoramic and show the whole town. Then the lens begins to zoom in on details. Houses and various rooms pass before our view; the church and its bell tower, both to be of great consequence in the story. We hear the voices of the village, we see food on the table. And we enter into the thoughts and actions of the people of this town, which we come to realize is fear-ridden and tottering on the brink of some dark calamity.

What keeps the town and all its people in such a state of tension and suppressed emotion is the dominance of an old, Spanish-style, now-outmoded concept of religion, a religious manifestation steeped in fear of damnation rather than love of God. The village church, as administered by its three priests, tries to cast a hermetic blanket over the town and to suffocate all dangerous thoughts, aspirations, and desires, most particularly any in the sexual realm. Through the "Acto preparatorio" we are enabled to visualize in detail the town and the life of its inhabitants. More importantly, we are imbued with the atmosphere which pervades the town and townspeople, and we know instinctively it is a situation which is unnatural and cannot forever endure.

These passages taken from the "Acto preparatorio" give a measure of understanding of this forlorn yet potentially explosive town.

> Village of black-robed women. . . . Village without fiestas, except for the daily dancing of the sun with its army of vibrations. Village without any music other than the clamoring of the bells, quick to toll for sorrows. . . . Parties, never. A sacred horror of dancing: not even by thought, never, never. . . . A village that is a convent. Shamefaced taverns. . . . Village without pool parlors, or phonographs, or pianos. Village of black-robed women. . . . Village of perpetual Lent. . . . Village of poor souls. . . . There is no pain in the village to equal that of honor stained: any agony, any misery, and whatever other form of torments is to be pre-

ferred. . . . Inns and taverns ordinarily empty. The village is not on frequented routes. . . . Conformity is the finest virtue in these people who, in general, aspire only to go on living until the hour of a good death. . . . Dry village. Without trees, orchards, or gardens. Dry to the point of hurting, to where there are no tears in weeping. . . . The separation of the sexes is rigorous. In the church, the Gospel side is exclusively reserved for men, and that of the Epistle for the devout feminine sex. . . . Life goes on among black-robed women. Death comes. Or love. Love, which is the strangest, the most extreme form of dying, the most dangerous and feared form of living death.[5]

His stage set and the mood evoked, Yáñez uses the next few chapters to populate the stage. By this time the reader surmises that he has met—or at least encountered mention of—a sizeable portion of the townspeople. While this multiplicity of characters may confuse some readers, it seems apparent that it is because Yáñez wants the town—and the town atmosphere—to be the protagonist of the novel, that he disperses the action of the story among a large number of principal characters, without permitting any of them to assume the leading role. The story draws life from the village itself and its brooding spirit.

The "Acto preparatorio" is relatively unorthodox and imaginative in concept and execution, but it does not involve the techniques which are to make *Al filo del agua* a truly revolutionary work in Hispanic-American fiction. However, Yáñez does not delay long thereafter in applying certain techniques used years before by James Joyce, Dos Passos, and numerous others in several languages but not yet employed to any meaningful extent in Spanish. In the first chapter we spend a good bit of time with don Timoteo Limón as he prepares for bed and tries to go to sleep. Gradually Yáñez lets him drift into interior monologue, which is of course a not-too-distant relative of the stream-of-consciousness and has been described as "the most effective technique for the presentation and simulation of the psychic processes."[6]

In the several pages of this monologue, don Timoteo divulges many things about himself, his emotional hang-ups, and about his son Damián, all of which will assume more significance in later stages of the story. His thoughts are set down in the first person

with no intervention by the author, and the sequence of the monologue is unpredictable. One thought tumbles over another with no
logical association, just as happens with all of us in such reveries.

From the beginning, then, Yáñez has shown us, through several
devices both of substance and form, his familiarity with psychology
and his dexterity in using this knowledge to explore the psyche of
his characters. This is an approach no previous Mexican novelist has
employed with the same degree of caution, skill, and professional
preparation. By the end of the first four chapters (124 of 387 pages)
we can see that *Al filo del agua* has broken sharply with the Mexican novel of the past and is charting a new course. It has already
departed, though only up to a point, from the old-style lineal
account of events. It is not a novel of action (in fact, there is no forward progress in the story in these first 124 pages!), nor a novel too
rooted in historical fact, as was the novel of the Revolution. And
whereas almost no prominent women characters figured in the
novel of the Revolution, in *Al filo del agua* there are at least five
highly important females.

In the remaining twelve chapters of the book the author carries us
through the "action" part of the work in successful and convincing
manner. Having briefed us so thoroughly on the moral, social, economic, and psychological makeup of the many main characters,
Yáñez introduces new events which trigger internal and external
reactions on the part of all these people. We are witnesses as the
three priests (Padre Dionisio Martínez and his assistants Padre Isla
and Padre Reyes) exert their well-intentioned efforts toward maintaining the status quo in the sin-obsessed town. We share Padre
Dionisio's concern over his two nieces Marta and María, who live
with him, and we come to know directly Marta's mixed-up state of
mind and María's growing spirit of rebelliousness. There clearly
are symbolic overtones in the author's choice of these two names
for the nieces, and perhaps also in the case of Victoria and even of
Gabriel. We move on through the emotional period of Holy Week.

The townspeople use the term "the northerners" (*los norteños*)
to refer to some young men who have broken out of the hermetic
town and gone north (to the U.S.) to seek more freedom, both
economic and spiritual. A chapter devoted to the unsettling return

of some of these "liberals," including Damián Limón, opens with more than a page of isolated comments by a number of unidentified persons, comments which reveal the fear felt by most of the towns-people in the face of these pernicious rebels. And there is no question that the *norteños*, with their money and uninhibited ways and liberal ideas of social justice acquired in the United States, do represent a threat to the established order. Most of the citizens view with greater disquiet the threat of disorder and change than they do the tense atmosphere of repression to which they are accustomed.

In a chapter titled "Canicas" [Marbles] Yáñez likens the characters of his story to the marbles in games of chance at village fairs. At any given moment there is no way of telling which way they will roll. There is a heightening of the air of apprehension on the national, local, and personal level. Political decisions of Porfirio Díaz concerning the approaching presidential elections of 1910 stir restlessness and resentment in many places. The padres (and others) strive to ward off an eruption stemming from the actions and attitudes of the *norteños*, and individual lives are drawing closer to a breaking point, all of which we learn more by way of their inner thoughts than through direct action.

An irritant as dangerous as the *norteños* appears in the town in the person of Victoria, a widow from Guadalajara. Like the *norteños* she brings with her the openness of the outside world, a much more liberal view of society. More than that, she brings in her own person a sensuality and a beauty quite capable of lighting the fuse of sexual desires kept repressed through fear of sin. A young seminary student, Luis Gonzaga, becomes so hopelessly enamored of Victoria that he loses his mind. Gabriel, the teen-age bellringer, also feels her attraction. This leads to one of the most interesting and most discussed chapters in the book.

Titled "Victoria y Gabriel," it is an interlude which in concept and execution departs from the rest of the story. One observer feels that it "disconcerts and displeases because of its melodramatic overtones" and finds it "narrated with the melodramatic language of the Romantics."[7] While the critics are at odds as to the artistic value of this chapter, it has importance in rendering subsequent events plausible. It also gives us two more fine examples of interior monologue, one in which Gabriel exposes his agitated state of mind and another in which Victoria shows surprise at her own daring in climbing the bell-tower to meet Gabriel for the first time.

The breaking point is finally reached in "La desgracia de Damián Limón" [The misfortune of Damián Limón]. One of the *norteños* has brought with him a Ouija board, and a growing group of "spiritists" gather clandestinely to be astounded by its revelations. The board predicts that Damián will go to jail because of a woman. It is assumed by Bartolo, and others, that the woman is his own wife, Bruna, who once was Damián's fiancée. And Damián does pursue her, but unavailingly. However, another woman is interested in attracting Damián's attentions. She is Micaela, once briefly in Mexico City, and no longer able to tolerate the town's social prohibitions. Her provocative actions lead to a blowup by Damián. The insecure and scheming Micaela turns her eye toward don Timoteo and the flattered old widower for a time gives signs of responding. Goaded beyond his limit, Damián murders his own father and then shoots Micaela down in the street.

This outburst of violence is a stunning experience for the town but at the same time is almost like the opening of a valve. The premonitions of calamity have been fulfilled and the collective tension reduced a bit. Clearly, the narrative pace has quickened in these last few chapters, and Yáñez shrewdly maintains the rate and lightens the sombreness somewhat at this point by describing the return of many of the village youngsters who have been away at school. They represent a distraction and a rather cheering element, although they also bring word of a political leader named Francisco Madero and sensational news about the return of Halley's comet. Another distraction comes in the form of a band of drunken musicians who play nearly all night, arousing varied reactions.

The final chapter, "El cometa Halley," is the longest and covers all of the year 1910 up to the outbreak of the Revolution in November. Lucas Macías, self-appointed chronicler and prophet, declares that the comet foreshadows the coming of disaster in various forms. As the year wears on, rumors in steady succession reach the village about the uncertain political situation in the country. Strange men from the outside pass through town, leaving behind increased speculation and fear. Released from jail by the new political director, Damián returns to town, oblivious to the open hostility of nearly everyone. On one occasion he is defended by María, whose intervention perhaps saves his life but leaves her the target of gossip and attacks. Rito Becerra, a friend of Damián, rises in support of the Madero revolt and comes back to occupy the town with his forces. There is confusion, the sacking of some stores, and endless rumors; the whole village fears for its women. María goes off with the revolutionaries to seek a freedom she had to have and the town would never give. At the end Padre Martínez, bearing profound grief and especially saddened that he has been unable to protect his flock, goes out to the altar to offer his Mass, the same as every day.

Not only is *Al filo del agua* a remarkably structured novel and an innovator with regard to a variety of stylistic techniques, it is in addition a work in which the characterization is truly outstanding. Although the town itself is the leading subject of the work, it is surprising how many of the dozens of characters stand forth in sharply etched detail: don Timoteo, María, Micaela, Gabriel, Luis Gonzaga, Damián, Padre Islas, Lucas Macías, Padre Reyes, Marta, Merceditas, Victoria, and Padre Dionisio Martínez. Of all of these, Yáñez appears to give somewhat more time and effort to the full development of the last-named, the *señor cura*, don Dionisio. Indeed, few characters in the Mexican novel are as thoroughly drawn as this parish priest.

A very acute critic of the Mexican novel observes that "the incorporation of modern psychological knowledge by means of narrative technique is the essential literary element enabling Yáñez to fashion complex characters—a feature which markedly distinguishes *The Edge of the Storm* from the novel of the Revolution."[8] And John Brushwood, another fine student of the Mexican novel, can say with good reason in 1964 that "*Al filo del agua* is the best Mexican novel to date, whether judged purely on the basis of its artistic worth, or on that basis combined with its merit as the expression of the nation."[9] There may be some challengers to this judgment but none, I believe, that can clearly prove their point.

Understandably, Agustín Yáñez has not written another novel that measures up to *Al filo del agua*, even though he apparently feels that he has done so in *La creación* [Creation], written while he was governor of Jalisco and published in 1959. When asked by Emmanuel Carballo about his reaction to the cold reception critics have given this work, Yáñez responded: "Without doubt, and this happened with *Al filo del agua,* within some years—it doesn't matter whether it is ten, twenty, or more—it will cause surprise that the critics of today have not seen in *La creación* its architectural and compositional values, its nuances, the implications, the care with which it is constructed."[10]

This is not immodesty but genuine conviction on the part of Yáñez. Deadly serious about his writing, he feels he has a right to speak about its value. But I think he is mistaken about *La creación.* It is not likely to be the beneficiary of the same sort of tardy recognition accorded *Al filo del agua.* The delayed reaction in the latter case was due in some degree to its innovations, its departure from existing norms, in very much the same manner that it took the critics a decade to appreciate the values of Azuela's *Los de abajo.*

One clue as to why *La creación* falls short of greatness can be found in the final phrase of Yáñez's defense quoted above: "the care with which it is constructed." While not exactly a contrived novel, *La creación* is in fact top-heavy in the attention given to its construction. Thus, we come full circle. In the novel of the Revolution, message always outranked art. *Al filo del agua* strikes a good balance between the two, and in *La creación* art tends to suffocate the message.

La creación has a special interest, nevertheless, for those who have read *Al filo del agua,* for here we meet again a number of the characters from the earlier work. All have now escaped the hermetic village and are seeking fulfillment in a different, far more open environment. Gabriel, the adolescent bell-ringer of the *señor cura's* church, is trying to establish the career in music first proposed to him by Victoria, who, along with María, plays a considerable role in Gabriel's adult existence. There are other characters, too, who appeared first in *Al filo del agua.*

Two new Yáñez novels appeared in 1960: *Ojerosa y pintada* and *La tierra pródiga.* In the former the author tries to give us a vision and an interpretation of Mexico City, using a taxi driver on twenty-

four-hour duty as the unifying element between many scenes, incidents, and people. Here again his ambition seems to have carried
him farther than his theme or its execution warrants, and the book
has had a rather uniformly poor reception. Carballo affirms that one
reason for the relative failure of both *Ojerosa y pintada* and *La
creación* (after all, if produced by a lesser figure they might have
been acclaimed as his best efforts) is found in their urban setting.
As Carballo words it, when Yáñez produces an urban setting, "inspiration quickly gives way to skill."[11] There is no denying that his
best realized works are those dealing with provincial life, one of
which is the other novel published in 1960, *La tierra pródiga* [The
prodigal land].

The setting of this novel is the tropical lowland region of Jalisco
along and near the coast, a land of lush wild vegetation, fertile but
at the same time unruly. *La tierra pródiga* is a novel of the land,
though not in the same way as many earlier examples of this type
of story in Spanish-American literature. They nearly always depicted
the struggle of the agricultural man against nature, with man frequently the loser. The Yáñez story finds man battling nature (in the
years 1924–29) to initiate a new era of industrialization in the
region, and man here is able to subjugate nature. As might be
expected with this kind of theme, the novel has a more dynamic
style, a faster pace than was the case with *Al filo del agua*. Yáñez
is a writer who believes that the style should bend itself to the
theme and setting. In this case, he says, "the dynamics of the novel,
the violent nature of the characters, the passions engaged in struggle, the very prodigality of nature demanded a rapid, violent form
of narration."[12]

The protagonist of *La tierra pródiga* is Ricardo Guerra Victoria,
"el Amarillo" (the yellow one), who comes down from the moun-
tainous regions of Jalisco and with gusto acclimates himself to the
very different coastal existence. With no scruples to hold him in
check, he contends for a long time with several others for control of
the region. Victory over his last rival, Sotero Castillo, is a sort of
symbolic conquest of the Indian by the white man.

The most recent novel published by Agustín Yáñez is *Las tierras
flacas* (*The Lean Lands*), published in 1962 and set in the high-

lands of Jalisco. They are parched, eroded lands, without irrigation, and the people live, singly or in little groups, in huts or houses called *ranchos*. Wresting a living from this land is an endless struggle. Here life is more austere and largely lacking in the gayety and easy manners which come naturally to the coastal people found in *La tierra pródiga*. The story takes place in a general area known as Tierra Santa (Holy Land) between 1920 and 1925.

Las tierras flacas is constructed around two myths of the Tierra Santa region: the myth of the land and the myth of the machine. In this case the machine is a simple sewing machine which now belongs to Rómulo and his wife, Merced. They owe a sum of money to Epifanio Trujillo, the *cacique* or boss of the region, and their dilemma is whether to give him the rest of their land or the treasured symbol of the new industrial age. Epifanio rules the area much like a patriarch, acquiring lands, controlling people and their lives, and fathering offspring all over the place. Gradually the simple people, combining some of their folk habits with some of their religious customs, nearly sanctify the sewing machine until it is regarded as something almost miraculous and also a symbol of opposition to the power and greed of don Epifanio.

Yáñez uses a technique in this work which cannot fail to surprise. He employs literally hundreds of refrains and proverbs, to the extent that they represent an amazing portion of the text (Carballo estimates at least 30 percent). Yáñez has explained this phenomenon by saying that "for one thing it is in keeping with the reality described and, for another, it is due to the need for achieving certain effects of expression and even of literary beauty."[13] This may be so, but I think the average reader will find the tactic overused and eventually somewhat tiring.

Yáñez regards *Al filo del agua, La tierra pródiga,* and *Las tierras flacas* as a trilogy of the land, of that provincial land he knows best, his native Jalisco. As would be expected, we find interiorization in these last two works as in his most famous one, though not quite to the same degree. In his last novel he adds an interesting new dimension in some of his interior monologues which project back to the past and bring into focus persons who are dead or who never actually appear in the story. This device of bringing the dead into apparently active participation in the story may have been picked up by Yáñez from Juan Rulfo, whose work *Pedro Páramo* will be discussed in the next chapter. There is little doubt that the novels in this trilogy constitute Yáñez's best narrative work. In fact, a strong case can be made for the belief that no other Mexican novelist has yet produced three works to equal their merit.

While it is quite probable that Agustín Yáñez has not yet produced his last novel, it is equally probable that any subsequent work will not surpass in quality what he already has done. This, indeed, is not to be asked or expected. In any event, there is no need to await further works before essaying a judgment on his place in Mexican literature. To my mind, the case is clear and rather simple. Had Yáñez written only *Al filo del agua* he would stand as a pinnacle in the history of the Mexican novel, since that work is, all things considered, the best novel so far produced in that country. Even if it were not for *Al filo del agua*, his place would still be very high on the strength of his remaining works, especially the two other volumes of his trilogy. At this moment he is unexcelled among the Mexican novelists.

NOTES TO CHAPTER 5

1. Joseph Sommers, *After the Storm: Landmarks of the Modern Mexican Novel* (Albuquerque, 1968). This excellent study by Sommers deals exclusively with Yáñez, Juan Rulfo, and Carlos Fuentes.

2. Emmanuel Carballo, *Diecinueve protagonistas de la literatura mexicana del siglo XX* (Mexico City, 1965), p. 295.

3. Ibid., p. 291.

4. Agustín Yáñez, *Al filo del agua* (Mexico City: Editorial Porrúa, S.A., 7th ed., 1967), p. 2. Subsequent quotes are from this edition.

5. Ibid., pp. 3–14. The suspensive dots are in all cases my own.

6. Samuel J. O'Neill, "Interior Monologue in 'Al filo del agua,'" *Hispania*, LI (1968), 447.

7. Elaine Haddad, "The Structure of 'Al filo del agua,'" *Hispania*, XLVII (1964), 525.

8. Sommers, p. 55.

9. John S. Brushwood, *Mexico in Its Novel* (Austin, 1966), pp. 10–11.
10. Carballo, pp. 294–295.
11. Ibid., p. 321.
12. Ibid., p. 307.
13. Ibid., p. 314.

THE NOVELS OF AGUSTÍN YÁÑEZ

Pasión y convalecencia, 1943
Al filo del agua, 1947 (Translated into English as *The Edge of the Storm.* Austin: University of Texas Press, 1963.)
La creación, 1959
Ojerosa y pintada, 1960
La tierra pródiga, 1960
Las tierras flacas, 1962 (Translated into English as *The Lean Lands.* Austin: University of Texas Press, 1968.)

SELECTED STUDIES ON AGUSTÍN YÁÑEZ

Alegría, Fernando. *Historia de la novela hispanoamericana,* pp. 252–257.
Brushwood, John S. *Mexico in Its Novel,* pp. 7–12, 45–48.
Carballo, Emmanuel. *Diecinueve protagonistas de la literatura mexicana del siglo XX,* pp. 283–324.
———. *El cuento mexicano del siglo XX,* pp. 45–54.
Connolly, Eileen. "La centralidad del protagonista en *Al filo del agua.*" *Revista Iberoamericana,* XXXII (1966), 275–280.
Ezcurdia, Manuel de. "Trayectoria novelística de Agustín Yáñez," *Memoria del Sexto Congreso del Instituto de Literatura Iberoamericana.* Mexico City: Imprenta Universitaria, 1954, pp. 235–242.
Flasher, John J. *México contemporáneo en las novelas de Agustín Yáñez.*
Gamiochipi de Liguori, Gloria. *Yáñez y la realidad mexicana.*
González, Manuel Pedro. *Trayectoria de la novela en México,* pp. 327–338.
Haddad, Elaine. "The Structure of 'Al filo del agua.'" *Hispania,* XLVII (1964), 522–529.
Lazo, Raimundo. "Agustín Yáñez, maestro de la narración imaginativa hispanoamericana." *Revista de Bellas Artes,* no. 17 (1967).

Martínez, José Luis. *Literatura mexicana siglo XX*, I, 201–212.

———. Prologue of 100 pages to *Obras escogidas de Agustín Yáñez*. Mexico City: Aguilar, 1968.

Morton, F. Rand. *Los novelistas de la Revolución mexicana*, pp. 223–228.

Ocampo de Gómez, A.M., and Prado Velázquez, E., eds. *Diccionario de escritores mexicanos*, pp. 413–417.

O'Neill, Samuel J. "Interior monologue in 'Al filo del agua.'" *Hispania*, LI (1968), 447–455.

Rangel Guerra, Alfonso. *Agustín Yáñez: Un mexicano y su obra.*

Sommers, Joseph. *After the Storm*, pp. 36–68.

Van Conant, Linda M. *Agustín Yáñez: Intérprete de la novela mexicana moderna.*

Vázquez Amaral, José. "Técnica novelística de Agustín Yáñez." *Cuadernos Americanos*, año 17, no. 2 (1958), pp. 245–254.

———. "La novelística de Agustín Yáñez." *Cuadernos Americanos*, año 24, no. 1 (1965), pp. 218–239.

6

Juan Rulfo, Novelist of the Dead

AMONG TODAY'S MOST NOTABLE MEXICAN WRITERS THE CASE OF JUAN
Rulfo is a quite remarkable one. Born in 1918, his total published
output up to 1971 consists of two slender volumes—one of short
stories and the other a novel. They appeared in 1953 and 1955,
respectively, yet his name and his influence are very much alive in literary circles today, both in Mexico and elsewhere. This is confirmed
in these recent words: "It is pleasant to observe when one travels
abroad—and, besides being pleasant, quite surprising—that on initiating a conversation on literary themes and personages with critics,
fellow writers, or readers in general, they immediately ask about
Juan Rulfo."[1] It almost seems that because he is not writing, Rulfo's
fame grows like a myth or a legend.

In 1970 Rulfo was awarded the Premio Nacional de Letras
(National Literary Prize). When one voice was raised against giving this honor to someone whose total printed works occupy fewer
than 250 pages and who has published nothing for fifteen years,
critic and writer Raúl Prieto responded at once that those 250 pages
or so just happen to represent a collection of short stories and a
short novel superior to any other such selections produced in Mexico
in the past seventy years. Mexican literary circles in general seemed
to be of the definite opinion that the award was an act of deserved
and just recognition.[2]

Considering the paucity of Rulfo's production and the enduring
influence of his works, perhaps no other writer has ever derived so
much from so few pages. This obviously is a substantial tribute to
the nature and quality of what little he has published. Yet we must

come to the question of why an author of Rulfo's undeniable gifts and interest in literature has not published more. Is he just another one of the "dead-end" novelists who dot the pages of literary history in Spanish America? These writers, a most numerous breed, turn out one or perhaps two novels, sometimes excellent ones, and then are never heard from again. Their disappearance from the literary scene generally is due to the hard economic reality that they and their families must eat and that they can't expect to do it on the pittance they receive from their novels. So they turn to politics, journalism, business, or whatever and their literary career ends almost at its beginning. But this really isn't the case of Juan Rulfo.

Rulfo considers himself an active writer, and so does everyone else. The truth is that he has been working for years on another novel, always promising to publish it soon. We know the title: *La cordillera,* and the setting: the villages of Jalisco, and Rulfo can occasionally be persuaded to talk about it. He reveals that the story traces the history, from the sixteenth century to the present, of a certain family who have large landholdings, concentrating on a female character who is the last descendant. He says that he wants "to show a reality that I know and that I want others to know . . ., to show the simplicity of country people, their candor. The man of the city sees their problems as country problems. But it's the problem of the whole country."[3]

But *La cordillera* has not yet been published, and even if it were to appear in print as these words are being written, the implications of his hesitant attitude remain. He has simply gone on year after year, promising the book and then reworking it, followed by more promises and yet further reconsideration. When and if it does appear it may be a masterpiece to outshine *Pedro Páramo,* or it may be overrefined and anticlimactic. Rulfo's vacillation is evidently a case of a great psychological hang-up. Perhaps there is a subconscious fear that anything he does from now on will not match *Pedro Páramo* or again, his hesitancy could be an extreme manifestation of his own personality, insecure, lacking in self-confidence, unable to take a forthright decision. Whatever else it is, it is a personal tragedy and a distinct loss to the nation in the literary realm.

Juan Rulfo, like Agustín Yáñez, is a native of Jalisco. Both of them have been singularly marked by the characteristics and life of the areas in which they grew up. But there is a great difference in the regions they know so well. Yáñez is a native of the "altos" or highlands of the north, a thickly populated and rather dynamic region. Rulfo, in contrast, comes from the lowlands of the south of Jalisco, once quite important but now a dusty, dying, depressed area. This fate of his native soil dominates Rulfo's mind and inspiration. He is obsessed with death, both of the land and of the people on it. Despite having lived practically all his adult life in Mexico City, the problem and atmosphere of his part of Jalisco constitute his one literary theme. The fact that he can make this desolate land with its dead or dying people come to life so realistically and hauntingly for his readers testifies to his genius and sensitivity. It may be, however, that Rulfo's sparse output is explained in part by his strict limitation of theme, as well as by his own personality.

Juan Rulfo is a shy man, unbelievably shy, an introvert, a "loner." Humble and lacking in self-assurance, he has never mixed in literary circles. He is a worrier—too concerned about too many things ever to relax. No doubt the experiences of his own early years have played a part in making him the way he is.

Rulfo's family, once apparently comfortably fixed, lost its possessions during the Revolution. He recalls moments and scenes from the days of the Cristero revolt in the late twenties. He lost his father in the first days of this struggle and his mother died only a few years later. For a time he was in an orphanage in Guadalajara, and in 1933 at the age of fifteen he went to Mexico City, where he studied accounting for a while and a little law, and then for more than ten years held a minor job in the Mexican immigration service. Following several years with Goodrich in Mexico, Rulfo worked briefly with the vast Papaloapan irrigation project near Veracruz. For a time he tried scriptwriting for the movies and some TV work in Guadalajara, and since 1962 has been with the Instituto Nacional Indigenista, an organization that compares in a general way with the U.S. Bureau of Indian Affairs.

Luis Harss gives us a vivid picture of Rulfo at his work with the Instituto:

It is tiring and depressing work that keeps him constantly on the move. He disappears for days at a time on some lonely mission into the misty backlands, and returns looking haggard, as if back from a lost weekend. Every trip is an added blow to him. On off days he sits humped over his desk in his antiseptic office on an upper floor of the Institute, starting every time the phone rings anywhere in the building and reaching for the receiver next to him as if the call were always for him. He is forever under the pressures of waiting. At any moment he might jump up and vanish. . . . Visitors who catch him on the way out, suddenly unavoidable, become honored guests. He makes an endless bustle, opening doors and pulling out chairs for them, excruciatingly shy, gazing at them out of frightened eyes. Installed at his desk in his dark suit, kneading his nervous hands, looking perpetually worried and disoriented, he is like a harried village priest at the end of a long day. . . .[4]

Yet it seems clear that Rulfo has been influenced little if at all by the several work experiences we have enumerated. Profoundly affected by his early years, he has never been able to shake the solitude he knew then, both in the orphanage and elsewhere. His inwardness and reticence seem to be characteristics of the poor country people of southern Jalisco. Of them, Rulfo himself has said: "Their vocabulary is very spare. In fact, they practically don't speak at all."[5] The desolation and abandonment and sadness of this region left a vivid and haunting impression on his mind. It is this—and all of this—that provides the setting, the motivation, and the tone throughout Juan Rulfo's two published works.

If Rulfo has trouble in putting his thoughts on paper to suit him, he likewise is slow to begin talking. In June 1965, when he was to appear in a series of informal talks by writers about themselves, Rulfo asked that Juan José Arreola, his long-time friend, come and sit beside him to help him get started. Arreola was born in the same year and the same part of Jalisco as Rulfo and is himself one of Mexico's foremost writers, principally of the short story. With his friend nudging him on, Rulfo gradually opened up. As is usual when he does so, he ranged back into the past of his Jalisco birth ground.

This sort of thing—the history of southern Jalisco all the way back to the days of the conquistadores and of the prominent families of the area—obviously fascinates Rulfo. It is a part of his abiding pre-occupation with the past. Actually, Rulfo has devoted a lot of time in an attempt to track down information on his ancestors and other families of his region. This effort has taken him to various libraries, banks, and museums in different parts of Mexico and as far north as California.

Rulfo's first novel was never published. He admits that he finally destroyed the manuscript, which was about life in Mexico City. Of this initial venture into writing and its aftermath, Rulfo tells us that it had "a somewhat rhetorical style" which he knew wasn't really the way he wanted to say things. "So," he continues, "practicing ways to free myself of all that rhetoric and bombast, I started cutting down, working with simpler characters. Of course I went over to the opposite extreme, into complete simplicity. But that was because I was using characters like the country people of Jalisco, who speak a pure brand of sixteenth-century Spanish."[6]

Then he tried his hand at the short story. It was some ten years, at one or two stories a year, before he had enough for his one collection, titled—after one of the stories—*El llano en llamas* (*The Burning Plain and Other Stories*), published in 1953. Here are fifteen of his stories, not all that he has written but most of them. Few though they are, they have been enough to give Rulfo an influence on the Mexican short story equal to what he achieved in the novel with *Pedro Páramo*. With regard to this collection, Luis Harss has written some rather poetic but very apt comments about Rulfo and his work:

> Rulfo is a man attuned to the primitive poetry of desert landscapes, dusty sunlit villages, seasonal droughts and floods, the humble joys of the harvest, the hard labor of poor lives lived out always close to plague and famine. His language is as frugal as his world, reduced almost to pure heartbeat. He has no message. He sings the swan song of blighted regions gangrened by age, where misery has opened wounds that burn under an eternal midday sun, where a pestilent fate has turned areas that were once rolling meadows and grasslands into fetid graves. . . . His theme is simply human sorrow in dispossession. He writes with

a sharp edge, carving each word out of hard rock, like an inscription on a tombstone.[7]

The reader is caught up in these stories of *El llano en llamas* and becomes an active participant, not through interiorization, density, or deliberate secretiveness as in many of the novels since Yáñez, but rather through the stark simplicity and directness, the somewhat astounding talent of Rulfo for relating his story in a way so faithful to the environment that the reader sees, hears, and feels everything as if he were physically present.

As an example we can cite "Nos han dado la tierra" [They have given us land], a satire on the land-reform program of the ruling Revolutionary Party. Narrated in the first person by cne of the campesinos, the story points up the fact that the distribution of land can sometimes be no more than a cruel jest. In this case four campesinos have been given a "generous" parcel of land, the only drawback being that it is all on the plain rather than down near the river where the water is to be had. As we walk across the plain with them, we experience in a vivid manner the reality they are living: the searing and unrelieved heat; the blinding glare; their parched, dehydrated state after hours of walking the plain; the desolation of the land, completely without trees or vegetation and so baked as not even to be dusty; the extreme dryness of their mouths; the sweltering frustration of it all. "So much land, for nothing," says our narrator. The starkness of everything, together with the simpleness of thought and word, magnify by contrast the cynical insistence of the agrarian administrator that they are getting preferential treatment.

In 1955, while still enjoying the recognition and popularity gained through *El llano en llamas*, Rulfo published *Pedro Páramo*. This work shot him into a foremost spot among Mexican and Spanish-American writers, a position he still retains. *Pedro Páramo* as a novel has evident kinship with the stories of the earlier volume. There is the same landscape, the same atmosphere, the same sparse language and overall brevity. Some of the characters could move easily from one book to the other and fit perfectly in either place. But obviously there is the difference too that here, instead of a series of stories, we have a plot revolving around the one central character, Pedro Páramo.

On first reading *Pedro Páramo* can be one of the most difficult and confusing works imaginable, especially if the reader has no advance knowledge about the story and its structure. A second and a third reading will bring the reward of seeing its complexity and obscurity dissolve into clarity if the reader has acquired the key for understanding. And the key is that Rulfo has done away with time. The living and the dead seem to mingle freely and dialogue casually. There is no way to tell the ones from the others. Later it appears that all the characters are dead and are talking among themselves about their days among the living. This somewhat startling discovery orients the reader perhaps more than anything else. Even so, the reading of *Pedro Páramo* is a challenging exercise.

This story of a local *cacique* named Pedro Páramo starts around the turn of the century and moves on through the Revolution and the Cristero revolt and beyond. When his father is murdered the young Pedro gives up being a playboy and begins to exact revenge on the village of Comala and all the area and its people. He makes himself the boss, the big landholder, the law. Nobody is spared and no method is too low if it adds to his power. To avoid paying off large debts left by his father, Pedro marries Dolores Preciado but soon his disinterest in her is such that she leaves him for good. He continues his ruthless way as lord of his estate, the "Media Luna," and ruler of the region until the Revolution comes, and then Pedro assumes that same role of opportunist that Mariano Azuela observed on all sides to his intense disgust. Like a character from an Azuela novel, Pedro Páramo professes to embrace the Revolution solely to save his own hide and his possessions.

The one thing Pedro Páramo wants and can't have is his childhood sweetheart, Susana San Juan. Her mother dies and she moves to other parts with her father. Yet Pedro remembers her, relives moments spent together, yearns for her. Clearly, she is a symbol of what he has lost: innocence, youth, love. There is also something Pedro has but can't keep. Of the several sons he has fathered, Pedro has eyes only for Miguel, who, still in his teens, has killed a man and violated many a girl. One night, riding off on his usual round of adventure, Miguel is thrown by his horse and fatally injured. Since Death knows no bribe, Pedro Páramo is helpless in the face of this blow. Other than the departure of Susana, this is the only setback he has known that can not be reversed by his money, his power, or his ruthlessness.

After many years of longing for Susana, it seems he is to get his wish. A deal is made whereby her father, now broken and in poverty, comes back to be maintained by Pedro Páramo, and Susana becomes Pedro's wife. But they don't live happily ever after. Susana, always a strange girl existing on the outer fringe of sanity, has grown worse with time and abuse by her father. Moreover, she has no love for Pedro Páramo and increasingly calls for Florencio, whom she loved in her adolescent years (before Pedro had him killed). When Susana dies, Pedro orders that the church bells be rung for three days without cessation, in his grief and frustration at losing the one prized possession he never really had. Then, angered at observing in the village a spirit of festivity while the bells are still ringing, he vows: "I will cross my arms and Comala will die of hunger."[8] It is a threat which he carries out.

Such is the story of *Pedro Páramo,* though the reader will be hard pressed to string together even this broad resume the first time through. For it is not presented in a neat chronological manner, but is given to the reader a bit at a time (there are no chapters, just a series of short sections). He must pick up little items here and there and try to fit them together, taking clues from gossip, rumors, thoughts, dialogue between the living and the dead—or between the dead harking back to different moments when they were living. Rulfo describes how he came to this approach: "I imagined the character. I saw him. Then, wondering how to handle him, I logically thought of a ghost town. And, of course, the dead live outside space and time. That gave me freedom to do what I wanted with the characters. I could have them come in, then simply fade out."[9]

The trouble is that on many occasions Rulfo makes a point of not identifying who is speaking. Gradually one becomes more adept in determining these and other unknowns, for there is always some clue if it can only be recognized. Another puzzling factor is that

Rulfo, perhaps necessarily, shifts the narrative viewpoint around a good bit, which is always a little upsetting.

A summary of the first portions will give a close-up view of the unique way in which Rulfo lays out the story. In the first section we find Juan Preciado approaching the village of Comala. Juan is the narrator and tells how he promised his dying mother, Dolores, that he would find Pedro Páramo and demand redress for Pedro's neglect of her. Juan meets a muleteer named Abundio, who says he also is a son of Pedro Páramo. Abundio adds that in the village they will be glad to see someone after so many years. Juan comments that the village seems to be abandoned, and Abundio replies: "It's not that it just seems that way. That's the way it is. Nobody lives here." When Juan asks, "What about Pedro Páramo?" Abundio says: "Pedro Páramo died many years ago."

Told by the muleteer to look for Eduviges Dyada, Juan is directed by a shadowy female figure (who appears, disappears, and reappears) to a certain house, where doña Eduviges meets him and remarks, to Juan's growing mystification, that his mother, Dolores, had told her he would come on this very day. There follows a section in which a young lad (only later can we identify him as Pedro Páramo) is daydreaming about Susana. A few pages later Eduviges reveals that Abundio also is dead, and when Juan looks more closely at Eduviges herself he realizes that her face is transparent as if lacking blood, her hands are withered and wrinkled, and her eyes can't be seen.

Later, doña Eduviges hears a horse galloping in the night—although Juan hears nothing—and identifies it as the horse of Miguel Páramo, roaming restlessly in search of its master. Then she tells how Miguel met his death on a night escapade. The two pages which follow tell how young Pedro's father was murdered, although nowhere is either actually identified. The somewhat pathetic figure of the village priest, Padre Rentería, next enters the story as he resists giving the blessing and final pardon at the funeral of Miguel Páramo; after all, Miguel was thought to have killed the padre's brother and violated his niece. The padre's inner struggle is heightened by his realization that it is only through the monetary support of Pedro Páramo that he is able to eat.

Damiana Cisneros, who had been Juan's nursemaid at birth, appears at his room in Eduviges's house and asks him to come and stay at her place, adding that poor Eduviges must still be wandering the earth in penance. A series of sections then show us Pedro Páramo and his scheming administrator, Fulgor Sedano, at work, specifically in the case of planning Pedro's marriage with Dolores for the sake of erasing large debts. We also are privy to Fulgor's amazement at finding the hitherto worthless Pedro so sharp and ambitious—and grasping. Walking across the deserted town, Damiana tells Juan not to be scared if he hears echoes in Comala, for it is filled with the echoes of departed souls still wandering the earth. She herself hears them all the time. When Juan asks her if she is alive, he is suddenly completely alone in the empty street. But he continues to hear voices, all revealing bits of the Pedro Páramo story: how he seized the lands of others, how Filoteo Arechiga's job was to find young girls to sleep with Pedro, and so on.

Juan is invited into a house where a man and woman (actually brother and sister living in incestuous relationship) let him sleep the night. Juan asks if they are dead. The woman smiles, the man looks at him seriously and says he is drunk. The woman thinks he is only scared. At dawn Juan hears them talking:

> From time to time I heard the sound of the words, and I noticed the difference. Because the words I had heard until then, and only then I realized it, didn't have any sound; they didn't sound, they were felt, but without sound, like the words we hear during dreams. [P. 61]

If this gives Juan the notion they really are among the living, other things which are said or which occur in this long and important section merely leave him in greater doubt, confusion, and fear. The woman tells him of the crowd of spirits that roam the streets by night, and later she calls it a pure wandering of people who died without pardon and for whom there is no way of getting it. By midnight of his second night in this house, Juan Preciado feels that he has to go out into the street to find air he can breathe.

> There was no air. I had to suck in the same air that escaped from my mouth, by stopping it with my hands before it went

away. I felt it going and coming, always less of it; until it became so thin that it filtered through my fingers forever.

I say forever.

I recall having seen something like foamy clouds swirling above my head and then of rinsing myself in that foam and of losing myself in all that cloudiness. It was the last thing I saw. [P. 73]

What appears to be logically the second half of the book (although there is no division or special indication of this in the physical format) begins at this point. From now on we have a sort of reverse focus as Juan Preciado speaks from his grave next to the old woman Dorotea, who in life was right in the middle of the whole Pedro Páramo picture. In fact, she was enlisted by Miguel Páramo to be his procuress. Susana is buried near them and they hear her thoughts and those of many others as the story of Pedro Páramo continues, piece by piece, to fill out the chronological sequence we already have presented. It even seems possible that Juan has been dead all along, in which case the first half of the book really was a case of his relating to Dorotea his arrival and stay in Comala and of his listening to the words, or thoughts, of the other souls buried near him as they recalled moments from life. Many of these are souls in anguish and, if they aren't exactly turning over in their graves, at least they are restless and squirming and remembering.

An interesting technique employed by Rulfo is that of returning several times to the same incident, but from different perspectives, so that it becomes well-rounded and the principal character of the episode assumes added dimension. The best example of this is the death of Miguel Páramo, which we see or hear discussed in four separate scenes. By the end of this we have a rather complete picture of the event and its implications in various lives.

And yet as we read—and reread—*Pedro Páramo,* we are aware that none of the figures in the story is developed exactly as we would expect in more conventional works. Not even Pedro Páramo himself, who in the aggregate clearly dominates the story, emerges as a flesh-and-blood person we could recognize if we met him on the street. And of course it is not intended that we should. After all, Pedro is dead and we see him only in a kind of afterworld way of recreating him: hazy, vague, less than three-dimensional, compounded of certain thoughts and memories of his own, rumor and comments about him by others, and something very much like myth. It is pertinent to point out the apparent symbolism intended by Rulfo in the choice of the name Páramo. The word *páramo* means "bleak or barren land," and its aptness in this case is surely apparent.

Almost as certainly as we can affirm that the true protagonist of *Al filo del agua* is Yáñez's village, we can conclude that Rulfo intends death to be the real protagonist of *Pedro Páramo* in the final analysis. Death is the overriding truth and presence in the story. We recall the line from Yáñez's "Acto preparatorio" saying that in his village the people had no other ambition than to go on living until the hour of a good death arrived. Here death has prevailed—even when these people were living, we might say—and it is evident that in few cases was it a good death. In this connection it is well to recall Joseph Sommer's comment that "the very substance of *Pedro Páramo* is fashioned from the concept, current in the folk belief of rural Mexico, of 'ánimas en pena'—souls in pain, condemned to roam the earth, separated from their corporeal origins."[10]

While *Pedro Páramo* is definitely not in imitation of *Al filo del agua*, it does not seem improper to say that *Pedro Páramo* carries the Mexican novel a step farther down the road. Some elements in the two works are in contrast: density and length in *Al filo del agua*, relatively few details and overall brevity in *Pedro Páramo;* full-bodied characterization of a number of figures in the former, as compared with no well-delineated character in the latter; the rich, poetic, artistic language of Yáñez, and the extreme simplicity of the folk language of Rulfo; the tense, pressurized, guilt-conscious town portrayed by Yáñez, alongside the much more relaxed though *cacique*-dominated village of Comala. Interior monologue plays a large role in *Al filo del agua*, together with a psychological probing in depth of the subconscious. In *Pedro Páramo* we may say that there is inner dialogue from the grave, and although psychology is of much less importance in this work, the whole story is narrated on the plane of the subconscious.

On the other hand, these two momentous novels coincide in some aspects. Each strives—and successfully—to create artistically an image of the rural reality in the same part of Mexico in the early years of the present century. Both books demand a high degree of reader involvement, more than any other Mexican novel up to their time. In achieving this, both Yáñez and Rulfo resort to the *hermetismo buscado* or sought-after confusion which forces the reader to look for clues, analyze everything, and make connections, in the manner of a literary detective.

As I see it, the extra step, which *Pedro Páramo* takes is Rulfo's negating of time and thereby more or less equating the natural and the supernatural, the living and the dead. He obviously is not the first writer to explore the supernatural and to give the dead a voice, but I know of no other modern novel that tells all or nearly all of its story from the grave. This is not something that is interesting merely because it is out of the ordinary. It is a daring concept, and it took unusual narrative skill to bring it off. In doing so Rulfo scores a signal success. Pedro himself is, of course, representative of a very common breed in the Mexican novel, but Rulfo's vision and treatment save him from being commonplace.

Naturally, *Pedro Páramo* was soon translated into various other languages (a total of seventeen up to now) and, as might be expected, the Mexican film industry was interested in the success attained by the novel. It was made into an ambitious movie in 1966, with the screen adaptation handled by Carlos Fuentes. For the exterior scenes they found a town in the state of Guanajuato which in recent years has dwindled in size from 40,000 people to barely a thousand. But in the film the story is allowed to unfold in chronological order before the eyes of Juan Preciado when he reaches Comala. This would seem to negate much of the value possessed by the novel. Apparently Rulfo felt the same way about it, for he is quoted as saying that they made *Pedro Páramo* into a sort of "western" which has no relation to the spirit of his work.[11]

Will we ever have more Rulfo works to enjoy and discuss? In the face of a publishing silence lasting nearly fifteen years and of the seeming psychological block which besets him, it would be easy to predict that Rulfo's significant literary output ended with the publication of *Pedro Páramo* in 1955. I believe, however, that he will one day release *La cordillera*. It is also known that he was working on some short narrative pieces which he promised to publish soon under the title of *Días sin floresta,* and there is mention too of another novel, called *La vena de los locos.* It is greatly to be hoped that this splendid novelist will return with other works as stimulating as *Pedro Páramo.*

NOTES TO CHAPTER 6

1. *Los narradores ante el público,* 1st ser. (Mexico City, 1966), p. 23.
2. *La Vida Literaria,* I, no. 10–11 (1970), 35.
3. Luis Harss and Barbara Dohmann, *Into the Mainstream* (New York, 1967), pp. 274–275.
4. Ibid., pp. 254–255.
5. Ibid., p. 256.
6. Ibid.
7. Ibid., p. 257.
8. Juan Rulfo, *Pedro Páramo* (Mexico City: Fondo de Cultura Económica, 1955), p. 147. All subsequent quotes from the text are taken from this edition.
9. *Into the Mainstream,* p. 270.
10. Joseph Sommers, *After the Storm* (Albuquerque, 1968), p. 88.
11. Quoted in the magazine *Tiempo* of Mexico City in its issue of December 19, 1966.

THE PUBLISHED WORKS OF JUAN RULFO

El llano en llamas, 1953 (Translated into English as *The Burning Plain and Other Stories.* Austin: University of Texas Press, 1967.)
Pedro Páramo, 1955 (Translated into English under the same title. New York: Grove Press, 1959.)

SELECTED STUDIES ON JUAN RULFO

Brushwood, John S. *Mexico in Its Novel,* pp. 30–34.
Carballo, Emmanuel. *El cuento mexicano del siglo XX,* pp. 60–73.
Embeita, María J. "Tema y estructura en *Pedro Páramo.*" *Cuadernos Americanos,* año 26, no. 2 (1967), pp. 218–223.

Harss, Luis, and Dohmann, Barbara. *Into the Mainstream,* pp. 246–275.
Los narradores ante el público, 1st ser. pp. 22–26.
Ocampo de Gómez, A.M., and Prado Velázquez, E., eds. *Diccionario de escritores mexicanos,* pp. 346–347.
Restrepo Fernández, Iván. "La cacería de Juan Rulfo." *Mundo Nuevo,* no. 39–40 (September-October, 1969), pp. 43–44.
Rodríguez-Alcalá, Hugo. *El arte de Juan Rulfo.*
———. Análisis estilístico de *El llano en llamas.*" *Cuadernos Americanos,* año 24, no. 3 (1965), pp. 211–234.
Sommers, Joseph. *After the Storm,* pp. 68–94.
———. "Juan Rulfo." *New Mexico Quarterly,* XXXVIII (Spring, 1968), 84–101.

Luis Spota: Self-Made Novelist

LUIS SPOTA, POSSIBLY MEXICO'S ALL-TIME BEST-SELLING NOVELIST, IS A restless, colorful figure, often the center of controversy in cultural and journalistic circles around the Mexican capital. Although abuse is commonly heaped upon him by some literary critics in his land, he is a good novelist, widely read in several languages. That he has achieved his present rank despite being a grade-school dropout simply makes his case even more fascinating to review.

Producing at the rate of almost two novels every three years (fourteen published between 1947 and 1968), Spota has kept the literary public agog in his country. He has always been what the journalists call "good copy," due in part to his own personality and extraliterary activities, but also because he approaches his writing in a manner that is uninhibited, imaginative, sometimes "flashy" and sensational, usually brash or brazen. He brings to his writing a mixture of cynicism, irreverence regarding just about all things and persons, an aversion toward insincerity wherever he sees it, impatience with the national ills, and a crusader's instincts.

In several of Spota's earlier works even the jackets, format, type, paper, and other physical characteristics were decidedly out of the ordinary, surely a calculated effort to capture the attention of the reading public. It is noticeable that in his later novels, after he had secured his place, neither he nor his publishers saw the need to lean on these promotional devices. Spota, whatever his theme or however he develops it, has the gift of provoking discussion and controversy on an impassioned plane. Rafael Solana, a highly respected literary voice in Mexico, puts it this way:

Luis Spota is not only one of the greatest novelists in Mexico but also one of the greatest writers in the Spanish language—no matter how much his books may displease us.[1]

Luis Spota was born on July 13, 1925, in Mexico City, the only son of a Calabrian merchant and an aristocratic Mexican lady. After six years of schooling he dropped out and began, as he tells it, "the adventure of living in absolute personal independence." He continues:

I learned very early about the rigors of hard work, and I had contact with the sea, the bullfighting art, and the weariness of passing out leaflets on the public streets or of wearing out shoes trying to sell encyclopedias from door to door. I was familiar with the disdainful gift of a tip as waiter in a cafe-drugstore on Avenida Juarez, and, in the fields of Texas, the resignation of the illegal wetbacks, and, finally, I worked as an office boy in a weekly magazine, which was then the best in Mexico.

He tells us too that he liked to read and that he did so "chaotically, without the counsel of a teacher, without a program, without differentiating the good from the bad." After enumerating a startlingly long list of authors of all types and nationalities, Spota adds:

As can be deduced from this list of authors which I read rashly, prematurely, and in disordered manner during adolescence, my cultural formation was chaotic, incomplete, and full of gaps. . . . I belong, consequently, to the insufferable group of the self-taught, who have to invent what they don't know. . . .[2]

While still in his teens, Spota was sent by his editors to Peru in 1943 to visit and interview José Mojica, internationally famed Mexican tenor, and long-time opera and movie star, who at the age of forty-five had turned his back on the world and gone off to become a Franciscan friar in Peru. Mojica's case was on everyone's lips in Mexico at that time, and Spota capitalized on this human-interest value by publishing that same year his first book under the title of *José Mojica, hombre, artista y fraile* [José Mojica: man, artist, and friar]. In no sense a great work, this hurried effort by the youthful Spota gives little promise of the vigorous and imaginative novelist to come. We can smilingly understate that Spota never again would come so close to pious writing.

Spota reveals that B. Traven once advised him that it is better to live before writing and that talent and imagination are poor replacements for reality.[3] This advice was given in 1948, when Spota, the aggressive young journalist, tracked down and "unmasked" Traven. Spota admits that he took Traven's advice to heart by writing of themes related to his personal experience. Most of his first books (published in 1947, 1948, 1950, and 1951) are strongly autobiographical. If we now examine these first works of Luis Spota as well as the more recent ones, we can observe how this self-taught novelist has matured and developed almost with the writing of each succeeding title.

It seems that when Spota left home he first took work on an old steamer in the coastal trade, and this experience is put to some use in the writing of his first novel, *El coronel fue echado al mar* [The Colonel was tossed to the sea], published in 1947. The novel tells of the strange eleven-day voyage during World War II of a U.S. ship, the *Anne Louise*, from a European port to the United States. Though it is really serving as a hospital ship, having been loaded with dozens of stretcher cases, this fact is not made known to the enemy. The huge painted crosses customary on the sides and decks of hospital ships are missing. Also, the grapevine reveals that some of the sick have died en route, but everyone knows there have been no burials at sea, except for a couple of sailors and also a colonel (hence the title of the book). This creates an air of tension and mystery which grows daily among the suspicious and superstitious crew.

When it is noticed that the chef sends out an overabundance of meat each time another patient dies, the horror-stricken crew refuse to eat. This hunger strike is broken after a few days by Speedy, a crewman who has surreptitiously achieved a more than passing intimacy with a redheaded nurse and from her has learned the truth. They have been transporting a boatload of soldiers wounded by some new weapon of the Nazis, and in the treatment and study of the wounded it is felt essential to hold for autopsy the bodies of those who die. In order to store the bodies under refrigeration, they must use up more and more of the food supply. Thus the mystery is dispelled.

El coronel fue echado al mar is not a very good novel, though it did win a minor literary prize. The youth and inexperience of the author are evident. The pace is not really sure or steady, and Spota doesn't pull the threads of his story together as neatly as he will a few years later. Yet two characteristics that are to become basic to his style are readily visible in this work: a true capacity for creating dialogue that is natural to the characters and the circumstances, and an equal talent for narration that holds the reader's attention from start to finish. The characters themselves are not strongly drawn, and description is largely ignored. Action is everything.

Spota's attention was then quickly captured by another cause. This time it is the so-called "wetbacks" who illegally enter the United States from Mexico each year by the tens of thousands. The result is *Murieron a mitad del río* [They died in the middle of the river], 1948, again a novelization of his own personal experiences. The principal character, José Paván, is a thin disguise for Spota himself.

Murieron a mitad del río is a book with no true plot. A strongly emotional account, chronological and episodic, it follows the wanderings, hardships, and experiences of some "wetbacks" in the Lower Rio Grande Valley of Texas. While not an outstanding novel, it marks another step in the evolution of Luis Spota as a novelist, for here he displays considerably more assurance and vigor in handling his material than in *El coronel fue echado al mar*. Moreover, his style shows improvement in such points as timing, effect, and pace, and his talent for dialogue and compelling action stands out even more notably.

A 1950 novel by Spota is *Vagabunda*, first written as a movie script. It has a strong kinship with his first novels in that it leans mightily on dialogue and action, so successfully that it is nearly impossible for the reader's fascinated interest to lag at any point. The "vagabunda" of the title is Flor, a captivating female devoid of morals and almost fiendishly capable of getting everything she wants.

The story has its setting along the Gulf coast of Mexico in the

1940s. The wandering Flor takes up with the Avila family (Pascual, the father; Miguel, a son, and his wife, Perla; another son, Mario, somewhat crippled). By story's end Flor has wrecked them all except Mario. Miguel has strangled his wife for Flor, Pascual has shot Miguel for Flor. Mario is interestingly enough one of the few Spota characters that we can genuinely like. At the final moment, when it looks like Flor is free to take all, she is caught up with in most ironical manner. Spota has a gift for creating a striking ending —not a real twist, generally, but just a good solid impact designed to carry the reader a long way after he has closed the book.

A second Spota novel published in 1950, *La estrella vacía* [The empty star], does little to enhance his career as a novelist. The theme this time is life in the film colony of Mexico City, and the "star" of the title is Olga Lang. We are treated to 537 pages of Olga's doings and are relieved of her only when Spota finally kills her off in a plane crash. It is neither edifying nor surprising to learn that the movie crowd in Mexico lives much like its counterpart in Hollywood: the norm seems to be for couples to live together without benefit of anything except physical desire. The keynote of the whole long struggle is aptly struck on the first page, where Olga is advised by her friend Teresa:

> Olga: if you want to be a star, if you want to make a name for yourself, go out with the wolves, go to their dens, be clever . . . and always carry a fountain pen in your purse . . . Do all of that. . . . And don't forget the pen. Movie contracts are signed in bed.[4]

Once again a novel with a minimum of plot, it simply traces down a great abundance of episodes concerning the activities and acquaintances connected with the rise and fall of Olga Lang. The dialogue here is good but not inspired, and the action is not sustained as in his other works. Spota likened *La estrella vacía* to a film, and we may agree that it is similar to a film for which the shooting has just ended. However, all the footage is still here. What Spota forgot or failed to do was edit, trim, pare, until he achieved a compact, swiftly paced product of about one-half the original length. It is hardly necessary to add that *La estrella vacía* soon appeared as a movie.

Más cornadas da el hambre, (*The Wounds of Hunger*), 1951, on the other hand is a distinct success and one of Spota's better works. It not only captured the Premio Ciudad de México for 1950, it also sold so well in its original edition that it was translated into half a dozen other languages. A bullfighting story, the title comes from the expression common among aspiring young *toreros* which says: "Más cornadas da el hambre que los toros" (Hunger gives worse gorings than the bulls).

As in his first two efforts, Spota is once more being autobiographical, for he went through a period of apprenticeship similar to that of the protagonist, Luis Ortega, in the book. There is, then, an air of assured authenticity in this work. Indeed, the whole story is reminiscent of some of the early chapters of the autobiography of the immortal Spanish *torero*, Juan Belmonte. This is a hard, rough story forthrightly told, with no trace of the sentimentality which splashes the pages of most bullfight literature (not excepting even Barnaby Conrad's own *Matador*).

Más cornadas da el hambre is much more fully realized, more carefully done than Spota's previous works. A little more of the meat of detail and description is wrapped around the bones of action. The pacing is excellent, the dialogue sparkling. Barnaby Conrad, a respected voice in this field, says: "This is the most powerful bullfighting novel I have ever read."[5] Again plot is unimportant, but the story never lags in interest. Luis Ortega and his faithful helper Camioneto are shown beating their way around the provincial bull-rings of Mexico for a year with many more reverses than triumphs. It is not until the final line of the last page that we find Luis stepping forth for the first time as a *torero* into the great Plaza México as the band blares and the clock strikes four on a certain Sunday afternoon.

The Premio Ciudad de Mexico for 1951 was again awarded to a Spota novel, *Las grandes aguas* [The big waters], published in 1953. The theme which commands Spota's interest on this occasion is the somewhat grandiose project to dam the Papaloapan and other rivers in southeastern Mexico to create what has been called the Mexican

Tennessee Valley Authority. Spota seems partially overwhelmed by patriotic fervor as he launches into this subject, first dedicating his book to Miguel Alemán (under whose presidency the project was launched), and then producing in Carlos Rivas (the number-one character who is superintendent of construction) a person whose passion for duty seems overdrawn, as though he is meant to symbolize the loyalty due to the *patria* in the case of such a gigantic national venture as that of Papaloapan.

To Carlos Rivas, duty is a god in the service of whose demands he renders tribute at all costs; it is an endless toll road with no exit. In the name of duty he risks his own neck, expects undue performance from others, turns his back on bribes, and pays scant attention to the needs and desires of his rather selfish and self-pitying wife and his ailing young son. No doubt Rivas would have continued on his colorless and duty-ridden way had he not been detoured by Mara, the most potent bribe to be offered by her father, Simón Kuri, whose shady business establishment has been declared off-limits to all the workers. At the same time Simón prevails on Lena (Carlos's wife) to accept such trifles as a case of whiskey and some bolts of cloth. All of this tends to make Rivas appear in more human light for a time, but a few fast crises toward the finish (notably the accidental death of Mara and the natural death of the Rivas boy) resolve the problem suitably and on the last page we find him back on the pedestal of duty—perhaps more firmly planted than before.

Las grandes aguas, though a work of some tenseness throughout, is not to compare in emotional buildup with *Más cornadas da el hambre.* We find here, however, additional evidence of Spota's growing maturity as a novelist. He has developed a better plot than in his previous works and depends less on his two great strengths of dialogue and action. He is still masterful in handling both, yet the story does not run on these two wheels alone, as with his earliest novels.

Probably the most controversial of Spota's novels—and definitely the most successful in the bookstalls—is *Casi el paraíso* (*Almost Paradise*), published in 1956. Here we have Spota's most effective plot yet, as well as a notable advance in the structuring of his novel. Here, too, his imagination, ingeniousness, and daring are pronounced. It is the lengthy, complicated, sordid story of a phony Italian prince who has taken the name of Ugo Conti and who operates in various parts of the world—always in the highest circles— with such skill that here he is on the brink of wedding the beautiful (and already impregnated) young daughter of a Mexican millionaire family when a mistake of his past catches up with him. Hence the title, *Casi el paraíso.*

The story is told from two directions: the past and the present. The past begins with his birth to an Italian prostitute; the present picks up some thirty years later as he first reaches Mexico at Acapulco in a yacht belonging to his paramour of the moment. Past and present alternate ingeniously in fifty-three extremely swift-moving chapters that lay bare the sham, hypocrisy, and false values of many among the highest echelon of Mexican society. Eventually, of course, as was inevitable from the start, past and present merge in the denouement of the final pages. It is not a pretty story, and many critics have lashed Spota for his lavish use of sex and sensationalism, yet it is all told with a mastery, an assurance, a pace which leave the reader limp at the finish.

The next novel from the Spota pen, *Las horas violentas* [The violent hours], was given to the public in 1958 and is one of Spota's better works. The twelve chapters of the book deal with the first twelve hours of a strike in a certain canning factory, hours in which tension builds up from a fast start and finally erupts in fatal violence. This is another Spota novel with a clear-cut theme (the control of Mexican labor unions by communist elements) and with drama, hatred, and violence, though with very little sex. The plot, though a lineal account moving through the twelve hours of the story (with some flashbacks to supply background), is skillfully handled. Several of the characters are more carefully delineated than is usual with Spota. And the pace is not so breakneck here as in nearly all his previous works. The twelve-hour time limit on the action makes it possible for Spota to flesh out his story with more detail and development than he has before.

In Marcos Luquín we have the first major Spota figure who is basically a good man. Simple, somewhat naive, at moments weak, Luquín is neatly depicted and gains the reader's sympathy and liking because of his innate honesty and fairness. In fact; he is too decent a person for his fellow labor leaders of the leftist stripe, who spurn a generous settlement offer by the management of the Empacadora Aguila and at the end gun down Marcos and his son Sergio (another of their own) solely for the sake of creating martyrs and inflaming the strikers to wilder demands and greater violence, all intended of course to enhance their own position and power.

In 1959 Spota published *La sangre enemiga* (*The Enemy Blood*). I am quite sure that he had high expectations for this work, that he considered it a "turning-point" effort, and that he hoped it would be hailed as his finest artistic and technical achievement up to that moment. If all this be true, then I think he produced a pretentious failure. My feeling is that *La sangre enemiga,* in the same manner as *La estrella vacía,* does little if anything to promote his literary prestige.

In structuring this novel Spota goes far beyond the alternating pattern that succeeded in *Casi el paraíso.* Here we have a more complex technique involving a multiplication of planes and points of view. But the effort falls flat. Spota fails to bring it off. It would be a better novel if written as a straight lineal account.

La sangre enemiga is a sordid story, not on the level of cafe society as in *Casi el paraíso* but rather on the level of slum society. The book is peopled with characters who, in their thoughts and deeds, reflect the haplessness, hopelessness, and degradation of their lot in life. The story revolves around several one-time circus performers, thrown on their own when the circus disbands following a serious train wreck. This little group roams through the poorer sections of Mexico City putting on impromptu performances featuring a bear and some dogs. Their leader is Esteban, left crippled and sexually impotent by the train wreck. He has a mentally retarded son, Sergio. Then there is Dimas, the blind drummer, his wife Cruz, and their teenage daughter, Alma, who runs off with a lover in midstory. Estela is the woman Esteban has lived with for some years. She is not Sergio's mother but does have a daughter of her own—Sara—who is young and beautiful and quite aware of the effect of her charms on men. When Estela dies Esteban forces Sara to share his bed, though he is incapable of satisfying her.

The rest of the story essentially is Esteban's struggle to keep Sara for himself and her efforts to escape this fate. Of course, there is also the struggle to survive from day to day. Sara has one chance to lift herself out of these sordid surroundings, but Esteban murders the serious young mechanic who is anxious to marry her. She has affairs with others but finds true sexual fulfillment only with Sergio. Esteban, on discovering them, sends Sergio off to water the bear, after which he beats and deliberately maims Sara. In the last lines Esteban and Sergio are wandering on off to other spots, where we know things will be no better.

Spota's next novel, *El tiempo de la ira* (*The Time of Wrath*), was offered to the reading public in 1960. This work impresses me as one of Spota's four or five best. It is a chronological account of César Darío's political career from the time of plotting the revolution which puts him in power until his assassination eight years later by his long-time aide Víctor. In this work Spota does not resort to flashbacks nor to the technique of alternating chapters of the past and of the present. Despite its length (557 pages), *El tiempo de la ira* never drags. The great narrative talent of Luis Spota, along with his ever-increasing concern with detail of the most down-to-earth and convincing sort and his obvious understanding of the subject, cause the reader to lay this book down only with regret, both during its reading and at its conclusion.

Perhaps *El tiempo de la ira* impresses more than most other Spota novels because he has handled so well a topic which is an almost universal Latin American theme: dictatorship. This endemic problem of the Latin American states has fascinated, quite understandably, many of their novelists, both good and bad. I believe it fair to say that few have truly surpassed Spota in their treatment of this subject. Because the approach differs so from novel to novel, it becomes difficult to judge their relative merits. In my own opinion, four of the most outstanding novels about dictatorship are *El señor presidente* (1946) by the 1967 Nobel Prize winner from Guatemala, Miguel Angel Asturias; the Mexican Martín Luis Guzmán's *La sombra del caudillo* (1929); the classic *Amalia* (1851–55) by the Argentine José Mármol; and Spota's *El tiempo de la ira*.

This narrative of the career of the dictator César Darío is dispassionately told from the vantage point of the omniscient observer. There is no overt attempt to defend or denounce Darío or anyone else in the book. Words and actions are objectively reported, and thoughts, too, for often during conversations we are given the unspoken feelings of the discussants. It might be argued that Spota obliquely favors dictatorship over democracy, since he has Héctor Gama, representative of an idealistic and intellectual approach to democracy, fail badly and swiftly once he comes to power as president in an election which César Darío scrupulously refrains from manipulating. It is true that the author depicts Gama as being thoroughly inept and incapable, favoring the traditional groups and interests, nullifying what he can of Darío's work in behalf of the common people, and then, when in trouble, resorting to those same measures of repression and absolute power which characterize dictatorships. Actually, *El tiempo de la ira* neither glorifies nor vilifies dictatorship. It simply shows both how good and how bad dictatorship can be and points up the lesson that democracy is not automatically better.

Nevertheless, it seems true that Spota's dictator is several cuts above the average Latin American tyrant. Darío is a dictator of the people, not of the rich. He is so fiercely determined to benefit the common man that practically every act he commits, whether laudable or lamentable, has this as its goal. In this stance he differs enormously from such real-life dictators as Rafael Leonidas Trujillo and Fulgencio Batista. Also, César Darío sees clearly what the national interest is and he defends it staunchly against any threat. He stands up to the foreign interests which have exploited his country and his people, though in doing so he places his government in a state of crisis, and each time he comes out on top.

Further, not even his enemies can deny that Darío is remarkably hard-working and honest. He is not addicted to drink or women. He leaves office as poor as when he went in. In truth, he is an exceptional dictator, even though he is not without many of the typical dictatorial traits: ruthlessness, love of power, increasing personal isolation along with growing distrust and fear of all opponents, a strong dash of demagoguery. (His ruthlessness extends even to the use of torture and cold-blooded murder when it comes to protecting his power.) But an honest appraisal of Darío's labors seems to point unerringly to the conclusion that, with all his faults, the common people and the country as a whole were decidedly better off because of his eight-year reign.

The characterization of César Darío is most effectively achieved. Long before the end, the reader understands him in depth and is attuned to his personality, his thought processes, his motivations, his moods. Almost as well delineated are Héctor Gama and the several characters of principal importance: Joe Flynn, Víctor, the Archbishop, Rómulo Real.

Suspense reaches climactic proportions in the last part of the book, when Víctor comes back from exile to kill Darío. The several abortive efforts, along with Víctor's own confused state of mind regarding his true feelings for Darío, keep the reader on edge up to the last line, even though logic tells him that it has to end with Víctor killing the dictator.

Luis Spota published two novels in 1964. The first of these, *La pequeña edad* [The tender age], was announced as the initial volume of a trilogy he planned to do on the Mexican Revolution. It deals with the so-called "Decena Trágica" (Tragic Ten Days) between February 9 and February 18, 1913, during which time government and rebel forces shelled each other in the heart of the Mexican capital, with immense destruction of property and high loss of life—both military and civilian. The violence ended with the overthrow and imprisonment (and, shortly thereafter, assassination) of President Francisco Madero, not by the rebel forces but actually by his own Minister of War, General Victoriano Huerta.

Spota permits his readers to view and feel this tragic period through the well-to-do Rossi family, whose home comes under artillery fire from the nearby military fortress, La Ciudadela (where the forces of rebel leader Félix Díaz, a nephew of the old dictator ousted by the Revolution in 1910, had holed up). The Rossi house is a natural and legitimate target, since a federal force (with a 75 mm. cannon) is operating outside and from the roof of the home.

In combining the story of the Rossi family with the actual facts of the "Decena Trágica," Spota of course seeks to breathe life into his historical treatment of this significant moment in the course of the

Revolution. By and large he succeeds in this objective. The narrative unfolds in straightforward manner, except that there are some flashbacks and references to the past by way of filling in the background both of the Rossi family and of the Revolution. The 562 pages constitute Spota's longest work (by five pages). There are ten chapter divisions, one for each of the Tragic Ten Days.

In *La pequeña edad,* and likewise in *El tiempo de la ira,* Spota swings away from the extreme dependence on action and speech of his early novels and heads toward the opposite extreme. While the two works contain a great deal of movement and dialogue, some spots seem almost too detailed, so that the action line is unduly clogged and the narrative flow is momentarily interrupted. Who would have thought that this great exponent of swift pace could come full circle, or even fairly close to it?

The plot of *La pequeña edad* is not complicated. Aldo Rossi is a prosperous, middle-aged, Italian-born merchant whose grocery establishment, "Sorrento," adjoins his house. He has a married daughter by his first wife, deceased some years before. For eight years he has been married to María Alard, of the old aristocracy which all but worshipped Porfirio Díaz, and they have a five-year-old son, Luis Felipe, who throughout the story is in bed recovering from smallpox.

María is rigid, frigid, and neurotic. All of this she has copied directly from her own mother ("Mamacita"). She gives Aldo such a bad time that it is no great wonder he has a mistress, Betina, in another part of town. The other characters are numerous and varied, including the following and many more: Alfonso (María's brother); doña Albina, Matilde, and Ausencio, servants; don Primo de la O, a genuine psychotic who lives across the street and who during the fighting takes sadistic delight in sniping at passersby with his rifle; Capitán Ojeda; Doctor Cobo; Conchita, Alfonso's common-law wife; Padre Paz; many soldiers and a goodly number of their women, the *soldaderas.* Alfonso, doña Albina, and even Aldo, are characters the reader can like—a rare harvest in a Spota work!

With these active characters and countless others who do not appear physically but who are talked about frequently because they are the figures involved in the revolutionary activity around the city, Spota guides the reader through a vivid narrative of that hectic time, made to come alive because it is happening to and all around the Rossi family and friends who are caught in the midst of the struggle. At one point in the story María, perhaps so shaken by the frightful events that she is dislodged from her usual way of thinking and acting, discovers true conjugal love and appears to have undergone a basic transformation. Not yet truly conscious of this, Aldo undertakes the dangerous trip across town to see Betina and is fatally wounded. María, aware of the choice he had made, can also be said to have been fatally wounded, at least figuratively. And so at the end Madero has fallen victim of Huerta's perfidy; Aldo is dead, a victim of the Decena Trágica and of his own infidelity; and María, back in her neurotic shell, is almost as good as dead. It is a good novel, a fairly strong novel.

La carcajada del gato [The cat's laugh], also published in 1964, relates a fantastic story, one that would normally strain credulity. In fact, it would be easy to say that Spota has gone too far in concocting such a plot were it not that he based it on a newspaper exposé of just such a situation. Taking that bare skeleton, Spota has filled it out with a multiplicity of ingenious detail. As with the great bulk of the Spota works, it is not a pleasant or happy story—indeed, in spots it is quite distasteful. Yet in true Spota style it is compelling. It seizes the interest and imagination of the reader and then crams his mind with so many artfully devised incidents and circumstances that the whole story in time becomes all too plausible.

In contrast with his earlier works, however, the pace here is never breakneck. The movement is measured and nearly always calm. Actually, from the first page until the last there is a lapse of barely one hour, though by means of flashbacks and inner monologues we are carried back to the real beginning of the story twenty years before and gradually led up to the final fateful hour. The book is also unusual in that there is not a single chapter division or other break from start to finish—just 406 pages of continuous text!

The action of *La carcajada del gato* is seen almost completely through the eyes of Claudia, who might well be classified among life's losers. In the first paragraph we learn that she and her two older children (Job, nineteen years old, and Yuri, seventeen) have just agreed to poison Lázaro, the head of the family, when he returns home an hour later. Claudia will season his soup with cyanide, which he will not notice because the years he has spent preparing insecticides have dulled his senses to the detection of the poison. Momo, another daughter now thirteen years old, is not in on the death pact.

If this all sounds a bit cold-blooded, its explanation is to be found in the background. Lázaro, now past sixty (Claudia is thirty-seven), is brilliant but so strange that he must be tagged as some kind of madman. He keeps his family utterly isolated from the outside world. The house, yard, garden, and small insecticide plant are surrounded by a series of walls, the gates and doors of which can be opened only by him. Inside, there are no clocks, calendars, mirrors, radios or TV, reading or writing materials. Claudia has not seen the outside world since she first came here to live with Lázaro twenty years ago. The children have never been outside the walls, have never seen another person besides themselves.

This would seem bizarre enough, but there's more. Lázaro, a thoroughgoing nonbeliever in matters relating to God and religion, is convinced that he is called to start a new strain of the human race, one that will be free of all our superstitions, prejudices, outmoded beliefs and traditions, vices and weaknesses. He has no doubt that he is superman enough to father such a new breed, but the mother must be someone uncontaminated by the world, a sort of germ-free guinea pig, as it were. So, he turns to Yuri as soon as she is old enough to bear children. The fact is that he had all this in mind even before he brought Claudia here to live. Yuri, who has no concepts of right and wrong, is a willing pawn. Claudia is horrified but long since quite cowed by Lázaro. Job is blind with jealousy. He once attempted to become passionate with Yuri (having spied on Lázaro and Claudia at night, he assumed that Yuri was for him), but Lázaro came upon the scene, beat the boy fiercely, and thereafter made Yuri his own.

But nature foils his mad plans. Five times Yuri becomes pregnant and five times suffers miscarriages. At this stage Momo is just old enough, and Lázaro turns his attentions to her. This brings us to the opening moment of the story. Claudia and the older children have strong reason to believe that Lázaro intends to possess Momo this very night. Hence, they have made the pact to poison him, though each party to the pact has a different motive. Claudia wants to put an end to the whole unnatural business, both the living in total isolation and the incestuous relationships. Yuri is consumed by hatred for Lázaro because he has abandoned her for Momo. Job smolders with rage against Lázaro, for mutilating his face in the beating over Yuri, for taking Yuri from him, and for being on the brink of doing the same with Momo, whom Job now covets.

During the hour of waiting for Lázaro to return to his doom, we see Claudia's past. Orphaned at three, she was raised by two pious maiden aunts in a provincial city. At seventeen, she was victimized by a prominent citizen who gloried in his female conquests. A few months later Aunt Amelia, horrified when she learned that Claudia was going to have a baby, insisted on an abortion for her neice. Claudia was then packed off to the capital to be shut up in a home for wayward girls. On the train to the city she met Lázaro and a couple of months later, after a doctor in the girls' home had tried to rape her and/or make her his mistress, Lázaro persuaded her to slip away and live with him.

For several months she was most happy, until the strange episode of a stray tomcat which came almost daily to sit in the garden and stare at her in a near-hypnotic manner. Sometimes when Claudia would appear, the cat frolicked with joy and actually gave forth with what sounded like a human laugh. (This would seem to explain the title of the book, though there is another implication which we shall mention later.) Anyway, Lázaro disliked the cat because of the fascination it held for Claudia, and one night he poisoned it—with cyanide.

In the course of the cat interlude Claudia began to keep a sort of diary, or at least to put down occasional thoughts in a notebook which Lázaro had, up to then, let her have. Included in the diary were a number of silly and romantic remarks about the "gato," which she always identified only by the initial G. Several years later Lázaro chanced upon this notebook and on reading the entries about "G." became absolutely furious and emotionally unstable in a manner that was to be permanent thereafter. He was certain she had been unfaithful to him by thought and desire with this person called "G." and from then on his hatred for her was lasting. As for Claudia, her life from that point to the poisoning of Lázaro can be labelled a martyrdom.

La carcajada del gato leaves us with several questions which we can not answer with certitude. Some of these revolve around the final implication of the title and the whole meaning of the cat business. When Claudia discovers the poisoned cat in the garden, she is horrified to see that its features appear to be those of Lázaro. And, when Lázaro becomes violently ill that same day through accidental self-poisoning with cyanide (he had forgotten to wash his hands the night before after setting out poisoned meat for the cat), she again is aghast to see that in his agony Lázaro's features are those of the cat. No doubt the psychologists can easily explain away such emotional reactions, but is Spota insinuating a pact between Lázaro and the devil? Is there a subtle intent in his giving the name Lázaro to this sinister character? Does Lázaro's apparent power of extrasensory perception tie in with this unnatural implication?

Again, when Job is born Claudia feels momentary revulsion because as she first looks upon him his face is that of the cat. Throughout the book we are reminded that Job is catlike (he has cat eyes, his ears are shaped like a cat's and he can make them move, his movements are stealthy, he sits and stares at Claudia—or Yuri or Momo—with the sinister patience of a predatory cat). Near the end we encounter these lines with reference to Claudia's failure to stand up to Lázaro at any earlier time through the years of enslavement:

> She justified the cowardness of her obedience by telling herself that it was her fate to suffer indefinitely and that it would be useless to try to escape from Lázaro, since, in keeping with what was written in the book of fate, she and her children would fall into the hands of another demon of the same species. Which will occur, in fact, as soon as Lázaro dies.[6]

The last sentence quoted has to be the most discouraging line in the entire book. In it we can find the veiled implication that the new demon of the same species as Lázaro will be his son, Job. Earlier we have seen him thinking that once Lázaro is out of the way, Momo will be all his—and Yuri and Claudia too. Does Spota tell us something through the name Job which he has given to this catlike figure who sits waiting and brooding? And is the title the tip-off that the final "carcajada del gato" is Job's laugh of triumph once Claudia has engineered the disappearance of Lázaro? Spota leaves it to his reader to decide.

The next Spota novel is *Los sueños del insomnio* [The dreams of insomnia] published in 1966. It is a story composed completely of interior monologue, as a middle-aged society playboy prepares to commit suicide. He is the only character actually to appear on stage in the whole book, though many others have their part as his reminiscences range back through his whole life. Not as outsized as some of Spota's works (only 350 pages), it is broken into fifty-one chapters or divisions in which the thoughts of the protagonist Flavio Millán alternate between his impending suicide and episodes of his past, mostly involving his women friends, including a wife who left him after eight years.

By the time Flavio gets around to taking the suicide pills in the final chapter, we have learned about all there is to know about him. The question does arise as to whether it is worthwhile to know Millán that well, for his life has not been of much value to himself or anyone else. Though he is intelligent and cultured and has made a name for himself in creative work (never identified), his life for many years has been basically meaningless, since he is self-centered and selfish, concerned only with pleasure.

Naturally, our reaction is as Spota intended. *Los sueños del insomnio* is another of his satires on Mexican high society and on corruption in public life, not alone in political arenas but likewise in cultural circles. It is typical of the Spota cynicism and pessimism displayed more than once previously, particularly in *Casi el paraíso*. As usual, his rare narrative talent is manifest throughout. Aside from Flavio himself, no other character is really developed, although the artist Julia Blandish does come somewhat to life.

Lo de antes [What went before], published in 1968, surprises from the outset, for its 205 pages make it the shortest Spota novel since *Vagabunda* in 1950. It is more alive and moves more expeditiously to its conclusion than any other of his recent works. Various interesting little experiments in form, style, and technique are utilized, and Spota (who knows the language of the street remarkably well) employs quite effectively the idiom of the common man in today's Mexico.

In this novel we find Spota making more than customary use of the inner monologue, flashbacks, the sudden and abrupt shifting of plane or place or time, the contrived ambiguity to compel the reader to enter into the story and into the mind of the main character. Also, as Carlos Fuentes does with Artemio Cruz, Spota has his narrator, Javier, speak in three different persons: "I," "you," "he" (all referring of course to himself and often within the same paragraph). I believe this is Spota's best novel so far.

Lo de antes is the story of Javier Lira Puchet, an ordinary person with no strong moral convictions. He has, however, risen above his twenty years of petty crime (mostly as a pickpocket—a "Tarzán") and has managed to go straight for five years. He has a modest though decent job as a loan and time payment collector for a Mexico City bank. Though he has a good home life with his wife, Berta, who has given him one child and is about to deliver another, he still has a somewhat roving eye. There is no doubt that Javier would have gone on being an ordinary person on the upper margin of the lower class had he not been pushed (bullied and blackmailed, in truth) back to his career of thievery by a police officer who had hounded him in his earlier years.

Javier is the central character, the only one carefully depicted. Everything is related through his eyes, or occurs in his presence—the technique of the single narrative viewpoint cherished by many fine novelists, particularly Henry James. The theme of *Lo de antes* is that the past is almost impossible to get away from finally and successfully, especially in the Mexican society of today. The setting of the story is Mexico City, though one flashback takes us to the penal colony on Isla Tres Marías where Javier spent three years.

Javier Lira Puchet is a believable character with whom the reader comes to sympathize rather fully, particularly in the later chapters when the corrupt Burro Prieto manhandles him and demands a daily payoff of one hundred pesos, which he tells Javier to get by once again resorting to his old trade. In several hours of wrestling with the problem, pondering the consequences of every possible turn, and desperately seeking an out, Javier reaches the only and inevitable conclusion, namely, that he can't escape his fate. Thus is spotlighted the problem and the plight of the man with a past which includes several convictions and a prison term. The fact that Javier's past returns to haunt and engulf him through the medium of a corrupt police officer merely adds to the irony and underscores the low esteem in which the police force has customarily been held in Mexico City.

Tracing the evolution of Luis Spota's novelistic paths and techniques is not in the least difficult. In his early years there is an urgency to get his story told and move on to the next. He relies too much on action and narrative skill, while building his story around a cause or theme, which he sometimes tends to overstate. These first novels (except for *La estrella vacía*) lean toward the brief side and do show the author's journalistic background and instincts.

Beginning with his sixth work, *Las grandes aguas,* there is a gradual turning which ushers in his intermediate stage. Action remains the foremost element but it seems a bit slowed by increasing attention to description and detail, with the books becoming somewhat longer and less of the journalistic touch. He develops more effective structuring in this middle period, which I feel terminates in 1959 with the publication of *La sangre enemiga.*

Spota's last five works (*El tiempo de la ira, La pequeña edad, La carcajada del gato, Los sueños del insomnio* and *Lo de antes*) represent a new era in his novelistic development, one in which he reaches maturity as a writer. Here he has slowed himself down on the action front, his structuring seems even sharper, his characterization finally achieves creditable rank, and he packs each of these works with believable and relevant detail to achieve the "density" so common now with serious novelists. Spota is no longer the journalist writing a novel, nor just a storyteller who pushes a set of thinly sketched characters through an ever-lively plot at too fast a pace. Now he lets the reader pause—even stop occasionally—and come to know and appreciate the characters intimately. Moreover, there is time to savor, indeed to revel in, a multiplicity of detail which gives the story body and depth and a satisfying fullness.

One prominent critic of Mexican literature has affirmed rather recently that "Spota really doesn't pretend to be enough of an artist to be included in the tradition of the deeply searching novel that was established by Yáñez in 1947."[7] I must disagree with this conclusion. I believe his last five works are precisely an effort to enter into the group of Mexican writers of the "new novel" that searches deep into the realms of the inner consciousness, the subconscious, the real and the unreal, the imaginary, the fantastic. Whether Spota succeeds in this intent to the degree that some others do is another question. I think it is obvious that he doesn't (though in *Lo de antes* he comes quite close) and that the reason for this is that his temperament and instincts are not of the sort that easily lend themselves to the new style. But to say that Spota doesn't pretend to write this type of novel ignores, to my mind, the evolution which he has shown in his most recent works.

Certain traits remain constant in Spota's novelistic output. For instance, he is preeminently a novelist of the urban scene. All except three or four of the earlier works are set exclusively or principally in Mexico City, which is Spota's own environment and he seems to know it as well as any writer can.

But, more significantly, he reveals in every work (except *El coronel fue echado al mar,* which stands apart from his other efforts) a cynicism and a preoccupation with bitterness, hatred, violence, and sex. In the great bulk of his novels we detect a tone of social protest, which leads us to wonder if Spota, the cynic, isn't also a reformer at heart. Not that he preaches (far from it!), and he never advocates any reform positively. But his characters are forever showing, by negative example or by their plight, many ills in Mexican life that call for correction. In this Spota plays no favorites. He finds sordid and seamy persons and situations wherever he looks, whether in the upper, middle or lower class.

In fact, an overview of the Spota novels points up the rather complete lack of moral sense or sensitivity on the part of most of his characters. Some are quite repulsive and most of the others neither admirable nor really likeable. Of the few who come close to being "simpático," Javier in *Lo de antes* stands out in my mind.

Furthermore, Spota has the almost unbroken custom of killing off one or more major characters in the final chapters or pages of his books, occasionally in the very last line. This could obviously be a defect in a novelist's capacity for structuring his work, for many a writer has been able to conclude his story only by exterminating the protagonist. Spota may fairly be accused of this in *La estrella vacía*, though in all other cases the plot leads unerringly to the point where it seems entirely logical (at times even desirable!) for the character in question to meet his end.

Not to be well received by the critics customarily would denote lack of talent in a novelist. Spota's critics, however, rarely deny his capability, especially his narrative gift. They denounce the repugnance of his plots, the meanness of his characters, the bitterness and hatred so prevalent in his works, and what they regard as poor taste in many Spota scenes. I doubt that Spota is as unperturbed by all this as he sometimes tries to indicate, for I conceive him to be highly ambitious as a novelist and immensely determined to achieve high rank among Mexican writers of this genre. Yet their criticisms seem not to deter him and even less to change him. He fires back at them in similar manner and goes his own way.

No doubt Spota invites some of the antagonism between himself and the critics, not only by the type of characters and themes he chooses for his books, but also through his somewhat aggressive, abrasive personality. He is something of a literary loner, and independent, and is not disposed to go about praising the works of others just so they will in turn praise his—a practice far from unknown in Mexico and elsewhere. And he isn't likely to win over many of the critics with comments such as these:

> My relations with the critics (with the group of critics that I make unhappy by writing and publishing) have never been good, nor do I expect them to improve now. I have absorbed so many of their barbs that I have become critic-resistant. Furthermore, seeing what those persons applaud and recommend, I would be alarmed, I confess, if I should begin to receive their praises.[8]

It is disturbing to observe that some critics (not all of them Mexican) dismiss Spota in rather cavalier fashion, judging all of his work on the basis of his first few novels. Granted that Spota was not an outstanding novelist in that early stage of his development; a consideration of his more recent works makes it much more difficult to brush him aside.

Several things about Luis Spota as a novelist command attention and respect. One is that no one has worked harder than he to attain competence in his craft. Another is that he has progressed enormously from his first efforts to his most recent works. And, whatever his accomplishments, they have been achieved almost totally by his own determination and hard work. No one can deny, either, that he knows remarkably well the things he writes about. Lacking the sheer talent and the literary artistry of a Fuentes or a Yáñez, he still has made a contribution to the present-day Mexican novel that is decidedly substantial.

It is safe to say that Luis Spota will be heard from again. Now approaching his mid-forties, he may be productive for another twenty years. At his pace since 1947, this means that we might expect a dozen or more Spota novels in the years to come! Whatever else may be said of him, I submit that Luis Spota, the grade-school dropout, has come a long way since *El coronel fue echado al mar.*

NOTES TO CHAPTER 7

1. Luis Spota, *Las horas violentas,* 2nd ed. (Mexico City: Libro Mex Editores, 1959), quoted on the jacket.

2. *Los narradores ante el público,* 1st ser. (Mexico City, 1966). All quotes in this paragraph are from pp. 76–77.

3. Luis Spota, *Murieron a mitad del rio* (Mexico City: Manuel Porrúa, 1948), foreword.

4. Luis Spota, *La estrella vacía* (Mexico City: Manuel Porrúa, 1950), in "Trailer" preceding the text.

5. Quoted in Luis Spota, *The Wounds of Hunger* (Boston: Houghton Mifflin, 1957), foreword, p. vii.

6. Luis Spota, *La carcajada del gato* (Mexico City: Joaquín Mortiz, 1964), p. 393.

7. John S. Brushwood, *Mexico in Its Novel* (Austin, 1966), p. 28.

8. *Los narradores ante el público,* p. 83.

THE NOVELS OF LUIS SPOTA

El coronel fue echado al mar, 1947
Murieron a mitad del río, 1948
Vagabunda, 1950
La estrella vacía, 1950
Más cornadas da el hambre, 1951 (Translated into English as *The Wounds of Hunger.* Boston: Houghton Mifflin, 1957; New York: New American Library, 1959.)
Las grandes aguas, 1953
Casi el paraíso, 1956 (Translated into English as *Almost Paradise.* New York: Paperback Library, 1964.)
Las horas violentas, 1958
La sangre enemiga, 1959 (Translated into English as *The Enemy Blood.* Garden City, N.Y.: Doubleday, 1961.)
El tiempo de la ira, 1960 (Translated into English as *The Time of Wrath.* Garden City, N.Y.: Doubleday, 1962.)
La pequeña edad, 1964
La carcajada del gato, 1964
Los sueños del insomnio, 1966
Lo de antes, 1968

Note: The *Diccionario de escritores mexicanos* indicates that there also are editions in English of *El coronel fue echado al mar, Murieron a mitad del río,* and *Las grandes aguas,* but I have been unable to find any other reference to them.

STUDIES ON LUIS SPOTA

Brown, Donald F. " 'Germinal's' Progeny." *Hispania,* LI (September, 1968), 424–432.
Brushwood, John S. *Mexico in Its Novel,* pp. 28, 35.
Brushwood, John S. and Rojas Garcidueñas, José. *Breve historia de la novela mexicana,* pp. 127–128.
González, Manuel Pedro. "Luis Spota, gran novelista en potencia." *Revista Hispánica Moderna,* XXVI (January-April, 1960), 102–106.
Los narradores ante el público, 1st ser., pp. 69–86.
Monsiváis, Carlos. "Luis Spota: novelista del futuro." *Revista de la Universidad de México,* XIV (January, 1960), 37.
Ocampo de Gómez, A. M. and Prado Velázquez, E., eds. *Diccionario de escritores mexicanos,* pp. 374–375.

8

Carlos Fuentes, "The Very Model of a Modern Major Novelist"

CARLOS FUENTES IS THE MEXICAN NOVELIST MOST WIDELY KNOWN and discussed internationally at the present time. While this is no guarantee that he is the best of the living novelists in Mexico, it does say something about the kind of person he is and the sort of book he writes. Fuentes himself is perhaps the most controversial literary figure in his country, and probably draws more attention in Europe than any other writer ever to come out of Mexico. The fact that he is constantly appearing and reappearing in the public eye can be attributed to his instinct for publicity and public relations and to his frank Marxist stance, which imparts an ideological slant to his works.

It is easy to reach the conclusion that, in terms of sheer talent and potential, Carlos Fuentes surpasses all other Mexican novelists. However, the great and nagging question about him is whether he has capitalized fully (or ever will) on this native ability. Lesser disputes swirl around the ideological intentions in his novels and the degree to which his success has been manipulated.

Becoming a novelist was, in a way, easier for Fuentes than for any other Mexican novelist of consequence in this century. Born in 1928 of "typical petit bourgeois stock," as he calls it, Fuentes spent his early and formative years in various New World capitals where his father, don Rafael Fuentes (who died early in 1971) was a career diplomat representing the Mexican government. Carlos grew into an urbane, cultured, sophisticated young man, at home in several languages and more than one culture. He took his law degree at the National University of Mexico in addition to a year in Geneva devoted to the study of international law.

With such a cosmopolitan background, it is not at all surprising that Fuentes is well read in several literatures. Distinctly handsome himself, he and his screen star wife, Rita Macedo, prior to their divorce in 1969, made a highly photogenic pair who moved in select social circles wherever they went and attracted much attention from the press. Given Fuentes's background, training, temperament, and interest, it was almost inevitable that he should engage in some sort of cultural activity. Since he had from childhood felt the urge to write, it was natural that he channel his efforts in this direction. Adding his extraordinary talent to the other advantages working in his favor, Fuentes very quickly propelled himself into the front rank of Spanish-American novelists. He carries off the whole thing so well that his friend Keith Botsford, the English novelist, dubbed him not at all inaccurately as "the very model of a major modern novelist." As Botsford points out, Fuentes is "exotic, erotic, experimental, and avidly plays the literary lion." While there is nothing inherently wrong in this, Botsford considers that it is dangerous and a waste of talent, as well as distracting, and that it causes the essential seriousness of the man to be lost.[1]

The ease with which Fuentes has always moved among the elite culturally, socially, and economically, both at home and elsewhere in Latin America and Europe, has provoked some sniping from less fortunate—or less endowed—colleagues. Some of the latter, mostly of the younger group, have hinted that much of Fuentes's success flowed from his social connections and his undoubted flair for attracting publicity. Prior to 1966 it was not beneath some to taunt him for not having won any literary prize, though such a feat by Mexican and other Spanish-American novelists was becoming relatively commonplace. But in that year the jeer was silenced when he was awarded the coveted Premio Biblioteca Breve, given by the Barcelona publishing firm of Seix Barral.

Even this triumph, however, was not without its controversy. The prize indeed was awarded to Fuentes, but Seix Barral did not succeed in publishing the novel *Cambio de piel* (*A Change of Skin*) in Spain. Spanish censorship banned the printing of the book on the grounds that it contained numerous obscene passages contrary to law and all good taste. Nonetheless, the novel appeared shortly in Buenos Aires and Mexico City, and in English and Italian translations quickly thereafter.

Along with much truly fine writing, Fuentes's works frequently turn to language that is offensive to many people. This type of writing, once rare, is of course very common in much of today's popular literature. The justification which Fuentes and the others would give is that some people obviously think and talk in this manner and that some of their characters, being of this type, likewise do so. Readers squeamish on the point are well advised to proceed with some caution in picking up a Fuentes novel.

Although never truly active in politics, Carlos Fuentes has always manifested a political concern (both on domestic and international issues). And he makes no secret of where he stands politically: on the left and in the camp of Marxism. He is an open admirer of Fidel Castro and his Cuban Revolution and equally frank in attacking what he calls the U.S. imperialist policy in Latin America, which he says he opposes because it gives visible support to dictators and outmoded political structures which would topple were it not for the backing of Washington.[2]

All of this, understandably, has not endeared Fuentes to the U.S. State Department, which has retaliated by denying him a visa on more than one occasion. When, in 1964, Fuentes was scheduled for some TV appearances in New York in connection with his highly successful novel *La muerte de Artemio Cruz* (*The Death of Artemio Cruz*), his arrival was delayed by the action of Thomas Mann, then Undersecretary of State for Latin American Affairs, who finally approved Fuentes's entry into this country for a stay of only five days. And in February, 1969, returning to Mexico on a Spanish ship following four years of voluntary exile in Europe, Fuentes was not permitted ashore in San Juan, Puerto Rico, because the U.S. authorities considered him an undesirable alien. This seemingly ridiculous and unnecessary action provoked the ire of Fuentes and a wave of protest from many other sources.

Yet our major concern is not the personal life or the ideology of Fuentes, but his literary career. The first appearance of his work in book form occurred in 1954, when he published a thin volume of six short stories under the title of *Los días enmascarados* [The masked days]. Here we see at once some things which are to characterize most of his creative work. For one thing, Fuentes reveals himself as an excellent writer with rare literary talent. These stories indicate too his deep concern over the social reality of the country. Most of all, however, they show his preoccupation with interpreting the past, with seeking the Mexican identity. In this search he frequently delves into what he calls Mexican mythology.

Fuentes wonders whether any other country, aside from Russia or Spain, has worried as much as Mexico about the sense of nationality, and he feels that the root of this true Mexican obsession lies in its myths.[3] Mexico's past, says Fuentes,

> weighs heavily, because although the Conquerors, the Spaniards, carried the day, Mexico, because of its particular political and historical makeup, has given the final victory to the conquered. That's what the statue of Quauhtemoc means. In Lima you have the statue of Pizarro, in Santiago that of Valdivia. Here the defeated have been glorified. Why? Because Mexico is a country where only the dead are heroes. If Francisco Madero, Emiliano Zapata, or Pancho Villa were alive today, with his finger in profiteering and graft, he wouldn't be a hero any more, would he? Our heroes are heroes because they were sacrificed. In Mexico the only saving fate is sacrifice. . . . The nostalgia for the past in Mexico is a direct result of the original defeat, of the fact that Mexico was a country that lost its tongue, its customs, its power, everything.[4]

He believes so strongly in this mythological complex of the Mexicans (in which they blend and confuse and transform legend and history) that he incorporates some elements of it in most of his short stories and several of his novels. In "Chac Mool," admittedly the best story in *Los días enmascarados,* a statue of Chac Mool, the Aztec god of rain, comes to life and takes over the house and possessions of the person who bought the statue. Discussing the stories of Carlos Fuentes, Emmanuel Carballo says that Fuentes invents a fictitious but credible atmosphere, fantastic but real.[5] The result is, then, one man's version of what has recently come to be called "magical realism."

The year 1958 witnessed the publication of Fuentes's first novel, *La región más transparente* (*Where the Air Is Clear*), which I feel sure is one of the six most-discussed Mexican novels of the present century. The others would be *Los de abajo, Al filo del agua, Pedro Páramo, Casi el paraíso,* and *La muerte de Artemio Cruz* (also by Carlos Fuentes). *La región más transparente* is an ambitious, sprawling, disjointed, extensive and expansive novel with an abundance of characters and a minimum of plot. The title comes from a phrase used by the famed nineteenth-century German scientist Baron Alexander von Humboldt to describe Mexico City: "the region of the most transparent air." The time of the story is mostly 1951, although the final chapters carry us up to 1954 and some of the earlier chapters trace the past of certain characters, or their families, back to the days of the Revolution.

Like many other Spanish-American novelists, Fuentes has written more than one film script and some of the techniques of scenario writing are visible here. Chapters often might better be called scenes, and they tumble one after another in such rapid succession and apparent lack of sequence that it takes a while to comprehend what is happening. This is particularly true at the beginning, when we are confronted by a welter of characters in quick order.

La región más transparente is Fuentes's vision of Mexico City on all levels of society and at the same time his interpretation of Mexico forty years after the Revolution. The great cosmopolitan capital is dissected vividly, dramatically, and convincingly. Fuentes knows well the groups he sketches: the upper middle class, which is living too fast and too selfishly; the remnants of the Porfirian aristocracy, still grasping at any straw which provides hope for a return to the old order; the teeming lower strata and its inevitable types; taxi drivers, prostitutes, "braceros" returned from working in the U.S.; ex-revolutionaries, some of whom have muscled their way into positions of great power and wealth, and others who have tried this and failed or who are content to gather together periodically to recreate the aura of those days of "glory."

As in many another Mexican novel in this century, the protagonist of *La región más transparente* is not one person but a whole society—in this case Mexico City in postrevolutionary times. Even so, the numerous characters in the book (with one exception) are convincing in what is seen of them, despite the fact that nearly all can be regarded as prototypes or symbols. Many appear only once, others briefly but on several occasions, a limited number form the backbone of the story, and one is almost ubiquitous.

The self-made financier Federico Robles is the most fully developed personality in the story. Of Indian origin, he participated rather obscurely in the Revolution and subsequently, by dint of ambition, business acumen, and absolutely ruthless financial operations, he rose to the pinnacle of worldly success. Status, power, and money are the personal gods he selfishly worships. To enhance his image he marries a stunning beauty in Norma Larragoiti, whose ideals are as vacuous and pragmatic as her husband's. Robles mintains a blind mistress, Hortensia Chacón, and it is through her that we see a more human side to this financial tycoon-machine.

Rodrigo Pola represents another type. Son of an idealistic revolutionary who ignobly went to his execution in 1913, and raised by a far too protective mother, Rodrigo grew up with a literary urge which sought poetic outlet but he has no fixed goal, no self-assurance, and is unwilling to face up to a life which he cannot manipulate. Typical of his ineffectual existence is the way he allows Robles to make off with Norma, for whom he has felt an enduring love.

There are many lesser yet important characters: Pimpinela de Ovando, daughter of a top family of the Díaz period, who with her mother persists in refusing to accept the new order and strives to preserve her family's one-time importance; the intellectual Manuel Zamacona, an ineffectual arguer for a better society; Roberto Régules, a somewhat shady lawyer who has climbed the social ladder and who eventually brings about the collapse of the Robles financial empire; young Gabriel, who has just come back from working in the U.S. and, like many of the lower ranks, is discontent with what Mexican life offers.

And then there is Ixca Cienfuegos, the unconvincing, ubiquitous character who carries the heavy burden of being everybody's conscience. It may be that Ixca also represents the attitudes of Fuentes. He appears to serve, too, Fuentes's obsession with mythical elements of Mexico's past. Whatever his function in the structure of the novel, it is too much, and Fuentes, with all his skill, doesn't bring it off. Ixca is too smug, too all-knowing, too much at home with all characters on all social levels, too prone to point the finger of reproach, too often intruding in countless scenes, always superior to the rest of the cast. Never a truly real person, he prods and probes and accuses, in mysterious and enigmatic manner, though a few times he becomes a distinct activist. In an out-of-character ploy (if it's possible for such a formless personality to be out of character), he whips off to Acapulco with Norma for a week of sexual abandonment. And it is Ixca who destroys Federico Robles by launching a whispering campaign against the latter's financial gambles. Without Ixca Cienfuegos, Fuentes would have had to structure his novel differently, but it would have been worth all the effort.

While *La región* doesn't have a genuine plot, there is no dearth of action in short bursts and a number of characters undergo drastic changes and varying fates. Norma dies in a fire in her own home and Robles, ruined financially, goes off to the north with Hortensia to start a new—and different?—life. Rodrigo, having sold out his principles and suddenly rich through the trashy film scripts he turns out, tries to buy a semblance of social respectability by marrying Pimpi de Ovando, who abandons her holdout and accepts Rodrigo rather than risk losing everything. Manuel Zamacona meets a sudden and meaningless (though perhaps symbolic) death, as do also Gabriel and the taxi driver Juan Morales. Roberto Régules meanwhile has climbed up to the financial spot Robles formerly held.

Besides fashioning these changes which lead the reader to a certain feeling of fulfillment, Fuentes at the same time weaves in various links between many of the families involved in the story. Thus, at one point toward the end, we learn that Federico Robles is in fact the father of Manuel Zamacona, though neither of them is aware of it. In this manner Fuentes gradually knits together the many loose threads of human existence which he scattered about in the opening chapters.

Fuentes does not suspend or negate time, as Rulfo does in *Pedro Páramo*, but with deft choice and genuine skill he presents his scenes without regard to a time sequence, in an order dictated by the narrative demand. Scenes and conversations of the smart social set and of the lower class are frequently and effectively juxtaposed. The striking differences in their interests, their thought processes, and their speech underscore graphically the distinctions and the chasm between the classes.

By interjecting an exchange of serious ideas in the midst of frothy chatter and frivolous gossip Fuentes obtains a good shock effect. These discussions, nevertheless, sometimes appear to be his vehicle for loosing his own ideas rather than a means of exposing the concerns of the discussants. In *La región* there is likewise a substantial amount of inner monologue, frequently in the form of introspective ponderings of the past provoked by a few sharp barbs from everyman's conscience, Ixca Cienfuegos.

It is not difficult to trace the outside literary influences which exert a pull on Fuentes in this work. He himself is quick to identify them: Faulkner, Dos Passos, D. H. Lawrence, and Aldous Huxley. He admits that Dos Passos was his "literary Bible" and that the technique of *Manhattan Transfer* naturally influenced him as he wrote about Mexico's great metropolis.[6] He feels too that the speech or jargon of his "international set" is something like Huxley transplanted from England to Mexico.[7] And he says that his handling of the time element is a sort of melange of Dos Passos's insistence on the past tense, Faulkner's use of the chronic present, and Lawrence's tone of prophetic imminence.[8]

Whatever else *La región más transparente* is, it must also be regarded as Carlos Fuentes's judgment of the Mexican Revolution some forty years after its inception. Viewed in this light, we find that it is mordant satire which indicts the Revolution in powerful terms for failing all the people except the few who grew rich off it by corrupt and ruthless practices. The basic theme is the same one at which Mariano Azuela hammered in more than a few of his postrevolutionary works, such as *El camarada Pantoja, Avanzada, Regina Landa,* and others. Note too that Fuentes in *La región* satirizes the new upper crust of Mexican society, shallow and pragmatic and opportunistic, just as Luis Spota did two years before in *Casi el paraíso.* But Fuentes does it better.

The next novel which Carlos Fuentes published, *Las buenas conciencias (The Good Conscience),* 1959, is radically different from his first effort. In truth, it is a letdown, both in conception and in techniques, although Fuentes answers in its defense that it was designed to be the first of a series of four novels and that, the project never being completed, it suffers through being considered alone. A traditional novel, *Las buenas conciencias* is set in the conservative provincial environment of Guanajuato and narrated, according to Fuentes, in the style of the Spanish novelist Galdós, a style chosen deliberately to mesh with the slow-moving environment.

This novel concerns itself with the Ceballos family, successful merchants, and particularly with young Jaime Ceballos, who already has appeared in the last pages of *La región más transparente.* Jaime, inspired by his mestizo friend Juan Manuel Lorenzo, is determined to break with the reactionary, pietistic stance of his family. But as time goes on this resolve gradually crumbles under the weight of the family tradition and pressure. He loses his last chance to avoid the family fate when he lacks the courage to back up his poor, weak father as the latter makes one gesture of rebellion against the stifling smugness of family control. It has been suggested that Jaime Ceballos incarnates the solid, secure adolescent years of Fuentes himself. The novelist admits that the path chosen by Ceballos is an alternative he once faced and rejected in favor of the one he has followed, which in elemental terms can be described as that of the liberal fighting the evils of the established order.

Though certainly not without its merits, *Las buenas conciencias* really does nothing to enhance the literary career of Carlos Fuentes. The same can not be said for his next novel, *La muerte de Artemio Cruz* (*The Death of Artemio Cruz*), 1962. This work, whether or not a greater novel than *La región más transparente,* is undeniably the one which catapulted Fuentes into international renown.

Like *La región, La muerte de Artemio Cruz* is a novel of broad sweep and clear ambitions. Both of them embody the personal philosophy and commitment of Carlos Fuentes. In *La región* the intent is to expose and examine all levels of society in Mexico City at mid-century, viewed through the words and actions of an extensive cast of characters and as the social end product of the Revolution forty years after its outbreak. The purpose in *La muerte de Artemio Cruz* is to enter the mind of one person, the moribund Artemio Cruz, and to recapture the twelve crucial episodes in his life, a life which supposedly epitomizes the course of twentieth-century Mexico. To attempt to synthesize in one man's existence the life of a whole nation for half a century is as difficult as it is ambitious. That Carlos Fuentes brings it off with patent success is a measure of his novelistic breadth and depth.

In this novel we figuratively sit by the bedside of the dying Artemio Cruz during the final twelve hours of his earthly existence. Through his memory, we review a dozen critical moments of his life, in each of which he has to face two or more alternatives and exercise an option. Each time the option he elects leaves in its wake the sacrifice of a person or of an ideal. Had he opted in the other direction at any point his future course would have been altered, with new alternatives and other options.

One is tempted to speculate on the different book Fuentes might have produced had he allowed his protagonist the freedom to choose the other alternative in one of the earlier incidents. But at once we realize the impossibility of this, for Fuentes intends the figure of Artemio Cruz to symbolize the Revolution itself and Mexico herself since the Revolution. The conflict in *La muerte de Artemio Cruz*, then, is the age-old yet ever fascinating duel between reality and conscience. But, symbol or not, Artemio Cruz *lives* in the pages of this work, in a vibrant, human, complex manner that wrings from the reader grudging or willing appreciation of the roundness and fullness of his personality.

Stripped of detail, pieced together in orderly time sequence, and without concern for the rejected alternative in each of the critical moments dealt with in the story, the life of Artemio Cruz is simple to summarize. Born in 1889 in a palm-thatched hut on a coffee plantation near the Gulf coast, he is raised until adolescence by the mulato Lunero (brother of his mother, Isabel Cruz). He fights as an officer in the revolutionary forces. During this time he has a brief idyll of love with Regina, whom he never sees after he is captured. He escapes execution by a cowardly act of collaboration, leaving a companion, Gonzalo Bernal, to his fate. Later he finds the Bernal family and, posing as Gonzalo's greatest friend, is warmly received, so much so that he wins the hand of the daughter Catalina in marriage. Soon he displaces the father in charge of the estate and before long is grabbing surrounding lands, by any and every means necessary. His local power leads him to Mexico City as a member of Congress, and more power accrues on a national level. He enters business and prospers even more, especially after allying himself with some U.S. entrepreneurs. His son Lorenzo is his joy, obviously a symbol for Artemio of his own youth, his aspirations, his revolutionary spirit. Lorenzo goes off to Spain to fight for the Loyalists in the Civil War and is soon killed. Artemio's decline and degeneration begins when he receives this word. His marriage, long loveless, still manages to survive, though for no apparent reason. A deep rancor exists between Artemio and Catalina, and she in effect leads a separate life along with their daughter Teresa. His current mistress is Lilia, with whom he is seen everywhere. Life comes to have very little meaning and Artemio becomes more cynical, more tyrannical, until his very name is feared and despised. There is really nothing left for him but death and it hovers in the wings as we are permitted to watch his life pass in review.

Naturally, the story is not narrated in the time sequence just summarized. As a novelist of the modern school, Fuentes is committed to reader participation and so he scrambles the order of the twelve critical episodes which define the life of Artemio Cruz. Manuel Pedro González has lashed out at Fuentes rather violently because of this approach and other techniques employed in the novel.[9] My own opinion is that Fuentes is right in electing to tell his story in this manner. Besides being more interesting, it seems both logical and convincing that Artemio Cruz in his dying hours should let his mind wander back over this wealth of detail from his long life (seventy-one years) and that he should recall it in just this haphazard sequence.

In *La región más transparente* Fuentes dreamed up Ixca Cienfuegos to serve a function as everyman's conscience and prod. Here he achieves the same end by having Artemio's conscience speak up repeatedly, addressing Artemio in the familiar second-person *tú* and always in the future tense. Luis Harss finds this to be "a curiously incongruous device consisting in a kind of voice of conscience

. . ., a disembodied accusative that tortures the syntax and disrupts the action."[10] Again, my feeling is quite the opposite. As a sort of Mexican everyman, Artemio's contemplation of the key moments in his life assumes certain aspects of a general confession. Certainly, confession was not his intention, yet nevertheless he is honest enough at the end to see himself pretty much as he is. It strikes me that it was a stroke of inspiration for Fuentes to give voice to Artemio's conscience in this manner. It definitely is more convincing than the part of Ixca Cienfuegos in *La región*.

Throughout the work, then, we find the story narrated in three persons (aside from the entry of other characters in direct conversation). They are the first-person *yo* (I), used by Artemio himself, who always narrates in the present tense; the second-person *tú* (you), which as we have seen is the voice of his conscience speaking in future time; and *él* (he), which is the narrator telling about Artemio and always in the past tense. Every chapter or major division of the book begins with one or another of these personal pronouns. To control and balance this triple (and original) perspective is a sort of technical tour de force, which not every writer could handle successfully. To my mind, Fuentes succeeds without question and in so doing adds to the stature of the work.

Artemio Cruz is a literary figure who will live long in the history of the novel of Mexico and Spanish America. His spiritual kinship with Fernando Robles is readily apparent to anyone who has read both of Fuentes's outstanding works. Like Robles, Artemio Cruz has a very humble beginning in life, plays a modest part in the Revolution, and becomes a feared financial tycoon by virtue of hard work, unrestrained ambition, and smart and sharp dealings in which it is permissible to trample anyone and everyone under foot. Each of them has a mistress, a neglected wife, and lackeys galore. And each is deadly bored with life (even if Artemio Cruz does struggle to the end against the idea that death is overtaking him). The principal difference between these two protagonists lies in the author's handling of them. Robles is seen as much through the eyes and words of numerous other characters as he is through anything he says or does. On the contrary, Artemio Cruz is largely allowed to tell his own story and remains at all times the axis on which the narrative spins.

No other character in the book is completely developed, and there are probably two motives for this: since the story is panoramic and most everything is seen through the thoughts of Artemio Cruz, no one else is on stage enough to become a life-size character; and, given Fuentes's determination to have Cruz symbolize the fate of Mexico herself in this century, the spotlight must remain focused on him. It may be remarked that his wife Catalina is the only person close to him who has not been broken to Artemio's will. In the beginning she feels for him a strange mixture of scorn, guilt, and physical desire. She regards the latter sensation, which overcomes the others by night, as a degrading weakness. Later, the desire disappears and in time the guilt too, leaving only the scorn and rancor. Of minor interest is the fact that Jaime Ceballos appears again in this novel. Having married Betina Régules, to whom he was engaged at the close of *La región más transparente*, he now is an important figure in the bourgeois set, and cynical, but his provincial, reactionary heritage keeps him from becoming really sophisticated.

Keith Botsford, in discussing *La muerte de Artemio Cruz*, is more severe with Fuentes than most other critics. He says that Fuentes loves what he is not himself and writes about what he is not, because he still considers writing an act apart from himself—something one *does*, rather than *is*. He also feels that in this work "the experimentation is not truly Fuentes' own, but part of a foreign tradition that he has only partly assimilated. . . . *But*, a novel is a variety of experience collected under a single view, a world ordered precisely because it has been seen in such-and-such a way and no other. This unity is what I do not see in *Artemio Cruz*."[11]

On the matter of assimilating his influences, the majority opinion (which is also my own) seems to be that these influences obtrude far less in *Artemio Cruz* than they did in *La región*. This time James Joyce and Malcolm Lowry (especially in his novel with a Mexican setting, *Under the Volcano*) appear to be the predominant ones. The strongest philosophical influence upon him, here and elsewhere, is the Mexican poet and essayist, Octavio Paz, for whom Fuentes shows a long and deep admiration, especially the ideas elaborated in *El laberinto de la soledad* [The labyrinth of solitude], 1950.

In 1962, the year in which Artemio Cruz became a household name among Mexico's literate public, Fuentes also published *Aura*, a very short novel which finds the author ranging rather deep into the realm of fantasy. It is a mystery story of the kind told more than once. A young scholar is engaged by the mistress of an old rundown mansion to do some work on documents in French left behind by her departed husband. The owner is an elderly, unusual lady who once must have been a picture of elegance. So strong is this impression on the young man and so deep her determination to keep alive a departed age that she appears to him as a beautiful young girl named Aura. Note the remarkable appropriateness of this name, which has the same meaning in Spanish and in English. Naturally, the young man falls in love with Aura. Since it is he who narrates the whole story in the second person, it is more vivid.

The weakness in *Aura* is that the reader, any reader, sees from the beginning what is happening, and so the story is like a punctured balloon. Instead of tension and pressure all the way to the moment of revealing the secret, we have only a flaccid outer structure which sags more and more as the pressure decreases. The story is well told and an atmosphere is created which would have been highly effective if Fuentes had been able to keep his reader from distinguishing fantasy and reality at the very outset.

The next work by Carlos Fuentes is *Cantar de ciegos* [Song of the blind], 1964, a collection of short stories. In truth, it can be said that this is the only one of the works he has published since 1962 that has enhanced his career to any appreciable extent. Fuentes is one of the very few Spanish-American novelists who can work equally well within the exacting requirements of the shorter genre. *Cantar de ciegos,* along with his earlier collection (*Los días enmascarados*), proves beyond a doubt that Carlos Fuentes can hold his own with almost any practitioner of the short story art in whatever language. In this role as outstanding *cuentista* he is joined, in Mexico, by Juan Rulfo and Juan José Arreola. A number of other writers in the short story form match these three with an occasional effort but not in consistency of performance.

In 1967 two Fuentes novels appeared in Mexico. The first of these was *Zona sagrada* [Sacred zone], which I feel does less for his stature than anything else he has produced. Here Fuentes offers a shallow theme (that of a jaded, aging, dissipated Mexican movie actress of international fame and her weak, worthless, confused son) and attempts to inject life and meaning into it by linking it to Greek mythology. He purports to find an analogy between the circumstances and existence of the characters of *Zona sagrada* and the legends woven around Ulysses, Circe, Penelope, Telemachus, Telegonus, and other figures and places of mythology. In an attempt to make it all mesh a little better, Fuentes gives the rather pathetic son the name of Mito ("myth"), a shortened version of Guillermito, in turn the affectionate diminutive of Guillermo. And, apparently thinking to add a dash of sophistication, Fuentes sprinkles his pages liberally with phrases in Italian, French, German, and English.

The whole thing may be cleverly done (indeed, one of its defects is that it is too clever and that form too often is in the saddle), but, considered in terms of the author's talents, it is a major disappointment. Placed alongside the powerful and ambitious themes he tackled in *La región más transparente* and *La muerte de Artemio Cruz,* the subject of *Zona sagrada* is patently inconsequential. The book was converted into a film, with the lead role played by María Félix. Some have said all along that she is the person Fuentes had in mind when he dreamed up *Zona sagrada.* Be that as it may, most Fuentes adherents would have been happier if he had written this bit of froth as a film script in the first place.

The other novel of 1967, *Cambio de piel* (*A Change of Skin*), was mentioned earlier as the 1966 winner of the Premio Biblioteca Breve. It represents Fuentes's most ambitious effort since the appearance of *La muerte de Artemio Cruz* in 1962. The 442 pages of *Cambio de piel* offer some impressive—and occasionally depressing—manifestations of the virtuosity of Carlos Fuentes. We admire his evident familiarity with cultures other than his own (both in times past and at the present moment), his clear talent as a literary artist, his inclination toward experimentation in novelistic form and techniques. We accept his customary inclusion of mythological elements and his repeated use, sometimes even abuse, of symbols and allusions and analogies. We tolerate his rather-too-open efforts throughout to "sell" existentialism. We question the need for some of the vulgarity and especially certain sexual excesses.

The story occurs in Holy Week of 1965, mostly between Mexico

City and Cholula, as the four main characters take off in a Volkswagen to get away from the capital. Actually, their destination is Veracruz but they never arrive. The trip itself seems symbolic of the need of each of them to escape his past, shed an old life, and find some form of personal salvation. It is symbolic too (and a nod to local mythology) that they visit pyramids in Xochicalco and Cholula, which are enduring symbols of the ancient Indian history of Mexico. But the story is not restricted in time or space to the realities just outlined. By virtue of flashbacks and other forms of reliving the past, we are transported to many places and times: New York, Buenos Aires, Italy, Prague, Germany, Greece, Mediterranean isles, and elsewhere, in time periods ranging from the 1920s up to the present.

Cambio de piel, then, is the story of Javier, an unsuccessful Mexican writer now in middle age; his American-born wife, Elizabeth, who hungers for the true love she feels Javier has not given her; Franz, also around forty, a Sudetenland German who was in charge of erecting gas chambers and other buildings in one of the infamous Nazi concentration camps which exterminated Jews by the thousands; and Isabel, an uninhibited young Mexican girl in quest of new forms of enjoying life to the utmost. Both of the women sleep rather unconcernedly (though not openly) with each of the men. In fact, it is during some of these musical-bed sessions that we learn the background and the hang-ups of the characters. Franz unburdens his guilt complex to Isabel in much detail, after Javier has long bored her with accounts of his personal lack of fulfillment. Elizabeth, unable to believe she has been as happy with Javier as she has a right to be, seeks understanding and affection from Franz. Isabel, uncomplicated and without either neuroses or morals, is a sort of counterweight to the existentialist searching and seeking of the others. As can be seen, there is among all of them a lack of firm principles and stability, but no one can complain about being shortchanged on sex.

The whole thing is narrated by a mysterious, omniscient type who speaks always directly to the two girls (shades of Ixca Cienfuegos and the conscience of Artemio Cruz!). If Ixca was a sort of technical disaster and Artemio's conscience a distinct narrative success, this case falls somewhere between those extremes. This voice is even more omnipresent than Ixca was, but at the same time, although he never really appears on scene, he impresses as a more human and believable observer. He plays a role similar to that of Ixca in chiding Elizabeth and Isabel (and through them the men also) to be themselves and to throw off illusions. Fuentes shows an addiction to this device of the shadowy observer who sees all and knows all and revels in casting barbs at others. We come to feel that in each case it is the voice of Fuentes, who, quite properly, refrains from interjecting himself directly into the story but gets in his licks just the same.

Cambio de piel in most ways does not measure up to the level of *La región más transparente* and *La muerte de Artemio Cruz,* but it does outrank the other four novels so far published by Fuentes. Actually, it is his most urbane effort, and he gives it a projection that carries beyond the Mexican milieu. Here he is not probing the collective personality—good or bad, rich or poor—of Mexico Ciity as in *La región,* nor is he scrutinizing the Revolution and Mexico herself through the symbol of Artemio Cruz. This time he zeroes in on the inner struggles of four personalities who seek not so much identity as renewal or rebirth. But no one of these characters achieves anything resembling the stature of Artemio Cruz, or even of Fernando Robles. And *Cambio de piel* drags in spots, a defect successfully avoided by the other works in question. As would be expected, Fuentes displays in this novel the influences of his mentors, Dos Passos, Faulkner, and Lawrence, among others. But it may be time to acknowledge that by now their techniques are his own too.

Early in 1969 Carlos Fuentes suddenly abandoned his self-ordained exile in Europe and returned to Mexico. This in spite of his repeated protestations that he would not go back ("At times a fierce homesickness besets me, it's true, but I will not return. I would need to stay in Veracruz or in Morelos, in view of the mountains. I know that it is no longer possible.")[12] We can only conjecture what provoked his change of mind. One possibility might be the impending breakup of his marriage with Rita Macedo. In any case, he returned with more than one manuscript in an advanced stage of preparation, for in less than a year and a half he published no fewer than six new works. Three of these were in the form of essays (*París: La Revolución de Mayo*, 1968; *La nueva novela hispano-americana*, 1969; *Casa con dos puertas*, 1970). Two others were theatrical pieces, a form not previously essayed by Fuentes (*Todos los gatos son pardos*, 1970, and *El tuerto es rey*, 1970), and the remaining one was a short novel called *Cumpleaños* [Birthday], which appeared in 1969.

It would be interesting, though not pertinent to our study of Fuentes as a novelist, to consider the other works just mentioned. We can pause long enough, however, to remark that they confirm Fuentes's virtuosity. It is already clear that he has relatively few equals in the novel and the short story in all of Latin America. Possibly he will now garner a name for himself in the field of the drama, and it becomes quite evident that he is a master of the essay, both in form and content. His essay treatment of the new Spanish-American novel is penetrating, somewhat original, and surely valid. While not everyone will accept his approach and his evaluations, none can deny that they are insightful, stimulating, and cogently presented. In fact, Fuentes's capacity for handling the Spanish language would be difficult to surpass. One critic expresses it this way: "The Spanish of Carlos Fuentes is sharp, beautiful, sonorous, and balanced, attributes which make the reading of his literary production very interesting, quite apart from the plot interest which his novels may involve. His works are delectable to read, giving an internal and nontransferable pleasure to the reader who finds himself in front of some written pages and savors them one by one, relishing them as he would some tasty dish."[13]

Cumpleaños offers no great surprises nor departures in relation to Fuentes's earlier novels. Perhaps he is more committed here to symbolism and to fracturing the time unity than in his other works (with the possible exception of *Aura* and *Zona sagrada*), yet this brief novel falls well within the tradition that Fuentes has been forging and expanding ever since the appearance of *La región más transparente*.

The action of *Cumpleaños* begins with a brief opening scene in a bare cell where we see an old theologian, a pregnant woman, and a cat. Then follows another short scene in which we first meet George and Emily, on the tenth birthday of their son Georgie. Thereafter, practically the whole work is an illusion (perhaps intended as an allegory too) narrated by George, in which he finds himself in a strange edifice with a woman, Nuncia, and a boy (her son). Various bizarre developments pass in review: Nuncia making love with his father; his father's death on a ski slope (a death George caused to be ascribed to heart failure); the appearance of the narrator's other self, leading to the two Georges' quiet struggle with each other (even in their constant loving of Nuncia, who thus spends nearly all her time in bed), until Nuncia discovers the cell and brings the old monk out to take care of him and to translate, until he dies, his murmurings for the narrator. The theologian identifies himself as Siger de Brabante (an antagonist of Thomas Aquinas), who died in 1281. George comes back to reality while walking interminably around London, on the day his wife Emily expected him home in time for Georgie's tenth birthday dinner. Seated on a park bench, however, he is joined by a pregnant woman and a cat called (as in his vision) Nino.

Actually, *Cumpleaños* is not all this simple but tends rather to be confused and confusing, heavily charged with elements of mythology and antiquity, and with questions of life, death, reality, fantasy, truth, time, eternity, immortality. In my view, it is definitely not an outstanding novel, although much more satisfying than *Zona sagrada* and more convincing that *Aura* because the fantasy is not so quickly nor so easily discernible.

Some disagreement exists among the critics over how good a novelist Carlos Fuentes is or might yet come to be. All concur that he is one of the major twentieth-century novelists in Mexico and in Spanish America, at the very least. And he has succeeded in attracting more attention internationally than any previous Mexican novelist. Nor does anyone doubt that he can move on to greater heights if he knows how to utilize fully the rare talent he obviously possesses. His performance up to this time, however, does not inspire an absolute confidence that we can expect Fuentes to develop steadily into a mature and consummate novelist.

Numerous critics judge his first novel, *La región*, as his best work to date, which would imply that in more than a decade he has not moved ahead. Other observers (including myself) regard *La muerte de Artemio Cruz* as his major effort, unmatched by his more recent works. But he is still a young man. If in the years to come he can surpass the achievements of *La región* and *Artemio Cruz*, he seems quite certain to consolidate for himself a top position in Mexican letters and an important spot in world literature.

The doubters point to a variety of little things to justify their skepticism concerning Fuentes's future. He has, they claim, too persistent a tendency toward "slickness" in his writings, a charge surely not without basis. Also, there are times when form overwhelms substance. And his enduring preoccupation with the role of mythology in Mexican life does not appear to pay proportionate dividends in what it adds to the value of his works. Some suggest that his talent is being adulterated by a proliferation of efforts in directions away from the novel and by the attractions, which evidently he does not despise, of the life of a literary lion.

Fuentes apparently is the first Mexican author to reach one goal sought by many writers everywhere, namely, the satisfaction of being able to live by his pen alone. Note that it is by his pen he lives, not by his novels. In fact, it is his diversification that makes this triumph possible. Besides his short stories and novels (with all of the latter shortly appearing in several foreign translations), Fuentes produces a variety of essays, articles, movie scripts, and other items, in addition to his lectures and television and radio appearances. His fluency in other languages opens extra doors to him in all of this cultural and literary activity. And, as he himself points out, a single article printed in American, British, French, and German magazines often pays him more than the entire edition of a novel in Mexico.[14]

It is interesting and in order to make certain comparisons between Carlos Fuentes and some of the other Mexican novelists who have most influenced the course of this genre in their own country during the present century. Considering Fuentes first with relation to Mariano Azuela, it has to be said at once that the former possesses a natural (and cultivated) talent for the novel which Azuela does not approach. On the other hand, Azuela's impact upon the novel has been somewhat greater. This is by no means to minimize the influence which Fuentes clearly has had (and is having) on the development of the Mexican novel. The fact is that Azuela exerted more impact because the novel of his day was stagnant and ready for change.

Both of these highly significant novelists insistently attack the Revolution for its failure to pursue with fidelity and vigor the aims it professed to have, for its incapacity to oust the opportunists who grew rich and fat off the Revolution and drained it of much of its spirit of change. The techniques employed by Azuela and Fuentes differ markedly, due in good measure to the time lag between the two. Also to be remembered is the fact that Azuela's approach in his early revolutionary period represents perhaps more of a break with the immediate past than do Fuentes's works. However the themes of Fuentes (at least in his two best novels) are more far-ranging and significant than anything attempted by Azuela.

There is greater affinity between Fuentes and Juan Rulfo, particularly with regard to technique. Both do unusual things with the time sequence and each probes the inner consciousness of characters. In *Pedro Páramo* Juan Rulfo analyzes on the local level a *cacique* with a revolutionary background, while Fuentes does the same in *La muerte de Artemio Cruz* but on a national scope. There is another and basic difference between these two works. Whereas in Rulfo's novel life is conceived as merely a prelude to death, the Fuentes work gives meaning only to life and perceives death as its negation.

Similarities are apparent between Fuentes and Luis Spota. They have in common the fact that both they and their works frequently tend to provoke controversy. They are more inclined to the use of sex and vulgarity than are the other major Mexican novelists. Both rely heavily on satire, and each chooses the city as the setting for most of his works. And they are both reformers or crusaders. Fuentes is against the whole neocapitalist system, which he sees as dominating the Revolutionary Party for the past two decades or so. Spota attacks, not the system as such, but the variety of social ills which thrive under the system.

Agustín Yáñez is not as satirical or controversial as Fuentes. His finest works have a rural rather than an urban setting. While Yáñez plays with the time sequence in his novels, he goes nowhere near as far in this respect as does Fuentes. On the other hand, we remember that it was Agustín Yáñez who for the first time in the Mexican novel employed on a wide scale the devices for exploring the subconscious of his characters, for probing the human spirit. Fuentes uses his own refinements to attain the same end, but we cannot say that he goes much further. In assessing their own impact on other Mexican novelists, there is little doubt that the greater influence has been exercised by Yáñez.

In the overall view, only Agustín Yáñez stands as a rival to Fuentes for the honor of being labeled Mexico's finest novelist up to this point. Of the two, I would have to cast my vote for Agustín Yáñez, for I feel that *Al filo del agua* is a better novel than any Fuentes has published. Further, it is my belief that Yáñez's total output is still more solid than what Fuentes has given us. At the same time, it is quite plain to me that Fuentes may yet surpass Yáñez and wind up as the greatest Mexican novelist of this century.

NOTES TO CHAPTER 8

1. Keith Botsford, "My Friend Fuentes," *Commentary*, XXXIX (February, 1965), 66.
2. *Los narradores ante el público*, 1st ser. (Mexico City, 1966), p. 153.
3. Ibid., pp. 138–139.
4. Luis Harss and Barbara Dohmann, *Into the Mainstream* (New York, 1967), p. 284.
5. Emmanuel Carballo, *El cuento mexicano en el siglo XX* (Mexico City, 1964), p. 73.
6. Emmanuel Carballo, *Diecinueve protagonistas de la literatura mexicana del siglo XX* (Mexico City, 1965), p. 434.
7. Ibid.
8. Harss and Dohmann, pp. 294–295.
9. Ivan Schulman, et al., *Coloquio sobre la novela hispanoamericana* (Mexico City, 1967), pp. 89–100.
10. Harss and Dohmann, p. 301.
11. Botsford, p. 67.

12. Quoted in *Tiempo*, August 19, 1968, p. 45.

13. Samuel Guzmán, reviewing *Cumpleaños* in *Tiempo*, February 2, 1970, p. 84.

14. *Los narradores ante el público*, p. 151.

THE NOVELS OF CARLOS FUENTES

La región más transparente, 1958 (Translated into English as *Where the Air Is Clear*. New York: I. Obolensky, 1960.)

Las buenas conciencias, 1959 (Translated into English as *The Good Conscience*. New York: I. Obolensky, 1961.)

La muerte de Artemio Cruz, 1962 (Translated into English as *The Death of Artemio Cruz*. New York: Farrar, Straus, 1964.)

Aura, 1962 (Translated into English with the same title. New York: Farrar, Straus, and Giroux, 1965.)

Zona sagrada, 1967

Cambio de piel, 1967 (Translated into English as *A Change of Skin*. New York: Farrar, Straus, and Giroux, 1968.)

Cumpleaños, 1969

SELECTED STUDIES ON CARLOS FUENTES

Arana Freire, Elsa. "La libertad de los demás y el lector comprometido." *Visión*, February 27, 1971, pp. 27–29.

Baxandall, Lee. "An Interview with Carlos Fuentes." *Studies on the Left*, III, 1 (1962), 48–56.

Botsford, Keith. "My Friend Fuentes." *Commentary*, XXXIX (February, 1965), 64–67.

Brushwood, John S. *Mexico in Its Novel*, pp. 36–41.

Carballo, Emmanuel. *Diecinueve protagonistas de la literatura mexicana del siglo XX*, pp. 427–448.

———. *El cuento mexicano del siglo XX*, pp. 73–80.

Díaz-Lastra, Alberto. "Carlos Fuentes y la Revolución traicionada." *Cuadernos Hispanoamericanos*, no. 185 (May, 1965), pp. 369–375.

Harss, Luis and Dohmann, Barbara. *Into the Mainstream*, pp. 276–309.

Los narradores ante el público, 1st ser., pp. 137–155.

Mead, Robert G. "Carlos Fuentes, Mexico's Angry Novelist." *Books Abroad*, XXXVIII (Autumn, 1964), 380–382.

————. "Carlos Fuentes, Airado Novelista Mexicano." *Hispania*, L (May, 1967), 229–235.

Miliani, Domingo. *La realidad mexicana en su novela de hoy*, pp. 76–92.

Ocampo de Gómez, A. M., and Prado Velázquez, E., eds. *Diccionario de escritores mexicanos*, pp. 120–123.

Reeve, Richard. "The Narrative Technique of Carlos Fuentes: 1954–1964." Ph.D. dissertation, University of Illinois, 1967.

Rodríguez Monegal, Emir. "Carlos Fuentes: Situación del escritor en América Latina." *Mundo Nuevo*, no. 1 (July, 1966), pp. 5–21.

Schulman, Ivan, et al. *Coloquio sobre la novela hispanoamericana*, pp. 82–100.

Sommers, Joseph. *After the Storm*, pp. 95–164.

————. "The Present Moment in the Mexican Novel." *Books Abroad*, XL (Summer, 1966), 261–266.

West, Anthony. "The Whole of Life." *The New Yorker*, March 4, 1961, pp. 123–125.

————. "An Uncouth Grace." *The New Yorker*, August 4, 1964. pp. 87–90.

9

Vicente Leñero
-a Mexican Graham Greene?

THE YOUNGEST GROUP OF NOVELISTS IN MEXICO IS LARGE, GROWING,
productive, and impressive. They may be defined as those born after
1930, meaning that most are still under forty years of age. Even so,
to choose for our consideration a representative of this "generation"
poses a problem. In arbitrarily electing to study Vicente Leñero we
are forced with regret to slight such interesting and already successful writers as Salvador Elizondo, Tomás Mojarro, Fernando del
Paso, Gustavo Sainz, Juan García Ponce, José Agustín, and various
others.

The choice of Leñero can be justified on several counts. For one
thing, his novels began to appear earlier than any of those just mentioned, and he has more works to his credit up to this time, with
four novels and a book of short stories published between 1959 and
1967 (all prior to his thirty-fourth birthday), in addition to four
highly interesting and successful plays produced since then. Moreover, his second novel, *Los albañiles*, was awarded in 1963 Spain's
prestigious Premio Biblioteca Breve, making him the first of the
young Mexican novelists to capture an international literary prize.
(Carlos Fuentes subsequently gained the same award in 1967 with
his *Cambio de piel*.) Besides all this, Leñero has a special appeal
because of the daring experimentation found in his works and because he is clearly and significantly influenced by Graham Greene.

Born in Guadalajara on June 9, 1933, Leñero studied civil engineering at the National University of Mexico and received a degree
in this field in 1959. By that time, however, his interest in journalism
and creative writing had become paramount. In fact, he had already

been awarded, in 1956, a grant for cultural studies in Spain and in 1958 he won first and second places in a short story competition sponsored by the university. He spent a while in the workshop of Juan José Arreola, one of the real masters of our time in the techniques of the short story, and (like the vast majority of the rising young Mexican writers) he merited a fellowship from the Centro Mexicano de Escritores (1961–62 and 1963–64). He also was granted a Guggenheim Fellowship in 1967–68.

Since Vicente Leñero is not—as yet, anyway—one of the few Latin American literary figures who support themselves by their artistic works, he made his living for a brief time in the practice of engineering, then by grinding out radio soap operas, and finally by writing TV serials (called "telenovelas" in Mexico). While he doesn't consider this type of work as of value in his career as a novelist (except that his novel *Estudio Q* is a direct outgrowth of his experience in television), he points out that it has served as the means of supporting his family.[1] For the past few years he has been managing editor of *Claudia*, a highly important woman's magazine (a sort of Mexican *Vogue*).

Vicente Leñero is a man with a good face and kind eyes, and the manner and bearing of a philosopher. When I met him in November, 1968, he was nursing a broken rib, received—of all things!—when a friend gave him one of the bear hugs which they call an *abrazo*. If this is an indication of the affection his friends have for him, we can only conclude that he is very well liked. Yet, Leñero is decidedly not a gregarious type. Indeed, he confesses to having always been unbearably timid. He is a "loner" in Mexican literary circles, not belonging formally to any group, and has explained and defended his attitude on this:

> I work at defending my solitude. By nature I am not a chummy type and I shun the idea of talking literature at all hours of the day and night. Moreover, I am not versed in philosophy, I don't read foreign books in their original tongue, and the work I have done to earn a living has been of a sort removed from intellectual circles.[2]

And he has revealed these things about himself:

Neither am I good at writing essays or critical pieces. . . . Movies don't greatly appeal to me. . . . Between a book and a good film, I'll choose the book. I almost never go to the theater. I'm not a catalogue of music, nor of painting. . . . And, for my personal enjoyment, books; if you press me further, fiction, even more, novels. But one would go crazy if wrapped up in books day and night. By no means are they the most important thing in the world. More important, much more important, is my family: my wife and my two daughters.[3]

These words have the ring of sincerity, humility even, and a balanced outlook on life. Anyone conversing even briefly with Leñero is confirmed in these feelings and recognizes that here is a human being without sham or pretense, one who knows his limits and also knows what he wants to do and how he plans to go about it. He impresses as a thoroughly honest and sensitive man.

It is not surprising that a sincere Catholic of the temperament of Leñero would discover a powerful influence in the works of Graham Greene. He tells us that he had read rather widely from his early years, but that it was near the end of his engineering training when he came upon some of Greene's novels. The approach of Greene to Christian moral problems was a distinct revelation to Leñero, who tells of it in these words:

To Greene I owe above all the answer to a false dilemma in the moral order which I had absurdly and scrupulously created for myself at that time. Reading Greene, I found an obvious solution: there do not exist any themes which are taboo for a Christian writer. The themes that my ingenuous conscience was condemning were the very ones worthy of treatment by an author of faith. Through the novels of Greene, rather than in the catechism, I learned the meaning of the mystery of Grace.

Today, my religious convictions are a potent fuel activating my literary fever. In Christianity I find the indispensable charity—in its theological sense—which a novelist requires for observing, loving, and trying to understand the world which surrounds us, so as to be moved by and to respond to the ebb and flow of sin and redemption and then sin once again: the conflict of today and forever.[4]

Emmanuel Carballo says that Leñero "has created a new image

of what a Catholic writer in Mexico can be who abandons sectarianism for the sake of comprehension."[5] This appears to be a valid comment and has a particular meaning within the framework of Mexican literature, in which Catholic writers have not been prone to approach the moral problems of their time with the same technique which Leñero has cultivated. It is perhaps anticipating a bit too much to refer to Leñero as a Mexican Graham Greene. Leñero is still in a period of experimentation and development and quite probably will never equal the Englishman in overall artistry. In any case, no one would want to see Leñero tie himself slavishly to the Greene model. Yet in each of the four Leñero novels which have appeared to date there is visible the influence of Graham Greene in one way or another, always in relation to a Christian dilemma or a Christian approach to some issue of consequence in Mexican society.

Leñero's first novel, published in 1961, was *La voz adolorida* [The sorrowful voice]. The story is told entirely in the first person by Enrique, a mentally disturbed young man in his mid- or late twenties. He is pouring out his story to a doctor (either a psychologist or a psychiatrist), and to explain his situation of the moment he traces his personal history back to his earliest years. One critic has remarked that it is almost like a general confession.[6] It is so much so that the reader at some moments is apt to feel embarrassed at eavesdropping on such a personal and poignant story.

Until recently Enrique had been in a mental institution and then in a sanatorium for mental cases in Puebla, from which he was taken by his lifelong friend, Raúl Zetina, on the plea that he had to return to Mexico City just to take care of one matter. Later Raúl sent him to the doctor, who listens with much patience to the whole story. The doctor never speaks and we know he is there only by the manner in which Enrique addresses him from time to time. By this device Leñero preserves an unusual unity of viewpoint, even of mood.

Leñero likewise displays a sometimes startling insight into the thought processes of his mentally disturbed protagonist, an insight translated into a narrative which is convincing at every step. One of the more touching aspects of the story is that Enrique knows he is sick and yet realizes that at times he thinks lucidly. During his recital of his past he moves subtly in and out of these lucid periods. Although they are sometimes hard to distinguish, Leñero is always careful to give a cue which identifies the irrational moment. The reader must be alert to the frequent contradiction and change of mood, the childish insistence on minutiae and on the self-evident, the sudden shift of topic, the typical suspicion of the twisted and tortured mind, the obvious hallucination.

Enrique's father died when he was very young and the boy was raised by his aunts Ofelia and Carmen, who also kept his mentally deranged mother isolated in an upstairs bedroom. In his unbroken monologue Enrique takes us through his early years, the beginning of his friendship with Raúl Zetina, his difficulties in school until the aunts withdraw him, his gnawing desire to see his mother and his great disillusionment when he finally does. We see the arrival of Isabel Huerta to live with them, his marriage to Isabel and her death in childbirth, his stay in the mental hospital and then in the high-class sanatorium in Puebla. Enrique tells also of his determination to escape from the sanatorium and return to the old house to rescue his son, whom he is convinced the aunts have kept locked up in the basement for seven years (during the first three of which they told him the boy was still in an incubator in the hospital). Only near the end do we become fully aware that there is no son, that he too died with Isabel. We realize also that it was at the moment of Isabel's death that Enrique's mental disturbance really got out of control.

The influence of Graham Greene is less clear in *La voz adolorida* than in Leñero's subsequent works. Yet it appears to be present in a number of somewhat muted points turning on Christian principles. As already noted, Enrique's monologue takes on the aspect of a very detailed confession, and in it are raised some questions of interest. Thus, while *La voz adolorida* is presented as the troubled story of a young man with mental problems, it seems also valid to interpret it in another way.

This aspect revolves around the responsibilities of those burdened with the care of mentally ill relatives. In this case, who—other than God—can judge the motives and the actions of Ofelia and Carmen in their lonely and even frightening efforts to "do their duty" first to

Enrique's disturbed mother (clearly a much worse case than Enrique) and then to Enrique himself? In trying to assess their attitude and conduct in all of this, it must be remembered that we see them only through Enrique's biased and distorted view. Even so, they don't come off too badly if we discount his irrationality regarding some of their motives and deeds. The aunts are overly protective of him in his younger years, and just possibly they have contributed to his mental insecurity in keeping his mother locked up in a bedroom rather than sending her to an institution. But if they had sent her away, would this have saved Enrique? Or does Leñero intend us to understand that this mental illness was going to pass from mother to son in any case?

A peripheral question is that concerning the faith and redemption of a mentally disturbed person. Enrique is certain he is doomed to damnation, solely because of an incident that occurred in his teens. Waiting his turn for confession, he overheard a woman confessing her sexual sins. When asked in the confessional if he had heard this, he said he had not. He later concluded that his subsequent reception of communion was sacrilegious and that this sentenced him to an eternity in hell. It may be noted that a revised version of *La voz adolorida* was published in Buenos Aires in 1967 with the new title *A fuerza de palabras* [By dint of words].

At the present time Spain seems to be the country most addicted to literary awards, and one of the most coveted and prestigious of them all is the Premio Biblioteca Breve, which in 1963 was awarded to Vicente Leñero's second novel, *Los albañiles* [The bricklayers]. The competition for the Premio Biblioteca Breve attracted seventy-four entries that year, and it is noteworthy that three of the five leading contenders were by Spanish-American authors. (The Uruguayan Mario Benedetti was runner-up with his *Gracias por el fuego*, and *La selva gris* by the Chilean Jorge Edwards also figured in the final round.)

Los albañiles, published in 1964, is not only Leñero's best novel to date but also one of the outstanding Mexican novels of recent years. The setting is a construction site in Mexico City where a new apartment building is going up, and the story has to do with the investigation of the murder of don Jesús, the vicious and corrupt old watchman, except that on the last page of the book we are left with some doubt as to whether there really was a murder after all. The novel consists almost entirely of interrogations and statements by suspects as the police agent, Munguía ("the man in the striped tie"), strives to sift all the accumulating evidence—contradictory, overlapping, and confusing—and to identify the true criminal.

In a certain sense the detective Munguía might be called the principal character in this book. Although he bobs to the surface only periodically except for one or two chapters, the reader is always conscious of his presence. It is he to whom the several suspects are making their statements, and he is the one who skillfully extracts more and more details as they reveal themselves and their lives (in reality and in fantasy, sometimes almost as if hypnotized).

In the last chapter we find Munguía despondent over his failure to solve the case. As he goes through one last mental wrap-up of all the evidence, he fancies himself confronting each suspect with having had the motive and the opportunity for committing the crime. But he can't separate one from the other, and his imaginary accusations mingle in one global summation, a significant moment handled by Leñero with particular skill.

What Leñero seems to be saying in these pages is that each of the five suspects has on his conscience a share of the moral culpability for the murder, since each had a clear motive and each at one moment or another willed the death of the old watchman. By summing up all of the evidence (real or imaginary, conscious or subconscious) against the several suspects, Munguía (or Leñero) creates a joint indictment in which each of the five is guilty, no matter who really killed don Jesús—if indeed he was actually murdered at all.

Emmanuel Carballo feels that Leñero consciously leads his story to a dead end so as to leave "to the infinite mercy of God the judgment of human errors."[7] Carballo also says that "*Los albañiles* is a novel that puts the human race and its creator face to face: only the latter, Leñero seems to say, knows who these bricklayers are, what they want, and what end awaits these characters who willingly or otherwise are building in this world the city of God."[8] This evaluation is both logical and acceptable, and it also serves to point out the Graham Greene influence in this work.

This novel of Mexican urban life exposes many customs and facets of the existence of these construction workers, thus revealing some interesting social and even anthropological facts. In a very different way it is reminiscent at times of the sort of detail which fills Oscar Lewis's studies of lower-class Mexican families. At the same time *Los albañiles* is a psychological study in that it examines the actions, reactions, and motivations of the characters. What seems so simple on the surface turns out to be highly complex as we plunge deeper and deeper into the details of their lives.

We come to know why Isidro, the fifteen-year-old helper on the job, prefers to spend his nights at the building site with the *velador,* don Jesús, rather than at home with his mother and family, even though the old watchman is enslaving him to a homosexual relationship and eventually abuses Celerina, the young girl whom Isidro is beginning to court. We learn why the engineer's inept son, scornfully called "el Nene" (the baby), is put in charge of the construction job and the combination of background and attitudes and circumstances which explain his inferiority complex before the workers and, inevitably, his failure. His resentment is given a focus when his wallet with 3000 pesos disappears and he is convinced that don Jesús is the guilty party.

The case of Jacinto (the assistant foreman) is similarly laid open and found to be a tangled web of psychological conflicts. Since he is being blackmailed by don Jesús, who threatens to expose the fact that Jacinto has been making off with sizeable quantities of building materials, he is a prime suspect in the case. Then, there is the foreman, Chapo Alvarez, who hired don Jesús so that Chapo could sleep with the old watchman's young wife. Don Jesús is, of course, on to this and provokes a terrific argument with Chapo, who admittedly is not responsible when in the throes of one of his sudden and towering rages.

The character weighted down by the heaviest load of anxieties and hostilities is the plumber, Sergio García Estrada, called "el Cura" or "el seminarista" because he had spent some time in a seminary with hopes of becoming a priest. Besides being the most complex of the suspects (perhaps we could say the most in need of psychiatric treatment), "el Cura" is also the brother of Celerina. Her mistreatment at the hands of don Jesús would be motive enough, but an earlier incident with the old watchman on another job (steadfastly denied by Sergio) gives double reason for Munguía to grill him on the matter. If the reader had to choose the most likely suspect, I think his finger would point most insistently at Sergio.

Actually, the reader of *Los albañiles* might be pardoned for wondering if the killer didn't do society a good turn in removing from its midst a character as wholly repugnant as don Jesús—a heavy drinker, a marijuana user, a common thief, a homosexual addicted to filthy thoughts and obscene language, a real mental case who was for a time in a hospital for the deranged. Yet the probing into the thoughts and actions and motivation of several of the other main characters shows us that neither are they much of an asset to their society. While Leñero has not opted for fatalism in leaving us with this less than edifying stalemate, it does appear that he is subscribing to the belief that sociologically man is apt to be the product, or the toy, of his environment. And so, Leñero is inveighing not against these poor hapless individuals but rather against the system that spawns them.

In any case, it is all plausible and convincing, even though the reader is left wondering about a lot of things, especially what is real and what is imaginary in the thoughts and words of the suspects as well as of Munguía himself. The fact that we are kept guessing is a good part of the essence of the success of this novel.

The third novel published by Vicente Leñero is *Estudio Q*, 1965, a direct outgrowth of his association with the TV industry in Mexico. It is, however, much more than that. One critic has called it "a deft analysis of physic disintegration and a clever experiment in literary technique."[9] With devastating effectiveness Leñero satirizes the "telenovelas" so popular with Mexican TV viewers. Here the eye of the novelist is transformed into a camera, which is infinitely colder, more impersonal, more heartless than any novelist. Again, *Estudio Q* poses the old yet ever-valid question of what is life? How do we at times distinguish the line between reality and unreality? It even invokes briefly the Segismundo of Calderón's undying *La vida es sueño* (*Life Is a Dream*), a role which Alex Jiménez, the protagonist, once played for fifty performances. But for Alex life is not a dream but a TV drama, and the reader is caught (as Alex is) in the tangled threads of the script and of real life.

Alex is a highly popular though rather superficial and timeworn star of TV dramas. It is decided to produce a "telenovela" that will be a biography of his personal life. Much of the lengthy first chapter (of the five that comprise the book) is given over to an endless detailed analysis of the star's physical and psychological characteristics, as prepared by a woman scriptwriter. Starting with the earliest pages, Leñero skillfully introduces moments when the director is instructing Alex and others in the cast (as well as the cameramen) precisely how he wants them to effect each movement, each word, each shot.

From this point on the novel develops this intermingling of moments from Alex's real life and various scenes from his TV biography. The reader quickly becomes aware of two currents which are to merge and carry the story to its climactic though baffling conclusion. We see Alex struggling to maintain and control his own identity in real life as his TV identity inexorably hems him in. He fights to escape becoming a victim of the script, the camera, his filmed personality. We know he is losing the battle when, for instance, he is shaving and at the same time is mentally instructing himself in each detailed action with the same language the director uses. The scenes of the script become so identifiable with reality, and the real life moments so dominated by the film personality, that the reader is increasingly unsure which is which. Eventually the story ends with Alex committing suicide in rather sensational manner, but by this time Leñero has so manipulated the two currents that we don't really know whether the true intention of Alex was to kill Alex the TV star or Alex Jiménez himself.

Emmanuel Carballo thinks (and I agree) that *Estudio Q* is the most ambitious of the Leñero novels published to date and that its daring experimentation shows Leñero prefers knowingly to risk a failure than merely to repeat with slight structural variants the techniques which have already proved successful for him.[10] We can admire the courage, curiosity, and imagination which impel Leñero to explore new novelistic forms. Moreover, he again shows the talent already displayed in *Los albañiles* of forcing the reader to participate in the story, though perhaps not as totally this time as before. George McMurray, in referring to this facet of Leñero's work, feels that "Leñero views each of his novels as a kind of puzzle requiring the reader's active participation in order for it to be appreciated."[11]

The influence of Graham Greene upon Leñero in *Estudio Q* would appear to lie in Leñero's probings of eternal truths: What is real? What is imaginary? What is life? How can man remain human and individual in the face of dehumanizing pressures and influences?

The most recent of the Leñero novels is *El garabato* [The maze], published early in 1967. Once again his experimental instincts are given free reign and they have conceived a novel of unusual structure. And, as before, Leñero almost challenges the reader to stay with him and to put together the pieces and find the meaning of the story. Here too Greene's mark is present, readily identifiable this time.

Ostensibly, *El garabato* is a novel within a novel within a novel. It purports to be a work turned over by Pablo Mejía Herrera (before he went off to do graduate work in psychology at the University of Texas) to his friend Vicente Leñero who will attempt to find a publisher. Pablo Mejía's novel, titled *El garabato*, is narrated in the first person by Fernando J. Moreno, a critic who has long talked of the great novel he someday must write. That he has not done so previously may be due to an excess of self-criticism or simply an incapacity for creativity (either of which would explain his inner desire to downgrade the work of others). In any case, he promptly shows himself to be a bit stuffy by repeated citing of authorities (including some of his own essays). He has refused interviews with the press for the past few years on the grounds that he has said all there is to be said about Mexican and Latin American novelists.

Nevertheless, Moreno surprises even himself by granting an interview to a callow youth named Fabián Mendizábal who comes one day to see him. The same lad returns later and persuades Moreno against his will to read the manuscript of a novel he has written called *El garabato*. From here on we have alternating chapters in which on the one hand we read with Moreno parts of the somewhat ingenuous murder mystery by young Mendizábal, while on the other we share Moreno's mental criticisms—often picayune and carping—of the manuscript and also learn of the struggle he is having with his conscience over his private life.

After twenty years of married life with Norma (and children), Moreno had gone off with his mistress, Lucy. Norma secured a divorce and at the time of our story Fernando Moreno has had five happy years with Lucy. On second thought, they have been happy only in the sense of physical satisfaction. As a critic he has isolated and immobilized himself. He constantly strives to intiate creative work on his novel but can't get going. As a Catholic who believes in the doctrine of his faith, he fears damnation for the life he is leading. Seeking justification or a psychological rationalization of his behavior, he goes regularly to a psychoanalyst. It is in this area of the moral dilemma, of course, that we see the Graham Greene shadow hovering over Leñero. In fact, the moral problem with which Fernando Moreno wrestles is essentially the same one developed by Greene in *The Heart of the Matter* and *The End of the Affair*.

Before the end of the first chapter Moreno makes the decision to leave Lucy. Shaken by this unanticipated stand on his part, Lucy shortly thereafter flies off to Los Angeles. Through the rest of the book we see further chapters of Mendizábal's mystery and also witness Moreno's efforts to resolve finally his moral crisis. His emotions tell him to go back to Lucy (as does his psychoanalyst), while his reason and Christian faith support the move he has taken. Moreno does not finish reading Mendizábal's work before the latter returns and so the manuscript is given back with some most disparaging comments. For two or three weeks more, Moreno continues his inner struggle and searching of conscience until one day he quite unexpectedly finds himself drawn into a tourist agency where he buys a ticket and soon is on his way to Los Angeles and Lucy.

So, we never finish Mendizábal's story called *El garabato*, which is contained within Moreno's narrative titled *El garabato*, which is the work left by Pablo Mejía Herrera with Vicente Leñero for the purpose of finding a publisher. Leñero has given us a novel which is a jigsaw puzzle in more than just its structure.

My own interpretation of the work is that Fabián Mendizábal is Fernando Moreno's alter ego (note that their initials are the same). Indeed, Leñero gives us several clues to show that they are really one person. As Mendizábal he essays his long-promised "great" novel. As Moreno, the critic, he picks his own novelistic effort apart. Mendizábal's *garabato* or "maze" is the search for the solution of a murder, Moreno's represents his own quest for a way out of his moral dilemma. The decision of Moreno to fly back to Lucy ends both stories before a way out has been found. Thus Mendizábal's murder story is an allegory depicting and explaining Moreno's moral crisis, and a careful reading of the two narratives reveals how the former portrays the latter. The whole thing displays handsomely Leñero's experimental aptitudes and a distinct skill in bringing off such an imaginative novelistic effort.

El garabato may also be considered as a sort of satire on the writing of a novel, but genial satire with some telling touches of quiet humor. Leñero's concern with the artistic frustration of Fernando J. Moreno may be related to what he tells us about his own anguish in writing:

> It is difficult enough to undertake a novel. . . . Quite difficult, at least in my case: I don't write flowingly. I don't go from beginning to end, chapter after chapter. I fill pages and more pages, and I am forever going back over what is written to do it again. . . . I have an obsession for structuring the work so that it will function, I say, like a well-oiled mechanism. . . . I wish that it were easier, but it isn't. Perhaps if I didn't worry so much about the mechanism, which they tell me is my worst fault, or if I would write my novels straight through from start to finish, or if I would quit looking for new forms, or if I were more ambitious to achieve a truly transcendent work, if this or if that . . . I would obtain better results. My friends and my critics may be perfectly right, in their way, but I feel that I have my reasons and that, within my limitations, I do what I feel, what I want to, what I somehow can do. . . . Each novel is harder for me than the previous one.[12]

The fact that each novel proves more difficult for Leñero than the one before is, up to a point, something natural and reassuring. It denotes a growing maturity on Leñero's part and bespeaks the seriousness with which he approaches the creative process of writing novels with meaning. And I think it evident that his novels do have meaning. Knowing what we do about this young Mexican novelist, it seems that we can expect him to continue giving us works of significance, works of improving literary artistry, works with a moral dimension.

Leñero's obsession with the structuring of his novels, with the mechanics of putting them together so that, in his words, they run like "a well-oiled mechanism," constitutes for me a valuable aspect of his work and a partial explanation of his importance in the new generation of Mexican novelists. Too many of his fellow writers have neglected structural unity, too many have shunned experimentation of form and structure. Not all of them have the same compulsion—nor the same talent—as Leñero in this direction, and so it is all the more to be hoped that he will continue down this road.

In 1968 Vicente Leñero wrote his first theatrical piece, a timely and controversial drama called *Pueblo rechazado* [A people rejected]. It enjoyed a successful run in Mexico City (and, indeed, was one of the attractions of the Cultural Program of the nineteenth Olympic Games held in that city). *Pueblo rechazado* finds its direct inspiration in the widely publicized and slightly sensational case of the Benedictine monk Gregoire Lemercier, a Belgian who in 1950 founded a monastery in Cuernavaca (fifty miles south of Mexico City). In 1961 Lemercier, as prior of the monastery, began the experimental use of psychoanalysis for studying the vocational suitability of each candidate for the priesthood. In more than a few cases, the psychoanalytic study uncovered some motivation other than the strictly spiritual: a fear of responsibility and an inner desire to accept blind obedience; a dislike for ordinary human work and for the obligations of social existence; even an occasional tendency towards homosexuality.

Rather naturally, the matter soon came under the scrutiny of Church authorities in Rome, and after considerable discussion, an official ban was placed on the use of psychoanalysis in religious communities. As might be expected, the whole affair (both before and after the ban) caused something of an uproar in Mexico, with both sides of the issue finding articulate defenders. Eventually,

Lemercier left the monastery and the religious life but still lives in Mexico and remains the hub of a certain controversy.

It is easy to see, then, that Leñero, in choosing to base *Pueblo rechazado* on the Lemercier case, was touching a public nerve as well as staying in the Graham Greene groove of confronting Christian moral issues forthrightly. When I asked Leñero how he happened to resort to the dramatic form in this case, he replied that the play really was an offshoot of a novel on which he was working that will probe contemporary religious trends in Mexico, where—as everywhere else—the Church is caught in a profound tug-of-war between liberal elements and proponents of traditionalism. Hopefully, this forthcoming novel by Vicente Leñero will appear soon. We can count on it being a carefully structured and well-written work which will dissect some aspect of another Christian dilemma of our times.

Obviously encouraged by the success of *Pueblo rechazado*, in 1969 Leñero produced a dramatic version of *Los albañiles*, which was even more widely acclaimed. In fact, it brought him the Premio Ruiz de Alarcón, awarded by the Mexican Association of Theater Critics, as the author of the best theatrical play of 1969. At about this time, Leñero was quoted as saying that he would like to write plays with one hand and novels with the other.[13] He also confessed why he had turned to playwriting: "In 1965 I began writing a novel, of which I have about 200 pages completed. I am stalled on it and, to get away from it, I did *Pueblo rechazado* and the stage version of *Los albañiles*. This doesn't indicate writing capacity on my part but rather a lack of capacity to finish that novel. For me these plays have been a form of escape. That novel, then, is the reason why I am involved in the theater."[14]

Nevertheless, Leñero is openly impressed by the size of the audience he has been able to reach through his theatrical works. He points out that the first edition of the novel *Los albañiles* was of 8,000 copies, which took six years to sell, whereas some 10,000 persons went to see the dramatic version of the same work during its two months on the boards. "This reveals," says Leñero, "that the power of communication, at times, is more effective in the theater."[15]

Early in 1970 a third play by Vicente Leñero opened in Mexico

City. Its title was *Compañero* [Companion, or Comrade] and its subject Che Guevara, with Regis Debray also figuring prominently in the action, although no real names are used. One critic, in discussing Leñero's *Compañero,* spoke of "its dramatic range, of a high level, without demagogic nor partisan spirit."[16] By mid-1971 still another Leñero play was being staged in Mexico City. Called *La carpa* [The tent], it is a dramatization of *Estudio Q.*

Emmanuel Carballo has said that Vicente Leñero thus far has shown fully his ability as a writer of novels, his control over the materials with which he works, and that he needs only to convince us in subsequent efforts that he is capable of creating works ("verbal constructions") which begin to live when the reader closes their pages.[17] But in my judgment, in *Los albañiles* and to a lesser extent in each of his other novels, Leñero has already proved the point.

NOTES TO CHAPTER 9

1. *Los narradores ante el público,* 1st ser. (Mexico City, 1966), p. 187.
2. Ibid., p. 184.
3. Ibid., pp. 186–187.
4. Ibid., pp. 180–181.
5. Carballo in Leñero, *Vicente Leñero* (in the series Nuevos escritores mexicanos del siglo XX presentados por sí mismos [Mexico City, 1967]), prologue, p. 5.
6. Ibid., p. 9.
7. Ibid., pp. 6–7.
8. Ibid., p. 10.
9. George R. McMurray, "Current Trends in the Mexican Novel." *Hispania,* LI (September, 1968), p. 532.
10. *Vicente Leñero,* prologue, p. 7.
11. *McMurray,* p. 533.
12. *Los narradores ante el público,* pp. 185–186.
13. *Visión,* August 15, 1969, p. 76.
14. Ibid.
15. Ibid.
16. *Tiempo,* March 23, 1970, p. 100.
17. *Vicente Leñero,* prologue, pp. 11–12.

THE NOVELS OF VICENTE LEÑERO

La voz adolorida, 1961 (revised edition under the title of *A fuerza de palabras,* 1967)
Los albañiles, 1964
Estudio Q, 1965
El garabato, 1967

STUDIES ON VICENTE LEÑERO

Brushwood, John S. *Mexico in Its Novel,* pp. 49–50.
Clark, Lucie. *"Los albañiles." Cuadernos Americanos,* año 28, no. 1 (1969), pp. 219–223.
Los narradores ante el público, 1st ser., pp. 177–178.
McMurray, George R. "The Novels of Vicente Leñero." *Critique,* VIII, no. 3 (Spring-Summer, 1966), pp. 55–61.
————. "Current Trends in the Mexican Novel." *Hispania,* LI (September, 1968), pp. 532–537.
Nuevos escritores mexicanos del siglo XX presentados por sí mismos: Vicente Leñero.
Ocampo de Gómez, A. M., and Prado Velázquez, E., eds., *Diccionario de escritores mexicanos,* pp. 191–192.
Sommers, Joseph. *After the Storm,* pp. 177–178.

Sergio Galindo,
Novelist of Human Relations

ANYONE WHO READS WIDELY AMONG CURRENT MEXICAN NOVELS WILL soon discover that Sergio Galindo is one of the better novelists now writing in that country. Yet it seems easier to make that claim for him than to say why it is merited. He didn't start publishing works in his early twenties, as some of the youngest novelists now are doing. He is not a great innovator, nor is he remarkably prolific, and he has nothing which quite matches the best of Yáñez, Rulfo, Fuentes, or even Leñero.

But if Galindo does not impress through radical techniques or themes, he is still definitely outside of the commonplace novelistic patterns. Although his works lack some of the "obscurity" cultivated by many of his peers to coerce the reader into full involvement, this does not say that he is a traditionalist and thus simple to follow. Galindo has a few tricks of his own to achieve this purpose and others, and he utilizes them with skill and superb timing. One is his habit of dropping suddenly into the middle of an incident, and then as the reader grasps for meaning Galindo gradually feeds in the essential bits of background. Another is his fondness for moving the narrative viewpoint from third-person to first-person in a very unobtrusive and effective maneuver which provides the desired interiorization. Brushwood uses the term "outside-inside transition" to describe this technique, which is quite similar to that used by Fuentes with Artemio Cruz and by Spota in *Lo de antes*.[1]

Galindo's sensitivity to human behavior, particularly as seen through interpersonal relationships, makes for some very subtle delineation of characters. Sometimes his touch in this regard is so deft as to be truly delightful. And the net effect is to make the reader feel a closer identification with the characters themselves. It takes no great insight to conclude that this gift for creating, revealing, and interpreting human relationships is Galindo's most distinguishing characteristic.

It is this talent, too, which leads Galindo to a preoccupation with the attitude of his principal characters toward reality. In each of his works there is an effort on the part of one or more persons, consciously or not, to alter or sidestep reality, to make it conform to an imagined concept. This is a common human exercise, and one which rarely finds success, either in real life or in Galindo's novels. But he has a special ability to make the effort appear thoroughly human, true-to-life, and interesting.

Sergio Galindo was born in 1926 in Jalapa, the capital city of Veracruz. Although Veracruz is known mostly as a Gulf coast state, Jalapa lies inland some seventy-five miles from the port city of Veracruz and, because of its location in the mountains, enjoys a cool climate marked by frequent fog. While definitely a provincial town, Jalapa is known for its university and its intellectual atmosphere. Here Galindo has spent most of his life, until recently, and most of his short stories and novels have their setting in or near Jalapa. He evokes with affection and effectiveness the life and spirit and tempo of his native city.

After studying at the National University, Galindo spent a year in Paris. Shortly after he returned his father died and he became owner of a small factory, which soon failed. For a time he worked as an immigration agent. In 1955, having already published a collection of stories, *La máquina vacía* [The empty machine], 1951, he received a scholarship from the Centro Mexicano de Escritores. For several years he was in charge of publications at the Universidad Veracruzana in Jalapa, a position which included the editorship of the respected literary journal, *La Palabra y el Hombre*. He states frankly that this was the most pleasant job he has had.[2] He lives at present in Mexico City, where he is chief of coordination for the regional institutes of the Instituto Nacional de Bellas Artes.

Tragedy emerges in nearly all of Galindo's works, while humor only occasionally finds a place in his pages. And yet, in person, he seems to have a light touch and a ready sense of humor. An example of this is the presentation he made about himself and his work before an appreciative audience in 1965, as part of a series of such talks involving many of Mexico's current writers.[3] Almost the only Galindo work in which humor plays a part is *La comparsa,* where, because of the atmosphere and setting, it could hardly be otherwise. If in the majority of his published efforts Galindo writes in dead earnest, it is a reflection of his concern with the seriousness of life. His main strength, as already stated, is in penetrating human relationships and probing the driving motives of his characters as they wrestle with a reality which too often is more than they can handle.

Galindo's first published novel was *Polvos de arroz* [Rice powder], 1958. This is a story (really no more than a novelette) of loneliness and of human yearning for affection and understanding. The central figure, Camerina Rabasa, has come from Jalapa to Mexico City, ostensibly to visit in the household of her niece Julia. The true reason for her visit, however, is to meet for the first time a young man, Juan Antonio Ulloa, with whom she has for some time carried on a lonely hearts correspondence. Now that the moment of meeting seems near, Camerina's courage weakens, and we learn two reasons why: she is something over fifty years of age and is terribly overweight, facts never divulged in her letters.

Galindo lets Camerina's thoughts carry us back to the rather pathetic existence she has led in Jalapa. Life with her parents and her sister Augusta was prim and circumscribed. When her mother died, the father became a kind of lost soul, with the burden assumed by Camerina, who at that time was attractive enough to be courted by Rodolfo Gris, son of a once-affluent family. Because of her somewhat unsure and trusting disposition, coupled with his disinclination to seek a marriage date, the courtship lingered on for four years, at which time Camerina's romance was exploded by the shattering revelation that Augusta was carrying Rodolfo's baby.

From that day forward, Augusta never again spoke directly to Camerina or to her father, who withdrew more and more until his death. Augusta herself merely existed in a semimute state, practically devoid of communication even with her child, Julia, who was raised primarily by Camerina. At a young age Julia went off to marry one of her teachers, a decent man and an architect.

Now Camerina thinks she has found, in young Juan Antonio, the love and understanding so long denied her. In her isolation and loneliness she has built for herself an idyll through the letters exchanged with him. Rendered oblivious to reality by the force of her illusion, she arranged a visit with Julia (whose own children are already teen-agers) in order to meet her dream lover. But as she prepares to contact him, reality begins to break through and she awakes to the fact that her imaginary romance with Juan Antonio may end abruptly the moment he sees her for the first time.

And so through a good part of the novel she wrestles with her urge to call him and the conflicting intuition not to do so. She stalls and vacillates, and tries to transform reality by making herself think she can achieve a relationship of equals with Perla, the teen-age daughter of Julia. This seems a desperate attempt to put herself somehow on a plane of equality with Juan Antonio. Naturally, the illusion is fleeting. How much longer Camerina might have gone on both fooling and torturing herself is hard to say, for at about this point her dream world is broken apart, suddenly and cruelly. Without at first realizing what they are reading, Perla and Julia discover Camerina's secret through a bundle of letters written to her by Juan Antonio. When Camerina surprises them in the act, laughing and mocking, the bubble bursts and the harshness of reality reasserts itself.

A year after his somewhat tentative exploration of human relationships in *Polvos de arroz*, Sergio Galindo probes deeper into this same complex and fascinating realm in *La justicia de enero* [January justice], published in 1959. This time the setting is far from Galindo's native area of Jalapa, in Mexico City. The major characters are several immigration agents whose lives at work, at home, and in the past are brought into focus with sensitivity and a fineness of detail.

The action line of *La justicia de enero* is energized by the search for a Frenchman named Claude Rennie Vossler, whose activities and immigration status are both quite irregular. But this actually proves to be a rather slender thread which serves chiefly as the means for projecting on stage the assortment of immigration agents who are involved in this and other cases, and with one another. As Galindo begins to apply a sort of telescopic lens approach to each of

them, we come to understand in depth the private and official existence of each, and to witness how their lives as individuals out of
the office often influence their attitudes and actions as immigration
agents. Conversely, we see how the pressures, rivalries, successes,
and disappointments of their job tend to mark and shape their relationships with wives, families, and friends, as well as with each
other. This interplay of relationships on various levels, rather than
the search for the elusive Frenchman, is the real concern of *La
justicia de enero.*

One of these persons—Héctor Loeza—does emerge above the
others enough to become the most important single character if not
a typical protagonist. Loeza, twenty-five years old as the story unfolds, already has compiled a varied background. Leaving the home
of his widowed mother early (because of persistent conflicts with
her and with his two younger brothers), he has in a decade worked
as a sailor, stevedore, chauffeur, bartender, and insurance agent
before coming to his present work. As details gradually surface to
reveal the personality of Héctor Loeza, it is evident that sooner or
later he almost had to turn to some sort of police work, because of a
built-in compulsion to have a control over others. Not that he is
a brutish, bullying type. He does take a certain pleasure in the
dogged sort of detective work which forms a part of his job, and yet
his actions and words, and especially his inner thoughts, show a sensitive and lonely person, greatly in need of the warmth of love
which he seems incapable of reaching out for or even accepting.

Héctor is recently divorced from his wife Cecilia, who likewise
is a bundle of complexities and compulsions, although like Héctor
himself a thoroughly decent person at heart. It is evident that these
two people love each other deeply and need one another desperately, but their individual (and sometimes perverse) personalities
prevent them from sharing and enjoying the love and companion-
ship which would make each of them a warmer, better person. The
frustration—tragedy, even—of this couple overshadows all else and
we become painfully conscious of how little it takes to make or
break a union between two good persons. On more than one occasion, a single word, or the right action, by one or the other could
have brought them together again, though by failing to let this hap-

pen Galindo may be telling us that such a reconciliation couldn't be lasting.

So effectively and so intimately does Galindo involve his readers in the affairs of his characters that, when Héctor finally chances upon the elusive Claude Rennie one night, the sudden solution of this vexing case actually seems anticlimactic. Even Loeza seems to have this reaction. Remembering too that Sergio Galindo himself was for a time an immigration agent, we are perhaps afforded an insight into his personal feelings about this type of work through the fact that more than one of the agents in the novel are determined to leave their jobs by the time the story ends. In at least one case it is because the person no longer has any stomach for it. In another instance it represents the agent's imperative need to improve the economic situation of his family. Since January is thought to be the month of the most unstable weather, we can conclude that the title of the novel refers to the precarious sort of justice to be expected from underpaid agents whose work is often unpleasant and whose performance at least occasionally is influenced by the stress of personal affairs.

La justicia de enero is, in short, a really good novel and a distinct improvement upon Galindo's first effort, *Polvos de arroz*. Here we have a well-organized and well-achieved story of rather impelling interest, one which confirms Galindo's great strength in dealing with human associations. The next Galindo novel, *El Bordo* (*The Precipice*), 1960, finds the author's skill in this direction reaching an even higher degree of refinement. The critics split as to the relative merits of the two works. For Brushwood, *El Bordo* is definitely Galindo's best.[4] On the other hand, Rosario Castellanos feels that "the skillful counterpoint, the smoothness of the narration, the vigorous sketching of the characters, the internal coherence, and the inevitable ending place *La justicia de enero* several cuts above the other efforts of the same author."[5] The truth is that both are intriguing works, sensitively realized by this young writer gifted in exploring subtle as well as obvious psychological elements as his characters strive to confront (or evade) reality and to relate with others around them.

His study of these elements in *El Bordo* is somewhat more intense (or at least the reader feels he has a clearer view of them), in good part because Galindo reduces the field of action and the number of people who enter significantly into the story. The title of the book comes from the name of the property of the Coviella family, situated in the mountains just outside of Jalapa, in a spot that is cold, rainy, and fog-shrouded a good part of the year. It is a setting thoroughly suitable to the intense personality conflicts and psychological insights which Galindo develops and carries to a tragic conclusion.

As the story begins the aged and failing widow doña Teresa de Coviella together with her elder son, Gabriel, and his wife, Lorenza, await the arrival of the younger son, Hugo, and his bride, Esther. Hugo has been a spoiled, headstrong young man and, like his departed father, Eusebio, a heavy drinker. Also in the group waiting to greet the newlyweds is Joaquina de Larragoitia, Eusebio's younger sister, who had escaped a miserable family existence in Spain by marrying her brother's boss, Luis Larragoitia, when the latter returned to Spain after making his fortune in Mexico. Only a year or so later, Larragoitia died suddenly. Thus, Joaquina inherited all his holdings and for over thirty years has administered them shrewdly.

Galindo places all of these persons in the main house at El Bordo: Joaquina, doña Teresa (widowed some ten years earlier), Gabriel and Lorenza (plus their little son), and Hugo and Esther. Though beautiful, the place is isolated and lonely, which serves to provoke and magnify all temperamental differences. Actually, the problems revolve around Joaquina and Hugo. While it is obvious that Joaquina really has a deep affection for this nephew, some inner perverseness forces her to criticize him at every turn, thus touching off frequent and sometimes bitter scenes. The others, unable to prevent or restrain these episodes, are in turn sucked into the emotional vortex.

It is hoped by all that Hugo's marriage will defuse this explosive situation, and for a time it seems that this is to be the case. Hugo's black moods and self-indulgent attitudes give way to exuberant happiness and a rather startling dedication to work. The inspiration for these changes admittedly is Esther, an intelligent, talented, and attractive girl who moves smoothly into the family group. But as the months pass it becomes evident that even she cannot penetrate the inner defenses of Hugo's complex and compulsive personality. Joaquina still finds fault in him, particularly his fondness for drink, and the tension grows.

Several other factors further complicate the overall picture, such as Lorenza's obsession that some day she and Gabriel will be able to buy back the once splendid old home of her parents in Jalapa and go there to live, leaving the property at El Bordo to Hugo and Esther. Aware of Lorenza's fixation on this subject, Joaquina coldly turns down a last-chance offer of the property at a bargain figure, even knowing that with her rejection the owners will raze the house and convert the property to other uses. When this indeed comes to pass, she is agonizingly repentant and asks herself what moves her to such uncharitable actions towards those she really loves. The reader has long since realized that Joaquina's temperament is fully as compulsively perverse as Hugo's. The conflict and eventual tragedy in *El Bordo* centers around and feeds on the fact that these two basically good humans are so much alike, are driven by such an ungovernable need to hurt even those they love, so that there is no possibility of an extended peaceful coexistence.

Perhaps a psychologist could sort out the specific problems besetting both Joaquina and Hugo. To a nonprofessional it seems that Joaquina, who has for so long led a lonely, frustrated existence after but a year or two of happiness with Luis Larragoitia, needs an outlet for her embittered feelings and has for some years turned on Hugo because of his indulgent, lazy, noncooperative attitude. Now that he is married and happy and working as hard as anyone on the land, an element of envy mingles with her frustration and bitterness. Having no other convenient target, she continues to pick at Hugo, concentrating on his evident weakness for drink. And Hugo, always wound up tight, reacts predictably by lashing out at his tormentor and by drinking even more.

Esther, who in the early chapters appeared to be the heaven-sent peacemaker who would dissolve this family feud, becomes the innocent victim caught in the crossfire. With all her love and comprehension, it is beyond her to reach Hugo when he is worked up or drinks to excess. In this mood he sometimes says things which hurt her deeply, yet she never stops trying to find the answer. One point of tenseness between them is that he is desperately impatient for her to give him a son. After months of disappointment on this front, Esther does become pregnant and joyfully seeks the right moment to tell Hugo the news. She tries to do so at one point but Hugo's mood prevents it. This proves to have been her last chance, for the following day Hugo, while engaged in some reckless practice with his pistol, arrives at the breaking point. He shoots down the old family dog, leaps in a car and roars off to his own destruction at the place called The Precipice, from which the novel takes its name.

This tragedy clearly brings to an end the story Galindo is telling of human relationships that are out of kilter or refuse to mesh, but the author spends another twenty pages (of the total of 210) trying to tie up the loose ends. While the effort is done with skill, it is anticlimactic and leaves the reader with the thought that Galindo is a little too concerned about wrapping up the aftermath and taking each character to a solution of sorts. Nevertheless, *El Bordo* is a gripping psychological story artfully told and stands far above the average. Although it may be said that the old widow doña Teresa (at best a peripheral character) is the only person in the book who has any real sense of fulfillment, the others courageously confront life in some of its harder and less rewarding moments and emerge from the ordeal as tempered and more compassionate persons.

In his fourth novel, *La comparsa* [The masqueraders], 1964, Galindo veers off on a new tack. Though still concerned with human relationships, he is observing them on a different plane. The tense, emotion-laden situations of *La justicia de enero* and *El Bordo* are put aside and, in fact, he lets the pendulum go far in the other direction. The story of *La comparsa* unfolds in Galindo's own city of Jalapa during the first weekend of Lent in 1959. The occasion is the period of festivities commonly known as Mardi Gras, which of course ordinarily is celebrated in the last few days prior to the beginning of Lent. Jalapa, however, observes the rather extraordinary custom of holding this festival during Lent, for the very practical reason that the usual Mardi Gras blowout in nearby Veracruz makes it quite unprofitable for smaller Jalapa to compete at the same time.

From start to finish this slender novel recreates the carnival atmosphere. In fact, Jalapa, delivered over to the mood of merry-making, has to be adjudged the protagonist of the work, since no one of the dozens of persons who romp through the story stands forth as the leading figure. In keeping with the spirit of the occasion, Galindo's style is light and as frivolous as the attitude of the revelers. The kaleidoscopic nature of those festive days, is presented in a ceaseless series of short episodes (some extremely brief) in which the many characters appear, disappear, and reappear. It is not unsimilar to a disjointed home movie in which no sequence is allowed to finish before another interrupts. In this case, serving the purpose it does, the technique impresses as being most effective. The variegated procession of images, incidents, and conversations provides, in the aggregate, a satisfying characterization of these numerous persons caught up in uninhibited celebration.

La comparsa is a fascinating view, often amusing and occasionally eyebrow-raising, of a whole town that has collectively "let its hair down." All taboos are forgotten as everyone turns to pleasure in one form or another. For a moment the reader wonders if Carnival doesn't reveal the true nature of everyone, the inner nature unfettered by the restricting and restraining attitudes, conventions, and regulations of society. We wonder if this isn't the true reality, with the inhibited front put on in daily life being the face of irreality. But reason quickly restores the right perspective which identifies these few days of spontaneous abandonment as just a time for escaping the tedium, cares, and duties of daily reality—a momentary spell founded on the denial of reality.

Sergio Galindo's most recent work, *Nudo* [Knot], was published in 1970. Some observers no doubt will label it his best effort yet, and in some respects it clearly is. Here, more than in his previous works, he moves into the "groove" of the new-style novel, consciously seeking a certain ambiguity in the narrative stream by confusing the present and the past in such a quiet and effective manner that only with the greatest attention can we keep the thread of the story from becoming tangled. From one line to the next the characters may turn from the present to an inner monologue of some moment of the past. Galindo also resorts, briefly, to cinematographic devices, to narration through diary excerpts and the exchange of letters, and to the introduction of a very brief piece in dramatic form. Perhaps too often he includes whole sentences and even conversational fragments in English (and a few times in French). To the Spanish reader who knows no English, this could prove upsetting, since at times the English elements are important to the story.

The "knot" referred to by the title is a group of five persons whose lives have been closely knit. Various other characters move into the story from time to time, either actively or in flashbacks, but the plot revolves mostly around the five principal figures. There is Nan Green, who as the orphan Nan Park came from Canada to Mexico at the age of fifteen to be raised by the parents of Daniel Duarte, then a boy of nine. For almost three decades they have been very close—at the outset like brother and sister, though less in that vein as time moves on. Nan went to England during World War II to serve as a nurse and there met Allan Green, six years older than she. After the war he came to Mexico to marry Nan and to stay, as an artist. A very special bond joins Allan and Nan and Daniel, a bond which Galindo portrays adroitly throughout. Daniel, encouraged by Nan and Allan, marries Yvonne, a beautiful, rich, and somewhat spoiled girl, whose mother's suicide in mid-story is one factor in the breakup of their marriage after eight years. The other factor is Tom Hardley, a handsome young Londoner of little account, who toys with Yvonne and goes his way.

The fifth member of "the knot" in this story is Laura. Cultured, beautiful, intelligent, and a good deal deeper than Yvonne, she and Daniel fall deeply in love and are married four years after his divorce from Yvonne. The Greens welcome her into the circle wholeheartedly, making it what Allan refers to as the "ménage á cinq." Everyone accepts this quite casually, since Yvonne has remained close to Nan and Allan, as well as to Daniel, and she achieves a good relationship with Laura, although beneath the surface there is a trace of tension between the two.

These five spend considerable time together at the Greens' place in San Miguel de Allende, rethinking certain moments of the past, exploring human values, and enjoying a pleasant existence marked at times by more than enough drinking. On one such occasion

Daniel and Nan suddenly decide to make love. The subsequent repentant spirit on her part provokes the climax of the story. Saying that she has betrayed Allan through her infidelity, Nan decides that she has to leave him, quite against his wishes. She goes to Mexico City and lives with Yvonne, and for an indefinite (though apparently not too lengthy) period Allan is lost and desolate, Nan is groping and quite unhappy. Finally, Nan has Yvonne drive her back to San Miguel.

Allan, more than a little drunk, receives a call that the girls have had an accident only a few miles from San Miguel and he arrives in time to see the ambulance carrying Nan and Yvonne away. Frantic, Allan calls Daniel and says that Nan has been killed. Daniel and Laura arrive in a few hours and are standing by when Allan awakens from a profound sleep. Daniel tells him then that the girls are not seriously hurt and will leave the hospital in a couple of days.

My reactions to *Nudo* are several and largely quite favorable. This work cements even further the well-established talent of Galindo for probing human relationships in a truly convincing fashion. While reading *Nudo* I had the thought several times that one forgets, from one Galindo novel to another, what a delightful narrative manner he has, how penetrating his explorations of the thoughts and motives of the persons in his works, how often he adds something quite significant through the smallest touch. Yet, in the overall, I find that *Nudo* has less impact than either *El Bordo* or *La justicia de enero*. This seems to stem from the fact that certain critical moments of the climax do not impress as being completely in accord with the buildup. They don't flow quite so naturally from all that has gone before.

Nevertheless, *Nudo* is a significant addition to the Galindo bibliography and one that does him credit. His narrative skill is so well-developed, so subtle, his insights into human circumstances and doings so genuine and on the mark, his craftmanship so careful and professional, that any new novel of his is certain to be a solid effort and a contribution to Mexican letters.

NOTES TO CHAPTER 10

1. "The Novels of Sergio Galindo: Planes of Human Relationship," *Hispania*, LI (December, 1968), 813.
2. *Los narradores ante el público*, 1st ser. (Mexico City, 1966), p. 103.
3. Ibid., pp. 99–104.
4. John S. Brushwood, *Mexico in Its Novel* (Austin, 1966), p. 44.
5. Rosario Castellanos, *La novela mexicana contemporánea y su valor testimonial* (Mexico City, n.d.), p. 18.

THE NOVELS OF SERGIO GALINDO

Polvos de arroz, 1958
La justicia de enero, 1959
El Bordo, 1960 (Translated into English as *The Precipice*. Austin: University of Texas Press, 1969)
La comparsa, 1964
Nudo, 1970

STUDIES ON SERGIO GALINDO

Brushwood, John S. *Mexico in Its Novel*, pp. 42–44, 48.
———. "The Novels of Sergio Galindo: Planes of Human Relationship." *Hispania*, LI (December, 1968), 812–816.
Castellanos, Rosario. *La novela mexicana contemporánea y su valor testimonial*, pp. 18–19.
Los narradores ante el público, 1st ser., pp. 99–104.
Ocampo de Gómez, A. M., and Prado Velázquez, E., eds., *Diccionario de escritores mexicanos*, pp. 123–124.
Sommers, Joseph. *After the Storm*, pp. 171–172.
———. "The Recent Mexican Novel: Tradition and Innovation." *Inter-American Review of Bibliography*, XVI (1966), 400, 402.

And a Dozen More

THE MEXICAN NOVEL AT THE PRESENT TIME IS DEFINITELY IN A boom period. Never before have so many established or promising novelists been producing, and the quality of the production is more professional, more in step with world trends in the novel than ever before. In addition to the writers on whom we have concentrated in this book, there are many others deserving special attention. In fact, it is fairly safe to assume that ten years from now some of these other names will have commanded such respect as perhaps to displace a few of the figures who have been the principal objects of our study here. It seems prudent, then, to give at least cursory treatment at this point to some of the other novelists currently active on the Mexican scene.

Dividing the more important names by the decade of their birth, we find the following novelists born before 1920 who still are publishing: Juan José Arreola, Héctor Raúl Almanza, Rafael Bernal, Gilberto Chávez, Mauricio Magdaleno, Ana Mairena, María Luisa Ocampo, José Revueltas, Ramón Rubín, Rubén Salazar Mallén, and Rafael Solana (in addition to Agustín Yáñez and Juan Rulfo). The 1920s produced all of these: Armando Ayala Anguiano, Raquel Banda Farfán, Emilio Carballido, Rosario Castellanos, Carlo Antonio Castro, María Amparo Davila, Emma Dolujanoff, Guadalupe Dueñas, Sergio Fernández, Elena Garro, Luisa Josefina Hernández, Jorge Ibargüengoitia, Jorge López Páez, Sergio Magaña, Carmen Rosenzweig, and Carlos Valdés (besides Carlos Fuentes, Luis Spota, and Sergio Galindo). The 1930 decade has given us these figures: Julieta Campos, Salvador Elizondo, Juan García Ponce,

Juan Vicente Melo, Tomás Mojarro, José Emilio Pacheco, Fernando del Paso, Elena Poniatowska, and Irma Sepúlveda (along with Vicente Leñero). Of the youngest writers, those born in the 1940s, we may mention José Agustín, Gustavo Sainz, and Raúl Navarette.

Obviously, we have no intention of considering this entire long litany of writers. But it does seem advisable to attempt a concise evaluation of the contributions which a number of these figures have made toward the Mexican novel of today. It is unnecessary, I think, to examine any of the oldest group, some of whom received mention in the chapter on the novel of the Mexican Revolution. But each of the three more recent decades includes names which require a bit of attention. We will start with those born in the 1920s and move toward the present.

Emilio Carballido (born in 1925)

Carballido has written and published steadily since 1950, with his literary reputation resting principally on his writings for the theater. In more recent years, however, he has produced some short works of fiction that earn him a place of certain importance among the current novelists. His four novels are brief but well done: *La veleta oxidada* [The rusty weathervane], 1956, *El norte* (*The Norther*), 1958, *Las visitaciones del diablo* [The devil's visits], 1965, and *El sol* [The sun], 1970.

Carballido's approach to human problems is realistic and even grim. The problems faced by his characters are more universal than purely Mexican: identification, self-determination, achieving satisfaction in spite of the barriers erected by man's own civilization. And he doesn't find much cause for optimism. His protagonists are not able to extricate themselves from the web of circumstances which restrains them and they do not find the formula for communicating in a way that will brush aside the spiritual isolation which is a core problem of contemporary society. It is most likely that Carballido will publish other novels, and his stature may grow with each succeeding effort.

Rosario Castellanos (1925)

Women novelists (and women writers in general) are not uncommon in Mexico, many with undeniable merits. There will be few persons, I suspect, to object to the statement that Rosario Castellanos stands above all the others at this time through the breadth and quality of her literary, cultural, and human achievements. Recognized and admired for her ability and perception as a poet, essayist, short-story writer, novelist, and critic, she is beyond that a beautiful person of true warmth and depth.

Although born in Mexico City, Rosario Castellanos was raised in Comitán, Chiapas (the favored terrain of B. Traven, in the far southeast of the country). In 1950 she earned her master's degree in philosophy from the National University and then took some courses in Madrid and traveled through several countries of Europe. She worked briefly in the Institute of Sciences and Arts in Chiapas before having to take more than a year off to recover from an incipient case of tuberculosis. A scholarship from the Centro Mexicano de Escritores allowed her to finish some projects in poetry and the essay form. Next she returned to Chiapas for two years in the Centro Coordinador del Instituto Indigenista, after which she spent a few years in their main office in Mexico City preparing textbooks for use with Indian children. For a time she was in charge of public information at the National University, where she also has taught courses.

Becoming a wife and a mother has not kept Rosario Castellanos from maintaining a remarkable level of activity. Since 1948 she has published at the rate of almost a book a year. These works embrace poems, short stories, essays, plays, literary criticism, and three novels. For years she has contributed reviews and other literary pieces almost weekly to the cultural supplements of Mexico City newspapers and magazines, and in addition she is a regular and much respected columnist of *Excelsior*. She received the Premio Xavier Villaurrutia for *Lívida luz* [Livid light], a book of poems published in 1960. Early in 1971 she was named by President Luis Echeverría to be Mexican ambassador to Israel.

Worthy of respect, then, for a variety of cultural achievements, Rosario Castellanos takes on a special importance for her role in bringing to its culmination point a new approach to the treatment of the Indian in the Mexican novel.[1] A good example of the old approach is to be found in B. Traven's series of six "jungle" novels set in Chiapas in the era just prior to the outbreak of the Mexican Revolution. Traven (and others who wrote on this subject) accentuated the inhuman existence of the Indian caused by the exploitation of white masters. But Traven's Indian characters never really came to life as human beings. He moved them as pawns to achieve the purposes of his proletarian theme, and he saw no need to involve the reader too deeply in the customs, traditions, myths, and cultural background of the Indians. Traven narrated the story, manipulated the events, provoked a confrontation, and led things to a solution of sorts through revolution.

The new approach toward the Indian in the Mexican novel, inspired by narrative-type works coming from some anthropologists, finds its ideal exponent in Rosario Castellanos. Raised in the midst of the Tzotzil culture in Chiapas, she began to realize in the mid-1950s her rather unique opportunity for providing a new interpretation to the long-stereotyped Indian theme. The happy result can be seen in four works she published between 1957 and 1964, two volumes of stories and two novels. The first of these was *Balún Canán*, a novel which marked the beginning of the new trend. Here she treats the Indians as humans rather than as types, and she recognizes—and makes excellent use of—the value and force of the cultural heritage of the Tzotzil tribe. Because of this her Indian novels are more complex, less superficial, decidedly more natural and convincing than Traven's.

While any one of her four Chiapas works would have established this trend and assured her of a prominent place within it, the one which has consecrated her position in this matter is the novel *Oficio de tinieblas* [Occult craft], 1962. Here Castellanos explores and explicates, on a truly human plane, the relationships between the Indians and the whites which color all phases of life for both groups. The action is set in the 1930s, a period in which the Revolution was attempting to find self-realization under Lázaro Cárdenas (especially through application of the agrarian reform laws), and takes place in and around San Cristóbal de las Casas. Since the Indian mind reflects a blend of reality with myth, in which time is of little account, the Tzotzil past is depicted as conditioning his acceptance and understanding of the present.

The principal Indian figure in *Oficio de tinieblas* is Catalina Díaz

Puiljá, who overcomes her great disappointment at being unable to bear a child by finding importance and fulfillment in the role of magic healer (hence the title of the book). She is a fictional creation that will live long in the memory of any reader. There are other well-etched Tzotzil characters and a variety of whites as well, such as the greedy and powerful Leandro Cifuentes. Castellanos makes use of a number of the modern techniques, including inner monologue and flashbacks to create full-dimensional personalities.

We can say, then, that Rosario Castellanos, through the four works of her "Chiapas cycle," has humanized and personalized the Indian in Mexican literature, that she has removed the idealizations and stereotypes of the past and replaced them with a down-to-earth and convincing presentation of the Indian role in present-day Mexican life. Not that she solves the Indian problem any more than Traven did, but she puts it into clearer focus and, by revealing the Indian capacity for absorbing the present into the myths and traditions of the past, she shows how he can look through his eternal role as the exploited and still have the strength to survive.

This is Rosario Castellanos's special contribution to the literature of her land, yet it is but one of the reasons for saluting this rather remarkable lady. We recall the distinct merits of her other literary efforts—poetry, essays, criticism, and fiction—and add the edifying effect of her many personal qualities—serenity, peace, love, leadership—and we reach the happy conclusion that Rosario Castellanos is easily one of the most important and admirable figures in the current Mexican literary scene.

Sergio Fernández (1926)

In a career devoted almost completely to teaching and writing, Sergio Fernández has established himself as a solid essayist, critic, and novelist. Up to this time he has published three novels: *Los signos perdidos* [The lost signs], 1958, *En tela de juicio* [Up for judgment], 1964, and *Los peces* [The fishes], 1968.

Like the bulk of novelists both in and out of Mexico, Fernández is concerned about man in his "human condition," and like Carballido he is bitter and disenchanted. His works do not rest on plot but rather on what he has to say about his characters and on how he says it. Along with so many other novelists of our times in various languages, he focuses on the loneliness of man in the midst of a teeming civilization. Fernández employs a rich and detailed manner of relating the little things, insignificant in themselves, that document the isolation of his characters in their struggle to coexist and communicate with others.

In both *Los signos perdidos* and *En tela de juicio* Fernández sets before us an assortment of characters, for the most part rather colorless, who are trapped in the insularity of modern living. A good part of their unhappiness can be traced to a kind of withdrawal and a gradual loss of communication, which heighten the banality of the everyday. One critic, commenting on the fact that language ceases to be a vehicle of communication in *Los signos perdidos,* says that "if it serves for anything it is for the individual consciences, in their soliloquies, to be able to give a name, more or less precise, to the psychological processes of which they are, at one and the same time, actors and spectators."[2] Fernández himself has said of these first two novels that they were exercises in front of a keyboard, executed with such lack of sureness that they are almost nothing but babbling. This self-judgment is clearly much too harsh, yet it reveals the author's higher aspirations and his determination to profit from experience.

Los peces breaks the pattern established by Fernández in his two earlier novels. Here tedium is cast aside and language and action are much in evidence. This novel is closer to the most modern trend with language that is rich but confusing in form and style, thus forcing the reader's close participation. His story fluctuates between reality and irreality, so that we must work to sort out fact from hallucination. The setting is in Rome and the story, which transpires in a matter of hours, is related in the first person by a woman who is obsessed by the flesh. The plot (which is not strong) revolves around the age-old struggle between evil and salvation. While opinions no doubt will be divided on the merits of *Los peces,* it is in several ways an advance in the novelistic development of Sergio Fernández, who can be expected to give us more and better things in the future.

Elena Garro (1920)

Although Elena Garro has but a single novel to her credit at this point, she earns brief mention here through the quality of that one effort and also for the diversity of her activities in the realm of letters and culture. She has at one time or another been a choreographer for the Teatro de la Universidad, a journalist both in Mexico and in the United States, a writer of movie scripts, and the author of a number of successful plays (some of which have been translated and produced in both the U.S. and Europe). In addition to traveling widely, she lived for a number of years in France and in the United States, and at one time was married to the famous Mexican poet and essayist, Octavio Paz.

Her one novel, *Los recuerdos del porvenir* (*Recollections of Things to Come*) 1963, was awarded the important Premio Xavier Villaurrutia and has been called by one perceptive critic as perhaps the best Mexican novel of 1963 and also as "mature, profound, sensitive, and written with professional assurance that is apparent from beginning to end."[3] *Los recuerdos del porvenir* is the story of a southern Mexican town, Ixtepec, and is actually narrated in the first person by the town itself (though in a manner not completely convincing).

The events center around the time of the so-called Cristero revolt against the government of the Revolutionary Party in the late 1920s, yet time—as handled by the town-narrator—is about the least consistent element in the work. This perspective, which combines realism with fantasy (or "magical realism"), proves at times somewhat difficult to follow and accept. Yet the novel has many undeniable merits—enviable imagination, poetic style, an adroit manipulation of reality and unreality and a compelling plot. And it is a story with a most serious intent, for Elena Garro is weighing life against death and asking whether life as lived by many of this world's inhabitants is not a form of death—or worse than death itself.

Los recuerdos del porvenir resembles in many ways the great novel by Agustín Yáñez, *Al filo del agua*. There is of course a difference in time (1909–10 for the Yáñez work and 1926–28 for the Garro story) and in the role of the town within the military struggle (the Revolution reaches Yáñez's pueblo only in the last moments of the story, whereas Ixtepec during the Cristero revolt is occupied and repressed in much of Elena Garro's novel). Yet the two towns are strikingly similar in their archconservatism, their closed-mindedness, their utterly provincial outlook. In *Los recuerdos del porvenir* the issue is not so much sexual instincts versus a religion which controls by fear of sin, but more the armed power of an anticlerical revolutionary government as against a Church which holds the people in check and resists all change. In each of these works the novelist faces the reader with the question of whether life is meaningful in such static, stagnant circumstances, or whether indeed it is not a living form of death, perhaps more deadening than death itself.

Luisa Josefina Hernández (1928)

Like Emilio Carballido, this prolific writer gained no little renown as a dramatist in the 1950s before turning to the novel. Then, in the years between 1959 and 1970, she published nine novels—probably too many for best literary results. Nevertheless, she commands attention not alone for the number of her works but for the form and content of what she publishes. She has been granted scholarships by the Centro Mexicano de Escritores and by the Rockefeller Foundation, and studied theater at Columbia University in New York. She writes for several of the cultural outlets in her country, as do most of the other authors in Mexico, and teaches dramatic art at the National University.

Some of the shortcomings of the earlier novels of Luisa Josefina Hernández have been singled out by certain critics. Thus, Rosario Castellanos, although she praises *El lugar donde crece la hierba* [The place where the grass grows], 1959, for its depth, pathos, and beauty, finds at the same time that the author uses language "as an instrument to hide the truth, to cover the facts, to make the silence more impenetrable."[4] Related in the first person, it is the morose story of a neurotic female protagonist who is the victim of strong guilt feelings and a compulsive need for self-punishment.

John Brushwood feels that Hernández had trouble at the start in adapting herself to the novel form. Commenting on her third novel, *Los palacios desiertos* [The deserted palaces], 1963, which he considers her best up to that point, he concludes that "it does not accomplish what the author apparently intended."[5] The novel traces the love relationship between a poorly adjusted couple, as related from the viewpoint of each of the persons. Brushwood feels it ought to inform the reader more fully but doesn't, with the result that the reader isn't able to see beyond the surface of the author's analysis.

Actually, Hernández's second novel, *La plaza de Puerto Santo* [The plaza in Puerto Santo], 1961, is more pleasant reading than either of the two just mentioned, although it does have the same seriousness of purpose. In this work we find spontaneity and humor, along with some strong realism and the author's usual sensitivity. In *La plaza de Puerto Santo*, as in all her other novels up to the most recent ones, the author has chosen a provincial setting in which the characters are circumscribed by a narrow and backward environment. Rather naturally, costumbrista elements are frequently visible in these works.

Other Hernández novels, prior to her two latest, are *La cólera secreta* [The secret wrath], 1964, *La primera batalla* [The first battle], 1965, *La noche exquisita* [The exquisite night], 1965, and *El valle que elegimos* [The valley we chose], 1965. Although technically sound and strong in dialogue, as might be expected of an experienced playwright, for the most part they fail to become a moving experience for the reader but are somehow a bit too controlled, too cold, too brittle.

Luisa Josefina Hernández breaks with her provincial and costumbrista approach in *La memoria de Amadís* [The memory of Amadís], 1967, in a conscious effort to enter the main ring of today's novelistic circles and to produce something that falls within the framework of the so-called "new novel." The title comes from the recollection of Amadís de Gaula which Cervantes makes in *Don Quijote*. In *La memoria de Amadís* it is the memory of the protagonist Adelina, provoked by a deep crisis, which the author explores through introspection, interior monologues, and other devices common to most of today's better novelists. While *La memoria de Amadís* does not equal the best of such works written in Mexico in the past decade or so, it is a solid effort in which we can appreciate the author's fine language and sometimes lyrical style, as well as her success in injecting warmth and humanness into her characters.

The most recent Hernández novel is *Nostalgia de Troya* [Trojan nostalgia], 1970, perhaps her best work to date. The story revolves around René, whose fixation or "nostalgia" is to retain at all costs his own freedom in everything. Six critical moments of his life are related to us in six monologues which make up the chapters of the book, each set in a different place: Cuba, France, the Mexican resort Ixtapan de la sal, Rome, Canada, and Mexico City. In addition to the main characters of the story, there are several secondary figures who really come to life and impress.

Jorge Ibargüengoitia (1928)

A native of Guanajuato, Ibargüengoitia is a late starter in the field of the novel. He first embarked on a career in engineering and then in 1949 opted to make the shift to dramatic art. He studied theater in New York on a Rockefeller Foundation grant in 1955 and also had a scholarship from the Centro Mexicano de Escritores for two years. Like Carballido and Hernández he achieved distinct success as a playwright, several of his plays being awarded prizes in various competitions. He has also published a volume of short stories, *La ley de Herodes* [Herod's law], 1967.

His first novel, *Los relámpagos de agosto* [The August lightning], 1964, captured the respected Premio Anual de la Casa de las Américas in Cuba. The theme is a common one in Spanish-American literature, namely, the venality, irresponsibility, and corruption of some Latin American military leaders. But Ibargüengoitia's treatment of the subject differs greatly from the way it is usually handled. He turns his back on the tragic or dramatic approach to this topic, giving us instead a delightful satire that is light and humorous at every step yet still carries significant impact beneath the surface.

Spanish-American literature is not noted for an abundance of humor and satire. Obviously, efforts of this kind do exist, some of them quite successful, but the vast majority of writers of those lands are committed to an interpretation of man's role in an underdeveloped society plagued by multiple problems and social injustice. Life for the average person in Hispanic America is hard, humorless, often extremely grim, and this is the picture the writers commonly project. Yet there is decidedly a place and a need for humor and

effective satire, so that the occasional exception like Jorge Ibargüengoitia is more than welcome.

Los relámpagos de agosto places a number of generals and other
military and political figures against the backdrop of the Mexican
Revolution. While they may be fictional characters, they match perfectly the common image of the Revolution's military class and
several are clearly caricatures (or faithful portrayals?) of certain
historical personages. Purportedly the memoirs of General José
Guadalupe Arroyo, this little novel (125 pages) focuses in on the
political conniving of a small group of top generals in 1928 and
1929, following the assassination of the president-elect, who patently
represents Alvaro Obregón just as Vidal Sánchez is intended to be
Plutarco Elías Calles.

José Guadalupe Arroyo offers his memoirs expressly as a means
of clearing his much-besmirched good name. But Ibargüengoitia,
with a consummate skill for parody and mockery, causes Arroyo and
all the other figures in the story to reveal at every turn their egoism,
incompetence, opportunism, weakness, innate cruelty, lack of principles, and even cowardice. The general of the story writes in a style
that is a delight throughout because of its unintentional humor. Yet
this is not just a recital of a comedy of errors but bears a serious
message, and this is what comes through to the reader after he
turns the last enjoyable page of *Los relámpagos de agosto*.

Ibargüengoitia's only other novel to date is *Maten al león* [Kill
the lion], 1969, which continues in much the same vein the style he
established in his first work. This time he creates an imaginary setting—the island of Arepa (presumably in the Central American
region), which has been for untold years in the personal grip of a
military dictator, Field Marshall don Manuel Belaunzarán, "the
Child Hero of the War for Independence." Using the same roguish,
ironic, even festive tone he unveiled in *Los relámpagos de agosto*,
the author devotes the book's 178 pages to the perilous plans and
plots of a group of patriotic citizens of Arepa to do away with the
dictator. *Maten al león* is just as pleasant to read as his earlier novel,
with somewhat less satire and more outright humor, although the
reader doesn't fail to grasp the underlying seriousness of the theme.

Jorge Ibargüengoitia is quoted as saying that he abandoned the dramatic genre in favor of the novel because he found that theatrical producers are interested only in works which have already triumphed elsewhere and because in the theater praise is given just to the director and the actors, with the author all but forgotten.[6] So far as I am concerned, it would have been a welcome event if he had made the jump much earlier, for the Mexican novel can always benefit from the work of a satirist and humorist of the capabilities of Jorge Ibargüengoitia.

Salvador Elizondo (1932)

This young Mexican author has been described as "one of the most distinctive writers to appear on the Latin American scene in the past decade."[7] Salvador Elizondo is a case apart, certainly nonconventional and nonconformist, so much so that Carballo has said of him: "I do not find in the Mexican prose of today any antecedent which explains his work: in our setting, Elizondo is a point of departure, a most uncommon writer."[8] George R. McMurray finds that "Elizondo's principal concern as an author is to experiment with language, its mechanical complexities, philosophical implications and psychological effects."[9]

Perhaps it is not surprising to note that Salvador Elizondo has spent much time (and has carried out certain studies) in Canada, Italy, France, England, and the U.S., and that he knows European and U.S. literature better than that of his own country. Indeed it is difficult to find anything typically Mexican in his novels to date. Further, Elizondo does not write for the average reader. His works make an appeal to a special type of intellect. This is even implicit in the fact that he was a cofounder of the short-lived yet most interesting literary review *S.nob.*

The potential so clearly visible in Elizondo has helped him qualify for more than one grant: in 1963–64 he was a *becario* (scholarship grantee) of the Centro Mexicano de Escritores, and it was in this year that he completed most of the work on his novel *Farabeuf.* In 1962 he was a *becario* of the Colegio de México, while in 1965 he came to New York on a grant from the Ford Foundation. During that year he became intimately acquainted with more than one important American writer, but at the same time he fell into such a state of alcoholism and generally confused thought that on his return to Mexico he suffered a breakdown and was under psychiatric care for a couple of months.

Salvador Elizondo's interests have not always centered on writing. At first he considered himself an artist and dedicated his efforts in this direction for a few years. While in Europe he developed an overpowering interest in the film and in film making, and in 1965 he produced in Mexico a film called *Apocalypse 1900*, which attracted no little attention. He went through a period in which poetry was his great concern, finally turning to the novel and the short story, and it is most likely that he will continue to pursue this interest indefinitely. For years he has read voraciously in the world's principal literatures, and today he is professor of modern poetry at the National University. Thus far Elizondo has published a volume of poems in 1960, the novel *Farabeuf* in 1965, his autobiography (in the series Nuevos escritores mexicanos del siglo XX presentados por sí mismos) and a collection of his short stories titled *Narda o el verano*, both in 1966, another novel *El hipogeo secreto* in 1968, and the following year more short stories under the title of *El retrato de Zoe y otras mentiras*. Naturally, our interest is mainly on the two novels.

Farabeuf o la crónica de un instante [Farabeuf, or the account of one moment] is easily one of the strangest works to appear in Mexican literature. It reveals a direct kinship with Rulfo's *Pedro Páramo* in that in neither of them does the time element exist. Otherwise, it seems to me that *Farabeuf* and *Pedro Páramo* could hardly be more different. Whereas Rulfo is Mexican to the fingertips in his theme, setting, characters, and language, Elizondo's work has nothing in it to identify him as a Mexican writer. For my taste, being openly addicted to the *Mexican* novel, this is a plus for Rulfo and a minus for Elizondo, though I am aware that others might view it in a reverse light. Elizondo was awarded the 1965 Premio Xavier Villaurrutia (one of Mexico's most respected literary prizes) for *Farabeuf*, but I venture that it will never achieve anything resembling the widespread acceptance and influence of *Pedro Páramo*.

It is hard to explain *Farabeuf* and harder still to classify it as a novel, for there is very little action, no particular development of personages, no true mystery, little or no psychological penetration. I suppose the surest thing to say about it is that it is a most unusual experimental novel. Certainly, it leans on many of the techniques of the French "new novel" and also reveals the influence on Elizondo of Husserl's ideas on phenomenology.[10]

Only two characters have any importance in Elizondo's story: the author's adaptation of Dr. Farabeuf, a well-known French anatomist in the last century, and a woman, apparently—or possibly—mad. At various times they are *yo* and *tú* ("I" and "you") and at others *él* and *ella* ("he" and "she"), the distinction perhaps representing periods years apart, and this may be Elizondo's substitute for time. What little action there is turns largely upon a very graphic photo of the torture by dismemberment of a Chinese Boxer in 1901. There is a repulsive description of the victim's suffering, with emphasis on the combined pain and ecstacy visible on his face. The two characters find the photo and, studying it, are aroused physically and engage in sexual intercourse. At the end of the novel we find the woman, now apparently mad or suffering from loss of memory, and the doctor in a strange scene which ends with him taking her into his laboratory, rather clearly for the purpose of dissecting her alive. And so the reader is left wondering who is mad, after all. He also is left limp, bewildered, and upset. If he rereads the work until he comes to a fuller understanding of all the author is attempting, he may gain in admiration for the technical skill of Elizondo and so achieve a certain aesthetic appreciation of *Farabeuf*.

El hipogeo secreto [The secret underground burial place] is in its own way just as disconcerting as *Farabeuf*. At least, it is as unconventional and experimental and sure to baffle the reader who is not fully attuned to the extremes portrayed by the exponents of the *nouveau roman*. Elizondo's skill in the short story form was well established through his collection called *Narda o el verano* [Narda, or summer], but his recent book of stories, *El retrato de Zoe y otras mentiras* [The portrait of Zoe and other lies] is decidedly uneven in quality, as well as unusual in nature. Salvador Elizondo's brilliance and promise are beyond argument, but his final position among Mexican novelists will have to be determined by his future works.

Juan García Ponce (1932)

Born in Mérida, Yacatán, García Ponce completed his studies in Mexico City and subsequently was awarded scholarships by the Centro Mexicano de Escritores and the Rockefeller Foundation to further his literary career. Besides his prose fiction, he has written a number of plays and has achieved reputation as a literary critic. He also is editor of the *Revista Mexicana de Literatura*.

His initial two small volumes of short stories, published in 1963— *Imagen primera* [First image] and *La noche* [The night]— quickly gave him status as one of the better short-story writers in Mexico. These were followed in 1964 by his first novel, *Figura de paja* [Straw figure], which was no enormous success although (as in his stories) he demonstrated some capacity for psychological penetration and the creation of characters with dimension. In *La casa en la playa* [The house on the beach], 1966, García Ponce goes back to his native Yucatán for the setting and produces a structurally better novel, but still the work of a novelist in evolution. *La presencia lejana* [The distant presence], 1968, provided further evidence of his development, and with *La cabaña* [The Cabin], 1969, he emerged as a novelist of stature.

García Ponce's earlier works were really lineal narratives, starting usually with some unimportant moment and then switching to a certain point in the past, from which time the straightforward relation of events would begin. But in *La cabaña* we find more introspection together with other modern novelistic techniques. One critic has labeled his approach in this work as being "lineal in vertical depth."[11] There is no great plot in *La cabaña* and the movement is slow. In fact, there are chapters absolutely lacking in dialogue, yet most readers will probably find the pleasant style and the modest plot of this work attractive and satisfying. *La cabaña* is the story of Claudia, a strong protagonist who remembers and relives an unhappy love and finally achieves a peace of spirit and the strength to view the future with hope.

A prodigious writer, since 1963, all told, García Ponce has published two volumes of short stories, six novels, three volumes of essays, a short autobiography, the translations of two plays from

English, and probably some other things that have escaped my attention. As is nearly inevitable with all this quantity, he has not maintained the highest quality in each case. While he writes well and pleasantly, it would seem that he does not spend enough time in polishing and refining his prose.

In 1970 Juan García Ponce produced two novels, *El libro* [The book] and *La vida perdurable* [The enduring life]. The latter, a thin work of 135 pages and definitely not a major effort, concentrates on the rather vague search of a young man for the means of truly reaching his lover and, later, wife, Virginia (the only character in the book who is given a name). This ideal of the perfect spiritual and physical empathy is what he envisions as "the enduring life." As things are presented, however, in this traditional, linear account (with certain hangovers from romanticism), the problem appears to exist more in the mind of the author than in the protagonists, and the seeming resolution of the dilemma in the last lines is abrupt and unconvincing.

El libro, on the other hand, is a serious effort worthy of more attention. A university professor of literature (Eduardo) enters into a love affair with one of his students (Marcela), an alliance provoked by the study of a story by Musil called "La realización del amor" [The fulfillment of love]. According to Eduardo's interpretation, Musil has no interest in the story itself, nor even in literature except for its beauty, but is obsessed by the other thing, by what is beyond the story. So, Marcela and Eduardo seek that which is beyond and carry on a passionate romance for several months, at the end of which she tells him she is going to marry the young man to whom she is engaged, remarking that she now understands the truth of Musil's book and what truth really is.

In *El libro* García Ponce adopts what may be called the cubistic approach, in which the same reality is observed from several angles. The book has its good points (an effective style and a credible tracing of psychological changes in the characters, for instance). Yet my final impression is that it is all a bit too intellectualized, as is true of other García Ponce novels, such as *La vida perdurable.* Perhaps the influence of Albert Camus is present. If so, the pupil manifestly has not grown up to the stature of the tutor. But this Mexican author is still young and hopefully will mature and improve as he writes, particularly if he learns how to select and refine his materials.

Tomás Mojarro (1932)

Born in the state of Zacatecas, Mojarro moved on to Mexico City by way of Guadalajara. He was a *becario* of the Centro Mexicano de Escritores for two years and also of the Colegio de México. A modest, unassuming, relatively uncomplicated person and largely self-educated, he has read extensively in other literatures, although apparently not so widely as some of his fellow writers of the moment. For eight years Mojarro worked as a mechanic at a Mexican air force base, an experience which provides the setting and background for his second novel, *Malafortuna*. His first novel, *Bramadero,* and an earlier collection of stories, *Cañón de Juchipila,* have the provincial setting which he also knows well.

Mojarro is commonly regarded as a disciple, wittingly or otherwise, of Juan Rulfo. In fact, someone once began the rumor (in jest, surely) that Mojarro had found some unpublished pages of Rulfo's in a truck and launched his career by getting them into print. Mojarro jokes about this a bit, though one has the notion that he doesn't find it too funny.[12] At any rate, Tomás Mojarro has cultivated the simple style, spare and stark, which Rulfo employed so effectively in his two works. The essence of this style is, as noted by Joseph Sommers, "sensitive stylization—not reproduction—of provincial speech patterns."[13] His themes, also like Rulfo's, are sombre and brutally realistic.

Bramadero, 1963, is an account of the social, economic, and emotional changes forced upon a small rural town by the completion of a new highway. Wrested violently from the closed-in life and mentality it had known, the village is now confronted by new forces from the outside world. As "foreign" elements enter into Margil de Minas, we view the town in a period of transition and crisis. Long-existing patterns are upset, the established local powers are threatened, the people are thrust into contact with modern ways. The effects of all this need not be imagined, for Mojarro reveals them in relentlessly realistic strokes and trenchant sensory images. Margil de Minas was already a town divided in the traditional struggle between conservatives and liberals, the former spearheaded by the local clergy trying to maintain prerevolutionary conditions and the liberals typified by the political boss whose corrupt and personalist policies belie all the ideals of the Revolution. It is not the doings of the individuals but the suffering and transformation of the town itself that carries the impact in *Bramadero*.

Rosario Castellanos, in discussing this novel, makes the justifiable observation that "reading it obliges us to cast into doubt everything to the effect that the Revolution has achieved its goals and that Mexico is a prosperous country, like the statistics tell us, like the reports of the experts keep repeating, like sociological research demonstrates, like the politicians' rhetoric pounds into us, and like the banner headlines of the daily press insist."[14] This harks back to the days of Mariano Azuela, whose words and works were saying the same thing from 1915 on.

Malafortuna, Mojarro's second novel, published in 1966, takes its title from the name of a fictional town near a military air base, described only as being remote and in the south. This work reflects a complete about-face in the novelist's approach. While his book of stories and *Bramadero* fall clearly in a category which we can label "costumbrista realism," *Malafortuna* moves on into the realm of "magical realism," where the real and the unreal, the rational and the irrational, the natural and the supernatural all become bed-fellows.

When a military engineer flies in from the outside world (the altiplano) to inspect the air base, we are given a vision of this incredibly depressing, hopeless place through a duality of perspectives. The engineer speaks in the first person and in the present; the novelist as omniscient observer relates the past in the third person. All that is objectionable and unpleasant about the air base is revealed and accentuated through a combination of reality and fantasy, which has the flavor of a bad dream. A mysterious aura seems to announce tragedy or despair and to suggest that time has stopped and everything is destined to go on forever in this same vein. Faced with the alternatives of escape or utter stagnation, some who plan to escape decide at the crucial moment not to go through with it, thus emphasizing the hopelessness of the situation. If symbolically

Mojarro intends the air base to be the world and the people on it to be mankind, as has been suggested,[15] then the author is giving us a bleak and despairing vision of the future.

The works that Tomás Mojarro has published to date show his sure and encouraging development. Further evolution of his evident novelistic talents could permit him to become one of Mexico's finer voices in this genre.

Fernando del Paso (1935)

The case of Fernando del Paso is particularly interesting. Having published nothing previously except some poems and a short story, in 1959 he set to work on a novel conceived in highly ambitious form. His preparation of this work continued for several years, and he was aided for a time by a grant from the Centro Mexicano de Escritores. So much talk and such high expectations were generated in literary circles, so high the expectations, that pressure began to mount on the author to finish the novel and get it into print. He relates how he began receiving telegrams urging a rapid completion and how his publisher printed early portions of the work while he was still writing later sections.[16] In 1966 this novel, *José Trigo*, finally appeared, but there is some question as to whether the expectations were fulfilled or betrayed. Although it did receive the Premio Xavier Villaurrutia for that year, critical response has been mixed.

The action of *José Trigo* is placed in an old area of Mexico City known as the Nonoalco-Tlatelolco zone and spans the centuries from prehispanic days to the present. As might be expected, it is an outsized work (536 pages). While the time of the story is mostly in the present, innumerable chronological inserts refer to various moments and events of the past, and occasionally the scene shifts from the Nonoalco-Tlatelolco area to other parts of the country, such as to the states of Colima and Jalisco during the Cristero revolt of the late 1920s.

José Trigo is principally the story of the railways (tracks, yards, stations, workers, families of the workers, unions, strikes) which were concentrated in the zone before it was transformed in recent years into the Plaza de las Tres Culturas. There is surely material here for a stirring novel, though some will debate whether Fernando del Paso has told it in the most effective manner. He essays a sort of epic (if not at times biblical) style, with enormous amounts of descriptive matter rendered in highly rhetorical terms and a lexicon that will keept most readers grabbing for the dictionary with regularity. On the other hand, in dialogue situations the common speech of the railroad people comes through strongly. He also employs a number of variations in the physical presentation of the story. There will be page after page of italicized print to serve a particular purpose. At times the author resorts to what can almost be termed free verse, and he frequently cultivates a poetic approach. We also encounter layout tricks to enhance a situation or achieve a certain effect. On several occasions the speaker is identified by name in capital letters on the line above what he says, much in the manner of a theatrical piece. The total number of persons who appear in the story is almost beyond counting, although the main characters can be followed without undue difficulty. Probably the biggest question about *José Trigo*, however, is whether so much verbiage and rhetoric and linguistic ostentation were necessary.

If Fernando del Paso produces other works in subsequent years we will be in a position to judge his true merits as a novelist. On the strength of *José Trigo* alone, ambitious as it is and with certain undeniable merits, he must remain something of a literary question mark.

José Agustín (1944)

The youngest of the novelists we are considering here, José Agustín (whose full name is José Agustín Ramírez) was born in Guadalajara in 1944. By the time he was twenty-two years old he had published his first two novels and his autobiography, had been twice married, and had received a scholarship from the Centro Mexicano de Escritores. Brash and outgoing by nature, he has more than once been referred to as "l'enfant terrible" of present-day Mexican letters. Along with his running mate and mentor of sorts, Gustavo Sainz (four years his senior), he has spearheaded the youngest crop of Mexican writers, which is sizeable, serious, talented, and articulate—to say nothing of unabashed. Of the whole group,

José Agustín is the one who has produced the most and at this point shows the most likelihood of maturing into a first-rate writer.

José Agustín studied at the National University (with special interest in the film), and later studied drama at the Instituto Nacional de Bellas Artes (INBA) and in the Asociación Nacional de Actores. In 1969 he was offering a course in the history of the theater at the INBA. Clearly, he is in every respect among the most active and productive of the young literary element. The gulf that separates these new writers from the older group born in the 1920s is well illustrated by the flippant reaction (irreverent, if you will) of one of the young writers recently when the name of an older, well-respected Mexican novelist was mentioned: "Carlos Fuentes? Who is Carlos Fuentes?"

José Agustín's first novel, published when he was twenty, is *La tumba* [The tomb], 1964. It is a lineal recital (told in the first person by the narrator, Gabriel) of the almost completely unrestrained doings of a bunch of teenagers from well-to-do families in Mexico City. The speech, actions, and attitudes of these adolescents, while still objectionable to any older group of readers, are quite in step with what their age group is doing and thinking and saying in many parts of the world these days. *La tumba* slashes vigorously at what José Agustín (and apparently his peers almost everywhere) regard as the hypocrisies and outdated conventions of modern society. His characters (in this work notably the protagonist narrator) indulge freely in sex wherever they find it, relish obscene language, drink inordinately, and flaunt their nonconformity. Of course, none of this is original with José Agustín, but it is interesting that he lets his protagonist become a victim of the pathetic futility of it all, to the extent that the surfeit of sensuality and indulgence turns him to suicide.

Two years later this young writer published another novel, *De perfil* [In profile], 1966. Cut generally from the same cloth as *La tumba,* this work is considerably longer, more mature and ambitious, and it puts the author's sense of humor delightfully on display. *De perfil* also has more front-line characters and explores a wider range of the narrator's existence (family life with his parents and younger brother, the goings-on at school, and philosophical discussions with his friends). Despite the fact it is in part satire and that its viewpoint is anything but impartial, this novel possesses a documental essence. It is, to use the Spanish word, highly *testimonial*. And despite too its excessive fondness for the colloquial speech of the teen-agers and its disdain for proper grammar and syntax, *De perfil* is fresh enough and dynamic enough to make one serious critic label it the best Mexican novel of 1966.[17] On the other hand, Juan Rulfo passed a more restrained and sobering judgment of this young novelist. After naming José Agustín first among a few young fiction writers that he felt showed promise, Rulfo went on to say: "He has great talent, although it still is not reflected in his work." Continuing, he said that these youngsters are still producing "adolescent literature for adolescents and I think they cannot go on with that literature forever."[18]

One thing no one can deny is that José Agustín is industrious, serious, and determined to leave his mark on Mexican literature. Since 1966 he has written a work on "rock" music (*La nueva música clásica*), movie scripts, critical reviews, some songs, a play or two, and has even done some translations, on top of which he brought out in 1968 a book of stories and in 1969 a work which is difficult to classify by literary genre.

Inventando que sueño [Inventing that I dream] is a book of four narrative pieces (which the author calls "acts"). Whatever they are, they move the author's career a bit farther along, as he plays more skillfully with language and, displaying his usual rich imagination and narrative capacity, he provides additional evidence that he is mastering the craft of fiction. José Agustín's latest work is titled *Abolición de la propiedad* [Abolition of property]. This is hardly a novel, in the traditional sense of formulation and presentation. It has more the appearance of a dramatic work masquerading in semi-novel form. Actually, it may be even more closely related to television, perhaps an imaginative version of a TV script. It is known that José Agustín in these days is becoming involved with Mexican television.

Whether novel, play, or TV script, *Abolición de la propiedad* takes its author definitely out of the track which he followed in his earlier narrative works. It has only two characters, who do a lot of dialoguing, sometimes on the plane of reality and then again on one of apparent irreality, with points of view that are in conflict on matters of morals and matters of ideology. If nothing else, this work proves its author's versatility and his willingness to plunge into experimental forms. With continuing development, José Agustín may well become one of the greater Mexican novelists of the next few decades.

Gustavo Sainz (1940)

Long regarded as the leader of the youngest group of Mexican novelists, Gustavo Sainz has worn the mantle rather well in terms of his broad literary culture and the success of his first work, *Gazapo*. Just when it seemed that José Agustín was outflanking him, novelistically speaking, Sainz came out with his second novel in the very final days of 1969 and he is reportedly well advanced on the preparation of another one. More solid and serious than José Agustín or anyone else in the group, Sainz appears to be a natural leader of this young element, yet his leadership might have been challenged had he gone much longer without publishing anything following his initial success.

Gustavo Sainz studied law for a brief time at the National University, and then humanities. He also studied the film at the Centro Universitario de Estudios Culturales (where, incidentally, he first came to know José Agustín), and he spent the academic year of 1968–69 as writer-in-residence at the State University of Iowa in Iowa City. José Agustín's *La tumba* appeared a year before *Gazapo* came out in 1965, but the latter received considerably more attention, possibly because it was more experimental and made use of many more of the stylistic tricks of the vanguardist European prose; for instance, the inclusion of tape-recorded accounts, diaries, phone conversations, letters, and detailed reports by several persons of the same happening. *Gazapo* was quickly translated into French, Italian, English, German, and Portuguese, and it has had four editions in Mexico.

Gazapo displays an obvious kinship with both *La tumba* and *De perfil* in theme and general attitude. It concerns the search of today's adolescents for personal freedom, self-expression, and ultimate meaning in an existence which they fervently seek to mold along their own lines. They regard the society which spawned them as being too hypocritical, morally bankrupt, and stagnant to be saved, and thus anything they do in violation of that society is justified. Too young to grasp their own shortcomings and limitations, their unsure psychic makeup leads them to fantasy, misapprehensions of reality, and imagination which distorts the world they try to build around themselves. As appears to be true of adolescents everywhere these days, uninhibited sexual patterns play a large role in the existence they create to replace the society of their elders. Actually, it can be said that *Gazapo* is basically the story of a seduction, planned through the course of the work and brought off in the final pages. It also is clear, through the revelations in Sainz's autobiography, that *Gazapo* is in good part the story of his own adolescent years. The protagonist, Menelao, is Sainz himself and the Gisela of the story is now his wife Rosita.

Gustavo Sainz's second novel, *Obsesivos días circulares* [Obsessive circular days], 1969, is a strange, involved, and (to me, at least) unsatisfying work. As one critic puts it, the obsession seems to be generated in the writer and passed along to the protagonist to be transmitted to the reader, who is trapped by the subtle thread of the narrative, broken at every step and then remade. The whole work is kept deliberately opaque, so that one can only guess what is behind it. "It is," he says, "one more sample of that antitraditional and antiliterary literature into which many writers of the present moment and the present world happily throw themselves in order to set down in the pages of a book their concerns, their anxieties, their phobias, their social or personal unrest over this or that matter. It is a literature that by virtue of denouncing so many things really doesn't denounce anything."[19]

Other critics, however, find many virtues in *Obsesivos días circulares* and other works of the same type. For my part, I must confess that my sympathies rest largely with the critical reaction quoted above. This is not to say that I am unresponsive to the experimental tendencies of many writers of the "new wave" in and out of Mexico. Yet some of the new works carry a good thing too far and knowingly restrict themselves to a small elite of readers, which I believe is not in the best interests of literature as a whole. I find *Obsesivos días circulares* to be one such work and, to that extent, a disappointment.

NOTES TO CHAPTER 11

1. An excellent study on this subject is Joseph Sommers's "Changing View of the Indian in Mexican Literature," *Hispania*, XLVII (March, 1964), 47–55.

2. Rosario Castellanos, *La novela mexicana contemporánea y su valor testimonial* (Mexico City, n.d.), p. 19.

3. John S. Brushwood, *Mexico in Its Novel* (Austin, 1966), p. 52.

4. Castellanos, p. 20.

5. Brushwood, p. 52.

6. *Tiempo*, December 8, 1969.

7. George R. McMurray, "Current Trends in the Mexican Novel," *Hispania*, LI (September, 1968), 533.

8. Emmanuel Carballo, prologue to *Salvador Elizondo*, in the series Nuevos escritores mexicanos del siglo XX presentados por sí mismos (Mexico City, 1966), p. 9.

9. McMurray, p. 533.

10. This aspect of *Farabeuf* is discussed in depth by George R. McMurray in his article "Salvador Elizondo's 'Farabeuf,'" *Hispania*, L (September, 1967), 596–601.

11. Abelardo Arias, "Madurez de una novelística," *Visión*, XXXVII (October 10, 1969), 108.

12. *Los narradores ante el público*, 2nd ser. (Mexico City, 1967), p. 171.

13. Joseph Sommers, *After the Storm* (Albuquerque, 1968), p. 172.

14. Castellanos, p. 21.

15. Emmanuel Carballo, prologue to *Tomás Mojarro*, in the series Nuevos escritores mexicanos del siglo XX presentados por sí mismos (Mexico City, 1966), p. 10.

16. Gustavo Sainz, "Diez años de literatura mexicana," *Espejo*, I, no. 1, (1967), 171.

17. McMurray, "Current Trends in the Mexican Novel," p. 535.

18. Juan Cervera, "Entrevista con Juan Rulfo," in *La Gaceta*, publication of the Fondo de Cultura Económica, Spring, 1967.

19. Samuel Guzman in *Tiempo*, March 9, 1970, p. 82.

SELECTED STUDIES

Brushwood, John S. *Mexico in Its Novel.* (Novelists of this chapter who are included: Carballido, Garro, Hernández, Mojarro, and Castellanos.)

Castellanos, Rosario. *La novela mexicana contemporánea y su valor testimonial.* (Discusses Fernández, Hernández, Mojarro.)

Lafforgue, Jorge, ed. *Nueva novela latinoamericana.* (Discusses Juan García Ponce and Fernando del Paso.)

Los narradores ante el público. (First series includes Castellanos and García Ponce; 2nd series has Ibargüengoitia, Elizondo, Mojarro, and Sainz.)

McMurray, George R. "Current Trends in the Mexican Novel." *Hispania,* LI (September, 1968), 532–537. (Discusses Mojarro, Elizondo, Sainz, José Agustín, and del Paso.)

———. "Salvador Elizondo's 'Farabeuf.'" *Hispania,* L (September, 1967), 596–601.

Nuevos escritores mexicanos del siglo presentados por sí mismos. (Included in this series are brief autobiographies of Elizondo, Mojarro, García Ponce, José Agustín, and Sainz, each with a valuable prologue by Emmanuel Carballo.)

Ocampo de Gómez, A. M., and Prado Velázquez, E., eds., *Diccionario de escritores mexicanos.* (All of the authors discussed are treated in this work.)

Sainz, Gustavo. "Diez años de literatura mexicana." *Espejo,* I (no. 1, 1967), 163–173. (Discusses Hernández, Garro, Mojarro, Fernández, Carballido, García Ponce, Elizondo, Ibargüengoitia, del Paso, José Agustín.)

Sommers, Joseph. *After the Storm.* (Discusses Castellanos, Garro, Mojarro.)

———. "Changing View of the Indian in Mexican Literature." *Hispania,* XLVII (March, 1964), 47–55. (Compares Castellanos's treatment of the Indian with that of B. Traven.)

———. "The Recent Mexican Novel: Tradition and Innovation." *Inter-American Review of Bibliography,* XVI (October-December, 1966), 398–402. (Discusses works by Mojarro and Garro.)

The Novel and the
Novelist in Mexico Today

ONE FACT OF LITERARY LIFE IN ALL LATIN AMERICAN COUNTRIES IS that creative writing is largely an avocation and rarely a vocation. The circumstances are such that almost no one gains his livelihood solely as a poet, a novelist, or a short-story writer. Until the most recent years, at least, no more than a handful of Latin American novelists ever supported themselves by their writing.

There is no difficulty in finding a partial explanation for this. To begin with, the reading public is restricted by the twin barriers of illiteracy and economic limitations. Up to now barely half of the Latin American states can boast that more than 50 percent of their citizens can read and write, a fact which obviously reduces the potential book sale at the very outset. And many of those who know how to read lack the economic means to indulge in book buying with any regularity. Because of this situation the publishers bring out small editions of only a few thousand copies, and these are preponderantly cheap paperback editions. Even when a book becomes a best-seller and runs through several quick reprintings, it is quite rare for the total number of copies to exceed 25,000.

But another aspect of the matter was brought neatly into focus some time ago by Max Aub, a Spanish writer long resident in Mexico. Beginning with the claim that Mexico has too few readers and too many critics, Aub observed: "Outside of Carlos Fuentes, Spota, and Sainz, all editions in Mexico are of three thousand copies. When the country had only twenty million inhabitants the editions were of two thousand copies; after the population went up to thirty million, the editions increased to three thousand. Now that there are almost fifty million Mexicans, the editions continue to be of three thousand copies. Isn't this ridiculous?" Aub asserted that the situation is due in considerable degree to what he regards as the worthlessness of literary criticism in Mexico, "There is a total lack of knowledge about literary works in Spanish. The preferred authors are those who, according to the newspapers, have had success in Europe. . . . The new authors are having no more success than that achieved by the writers of the thirties: no more than Martín Luis Guzmán, for example."[1]

But we still do not have a total explanation of why so many Mexicans are not interested in the works of their own countrymen. With the larger number of graduates coming out of the Mexican universities (the National University alone has close to 100,000 students) and with the economic upsurge in Mexico during the past decade, it seems clear that the country now has more literate and even highly trained persons with better economic means than before, yet —as Max Aub points out—they sell no more copies of the average Mexican novel nowadays than they did when the population was about half of the present figure. It isn't that the current novels are only half as good as the old ones. If this study has achieved its purpose, it must be evident that the reverse is largely true. And some of the best novels out of Mexico at this time are attaining no little success in foreign translation. The relative failure of the Mexican educated classes to read their own authors is perhaps in part a manifestation of the old Latin American inferiority complex, which causes everything imported to be more highly valued than the domestic product. In any case, it is a discouraging phenomenon.

Traditionally, even the successful Latin American author has had to work at one or more regular jobs to support himself and his family, and his literary career has been squeezed into such spare hours as he could snatch from his other work. Some writers have been able to maintain a certain steadiness of output, at least in their first years of writing. A few are independently well-to-do and can afford to devote most of their time and energies to creative production. A few more achieve enough economic success with their writing to permit their outside work to become part-time, and as noted, perhaps a handful support themselves by their writing alone. A distressing number, however, become discouraged with the struggle and abandon the effort, resting thereafter on what literary laurels they may already have earned.

Writing in the newspaper *El Nacional* of Mexico City back in the late 1950s, Alfredo Perera Mena lamented the fate of authors in his country, specifically the obstacles encountered by the young writer. Tracing a typical case, he shows how an intelligent young man with an urge to write will somehow manage to complete his first book, only to have the publishers turn him away because nobody knows him and "our publishing firm is very prestigious." By skimping and saving, he later is able to have the book printed at his own cost. The booksellers will handle it only if they get 60 percent of the sale price, and the critics ignore it because he doesn't belong to any literary group—or because they really aren't qualified to know if the book is any good or not. The aspiring author starts another book, but has to accept some kind of regular job to provide for the needs of his family. He may then slave away the rest of his life at a job which makes no use of his intellectual capabilities, and not even his second book is ever finished. Once he is dead, however, the booksellers quote his work at a fantastic price, on the grounds that it is out of print and the author has died.

Granting that the foregoing represents a caricature or exaggeration, it still is close to the mark. That there have been cases to fit this formula cannot be doubted. The situation is especially objectionable when a young writer with talent and literary instincts is shut off at every turn and given no true opportunity or encouragement to achieve his potential. Happily, the past decade has seen an enormous change in Mexico in this matter. Never before have the gates been opened so wide for the beginning author.

One thing which thrust a group of the youngest Mexican writers into the public eye was a series of pocket-size autobiographies promoted by the respected critic Emmanuel Carballo. This series (printed by Empresas Editoriales) bears the general title of New Mexican Writers of the Twentieth Century Presented by Themselves. Each of these little books carries a valuable introduction by Carballo to the personal stories of such young authors as Vicente

Leñero, Gustavo Sainz, Salvador Elizondo, José Agustín, Tomás Mojarro, Juan García Ponce, and others.

Another interesting idea to make the current novelists and their work better known was conceived in 1965 by Antonio Acevedo Escobedo, head of the literature section of the Instituto Nacional de Bellas Artes. He organized a series of frank and informal talks by the writers themselves. Open to the public, these talks were given at frequent intervals over a period of more than a year. Eventually a total of thirty-three Mexican authors came to talk about themselves and their involvement with literature and to read a fragment of some unpublished work. In every case these were writers who came into prominence in the 1950s and 1960s. Four of them were under thirty years of age, seven more were under thirty-five, and twelve others were under forty. Each of the talks was taped and subsequently Empresas Editoriales offered them to a wider public in two attractive volumes. Besides being a source of invaluable information for the student of Mexican literature, these talks—in both spoken and printed form—served to bring the thirty-three writers closer to their audience and to reveal their personalities, their aspirations, their literary habits, and the influences that have helped to form them.

If it is true—and without question it is—that today's novelists in Mexico are better craftsmen, more capable in their profession than any earlier generation, an appreciable part of the credit must go to the Centro Mexicano de Escritores. Founded nearly two decades ago at what was then Mexico City College (now the Universidad de las Américas) and directed from the beginning by Margaret Shedd, this writing center (which soon broke away from its college affiliation) has exerted a perhaps decisive influence on several dozens of young writers who now are among Mexico's best and most promising. Supported by several sources, including the Rockefeller Foundation and a number of Mexican business organizations, the Centro each year awards scholarships to several writers in different fields (essay, drama, poetry, novel, short story, criticism, etc.).

The *becarios* or recipients of this aid are generally quite young, although Juan Rulfo and Juan José Arreola were approaching forty when they went through the Centro. The grant, which covers one year but sometimes is extended for another one, is not enough to support the *becarios,* but it does lighten their economic burden and makes it possible for them to devote an appreciable amount of their time to a specific writing project (for which the award has in fact been made). In addition to the financial lift and the increased time for writing, the Centro provides other services of real benefit to the developing writers. The *becarios* come together frequently to read to each other portions of their work and to engage in mutual evaluation and criticism. Moreover, there is a permanent staff which meets with the recipients for discussions of their work and of literary theories and techniques in general. Nearly every young writer of promise and prominence in Mexico today has passed a year or two as one of the Centro's *becarios.*

It is not alone the younger novelist who is better off in Mexico now. The truth is that the novel and novelists in general have more encouragement (except perhaps in the total sales of their books) and receive more exposure than ever before. All of the things we have just reviewed substantiate this with particular reference to the young writers, but there also are encouraging signs of a more general nature. For example, in recent years an impressive number of new literary journals and cultural supplements to the metropolitan newspapers have sprung up. Included among the new entries are:

Diálogos, a review of arts, letters, and human sciences published bimonthly by El Colegio de México

"La Cultura en México," supplement of the weekly magazine *Siempre!*

"El Heraldo Cultural," Sunday supplement of the newspaper *El Heraldo de México*

La Palabra y el Hombre, journal published by the Universidad Veracruzana

"El Gallo Ilustrado," Sunday supplement of the newspaper *El Día*

El Rehilete, a quarterly featuring the output of several literary workshops

Revista Mexicana de Literatura, bimonthly journal devoted to literature (founded in 1955 by Carlos Fuentes and Emmanuel Carballo)

Revista de Bellas Artes, bimonthly cultural outlet of the Instituto
Nacional de Bellas Artes
Espejo, quarterly devoted to the letters, arts, and ideas of Mexico,
founded in 1967 by Luis Spota
La vida literaria, monthly organ of the Asociación de Escritores
de México (1970)

The cultural publications just listed complement others established
earlier, such as:

Revista de la Universidad de México, published monthly by the
National University of México
"Revista Mexicana de Cultura," Sunday supplement of the news-
paper *El Nacional*
"Revista de la Semana," Sunday supplement of the newspaper
El Universal
"México en la Cultura," Sunday supplement of the newspaper
Novedades
"Diorama de la Cultura," Sunday supplement of the newspaper
Excelsior

Mexican letters in general received an incalculable boost with
the publication in 1967 of the *Diccionario de escritores mexicanos,*
edited by Aurora M. Ocampo de Gómez and Ernesto Prado Velázquez. A project of the Centro de Estudios Literarios of the National
University, this handsome work is monumental in concept and most
adequate in execution. Suitable biographical and evaluative material, along with truly complete bibliographical information, is presented in very ordered manner for nearly five hundred Mexican
writers, from Bernal Díaz del Castillo in Conquest times right down
to José Agustín, the youngest of the current crop. For the researcher
this compilation is of inestimable value. To my knowledge, no other
country in Latin America has anything to approach it in terms of
being comprehensive and up-to-date.

Also, several new publishing firms in Mexico City have proved
quite successful in the past decade. Among the more active and
significant of these are Empresas Editoriales, Joaquín Mortiz, Siglo
XXI, Editorial Diana, Editorial Diógenes, Ediciones Era, and others.
The largest publishing house in Mexico, however, continues to be
the Fondo de Cultura Económica, although it does not dominate the

field to the same extent it did twenty years ago. The number of other respected publishers in Mexico is decidedly impressive, some of the older standouts being Editorial Porrúa, Compañía General de Ediciones, E.D.I.A.P.S.A., Ediciones Botas.

Despite this laudable upsurge in the publishing industry, Mexico City still trails considerably behind Madrid, Barcelona, and Buenos Aires in the business of producing books. In fact, only the Fondo de Cultura Económica has branches in other countries, although naturally books from all publishers are exported. It has been asserted that one reason why the Mexican publishers don't compete too successfully in the distribution of their books is that they lack the government backing granted to publishers in Spain and Argentina.[2] It is suggested too that some of the most prestigious names in Mexican letters will soon be inclined to let foreign publishers handle future editions of their works because of the lure of larger editions and superior distribution, with the consequent higher royalties.[3]

For example, early in 1969 Juan Rulfo signed a lucrative contract with Editorial Planeta of Barcelona, one of the best in Spain, for a one-volume edition of his two works (*El llano en llamas* and *Pedro Páramo*). It is more than likely that the Planeta edition will involve as many copies as the several printings of the Fondo editions totaled in the first ten years (which in the case of *El llano en llamas* reached 31,000 copies, a good figure in Mexico but modest in Spain).

In Mexico the usual first printing of two or three thousand copies may sometimes be exceeded if the author is already established as a "big seller," in which case as many as six thousand copies may be run off. Two Fondo printings (1960 and 1961) of Azuela's *Los de abajo* reached a total of 50,000 copies sold by 1963. Luis Spota's *Casi el paraíso*, regarded as something of a runaway seller, recorded 28,000 sales in its first seven years, while *La región más transparente* of Carlos Fuentes reached 19,000 in six years. With even the most popular works doing no better than this, it is easily seen that the Mexican novelists don't grow fat on their royalty checks. That is, not unless they strike it richer in translation. While the fate of most translated editions is usually unexciting, such authors as Azuela, Fuentes, and Spota have fared rather well.

Surprising to many visitors in Mexico City is the incredible number of small bookstores to be found all over the city, except perhaps in the real slum areas. Of course, these booksellers deal in all sorts of works and generally have a selection in other languages besides Spanish. And most of them obviously must be content with quite modest sales. Even so, the inflated number of bookstores gives the impression that everyone must be buying books.

Any discussion of the state of literature has to turn eventually to the question of the literary critics. In Mexico (and in other countries of Latin America) this is a question that can quickly arouse emotions. As we have seen, the Mexican critics ignored for some years both *Los de abajo* and *Al filo del agua,* probably in good part because these works, revolutionary in content and techniques, went beyond their rigid critical capabilities. And Luis Spota isn't the only Mexican novelist who has his troubles with the critics. His running feud with them may be the prime example, but plenty of writers (including Traven, Fuentes, and many others) indicate distress at one time or another over the state of literary criticism—or at least over the dictates of one critic or another.

Not long ago Rafael Solana, himself a versatile, talented, and much respected figure in Mexican letters and culture, had these comments:

> Lately it is evident that some cliques made up of some painters, actors, and writers of the new wave have taken over the cultural sections of certain publications, solely to promote themselves in the most barefaced application of the formula of a mutual admiration society. This is extremely dangerous, since it inflates persons whose work has no value. Such is the case with various young writers, who even have been awarded first prize in literary competitions and whose books are, sincerely, impossible to read because they are so boring.[4]

While champions of the "new wave" might want to toss aside this rebuke on the grounds that Solana is just an old traditionalist (born in 1915), his charges can't be dismissed that easily. This same sort of accusation has been hurled repeatedly in the course of Latin American literary history, without ever being fully disproved. And a reading of the cultural supplements does indeed leave one with the feeling that certain young-writers-turned-critic are uttering only praise for the efforts of other young writers.

John S. Brushwood, who surely qualifies as an objective outside observer, speaks to this point quite directly:

> It is perhaps unnecessary to say that treatment of the novel becomes more difficult as we approach the present day. Current criticism is not very helpful, because it is not really independent. Personal friendships or enmities, the pressure of literary cliques, and political and professional associations inhibit objective professional criticism. And since the number of novels published is increasing steadily, it is difficult to separate wheat from chaff, and even harder to say which of the wheat is best.[5]

Max Aub likewise has a few barbs for the literary critics. After stating, as seen earlier, that Mexico has too few readers and too many critics, he moves on to observe that criticism in Mexico serves no purpose, since a favorable review brings no more readers than an adverse one. As he sees it, part of the trouble is that the critic can't make a living from his critical pursuits, so that the most he can do is "half read the blurb and complete the panorama of the work on which he is going to 'comment' by thumbing through a few pages."[6] Aub feels that criticism in Mexico is not even at a good university level.

Despite the fact that there is some truth in all of this, it is of course not quite fair or correct to say that no good critics and no just criticism can be found in Mexico. Through the course of these pages repeated reference has been made to Emmanuel Carballo as one of the more respected critics in his country. This opinion is shared by many and is founded on the integrity and critical capacity of Carballo. Moreover, he is less subject to attack because his career in letters has been devoted almost exclusively to the field of criticism, and therefore he has no need to praise someone else's work so that he in turn may be praised. There are other Mexican critics, too, who have concentrated most of their efforts on criticism and are well regarded, among them José Luis Martínez, Antonio Magaña Esquivel, and Gabriel Zaid. Of the active novelists, at least Rosario Castellanos impresses as a perceptive and professional critic, and recently Vicente Leñero has been doing some critical pieces of evident value and objectivity.

Naturally, not all who attempt literary criticism are themselves creative writers. Many are journalists with no particular training or background for the role of critic. If the writer-critics are guilty of favoritism toward their own friends, the journalists sin in a manner characteristic of their clan. They try to be sensational, to provoke controversy. Even more, they reflect the inferiority complex which is present in the Mexican mentality in that they tend to downgrade anything native until it has acquired fame and acceptance abroad. Thus, the journalist-critics are prone to snipe at the Mexican novelists in a manner both unprofessional and unjustified.

The truth is that the art of literary criticism in Mexico (and elsewhere in Latin America) has not evolved to the same degree as fiction writing. This is a serious disadvantage for the creative writer, whose development could be faster and surer with the aid of perceptive and insightful criticism. The low level of critical writing, besides leaving the novelist without the guidance of a truly professional evaluation, also leaves the reading public in confusion and with reduced enthusiasm for the national literary output.

Luis Spota is far from alone in his antagonistic attitude toward the critics. Other writers share his feelings but generally are less vocal about it. Nevertheless, Carlos Fuentes spoke out sharply in justifying his several years of voluntary exile in Europe:

> What writer could come away unwounded from a breakfast with the Mexican press? . . . Acceptance or rejection are too easy there, to the point of abuse: he who goes to bed as Pope may wake up the following day an acolyte. The writer succumbs to bureaucracy, publicity, or journalism. And, to the contrary, in Europe he loses his emblematic character, he becomes an anonymous creature, alone with himself, free to plan his work serenely. They say in Mexico that I have destroyed a whole generation, they have been displeased because of some of my neckties or because I omitted the name of some critic on a guest list. In Europe I can't trample anybody: my books exist, simply. . . . And, besides, the options for earning a living are multiplied: I give lectures, write articles, movie scripts, give auditions for BBC, RTF, RAI.[7]

And it is partially because such writers as Fuentes have proved themselves on the European Continent that the Mexican novel, along with the Latin American novel in general, has of late established a respected place for itself in world literature. Whereas formerly only an occasional author or some individual work was known on the international scene, we find a steadily growing number of Mexican writers who are capturing world interest. All of the novelists considered in this book have contributed to the internationalization of the whole Hispanic-American novelistic effort. The invasion of the Spanish market has been particularly successful, but in translated form these novels have also penetrated the rest of Europe and the United States, as well as other regions of the world. Works by Azuela, Traven, Yáñez, Spota, Fuentes, and Rulfo are available in all the major languages and in many of the less common tongues.

There has been an upsurge of interest, too, in critical studies about the Mexican novel. In the past fifteen years or so a wide variety of serious studies in this field have made their appearance. Works have appeared, in English or in Spanish, on the Mexican romantic novel, the realistic novel, the nineteenth-century novel, the novel of the Revolution, histories of the novel, and so on.

Perhaps we should concern ourselves for a moment with Rafael Solana's disparaging comment, quoted earlier, concerning the youngest writers. While it is beyond dispute that they have produced works of consequence, it is equally undeniable that the fierce determination of all of them to publish almost constantly has not earned the admiration of every writer in the older generation. In addition to that of Solana, we find other important voices of caution being raised. Among these are Juan Rulfo and Vicente Leñero, each of whom is justifiably known as a friend of the young writer. In 1967 Rulfo, when asked about the youngest group of writers in his country, mentioned a few who show talent and then added: "But I have to point out that they are producing adolescent literature for adolescents, and I think that they can't keep on with that kind of literature forever."[8] Leñero offers these comments: "A child-genius cannot remain a child-genius all of his life. The adolescent-writer must become a young man-writer and an adult-writer. If this generation can do so, if it manages to evolve in such a manner, positively and productively, there will of course be no more talk about the 'young narrative of Mexico;' there will only be talk about *good* writers. And this is, after all, the only thing that is literally valuable."[9]

We can confidently affirm that the state of the novel and the novelist in Mexico today, although still not ideal, is patently much better than before. The number of active novelists publishing worthwhile works is decidedly larger than at any time in the past. And most of these writers are more widely read in world literature than their predecessors, more trained and skilled in their craft, more conscious of current trends in the novel everywhere. Starting with Yáñez, they realize that to achieve world stature the Mexican novel must change its focus from the land to the inner person.

The result of all the foregoing is that the Mexican novel has lifted itself during the course of the present century from a position of relatively slight consequence to a spot in the main arena, albeit still in the background. This has happened largely through the efforts and the published works of the writers we have considered here. They are the ones responsible for moving the Mexican novel dramatically forward and causing it to come of age in these times. Considering all circumstances, there is solid reason for expecting Mexico's novelists of the future to consolidate this hard-won position and indeed to move on to a higher place in the ranks of world literature.

NOTES TO CHAPTER 12

1. *Mundo Nuevo*, no. 39–40 (September-October, 1969), pp. 125–126.
2. In the "Letras" section of *Tiempo*, February 17, 1969, p. 52.
3. Ibid.
4. Quoted in the *Gaceta* of the Fondo de Cultura Económica, no. 160 (December, 1967), p. 5.
5. *Mexico in Its Novel* (Austin,1966), p. 34.
6. *Mundo Nuevo*, no. 39–40 (September-October, 1969), p. 125.
7. In the "Letras" section of *Tiempo*, August 19, 1968, p. 45.
8. In *Gaceta*, Fondo de Cultura Económica, Spring, 1968, p. 11.
9. Vicente Leñero, "Reflexiones en torno a la narrativa joven de México," *Mundo Nuevo*, no. 39–40 (September-October, 1969), p. 21.

BIBLIOGRAPHY

ABREU GÓMEZ, ERMILO. *Martín Luis Guzmán. Un mexicano y su obra.* Mexico City: Empresas Editoriales, 1968.

_____. *El pensamiento político de Martín Luis Guzmán.* Mexico City: Secretaría de Educación Pública, 1968.

AGUIRRE, RAMIRO. *Panorama de la literatura mexicana del siglo XX.* Mexico City: Ediciones UME, 1968.

ALEGRÍA, FERNANDO. *Breve historia de la novela hispanoamericana.* Mexico City: Ediciones de Andrea, 1959.

_____. *Historia de la novela hispanoamericana.* Mexico City: Ediciones de Andrea, 1965.

ANDERSON IMBERT, ENRIQUE. *Historia de la literatura hispanoamericana.* Vol. I, 4th edition. Mexico City: Fondo de Cultura Económica, 1964.

_____. *Historia de la literatura hispanoamericana.* Vol. II, 3rd edition. Mexico City: Fondo de Cultura Económica, 1964.

ARCE, DAVID N. *José Rubén Romero. Conflicto y logro de un romanticismo.* Mexico City, 1952.

AUB, MAX. *Guía de narradores de la Revolución Mexicana.* Mexico City: Fondo de Cultura Económica, 1969.

AZUELA, MARIANO. *Cien años de novela mexicana.* Mexico City: Ediciones Botas, 1947.

BRUSHWOOD, JOHN S. *Mexico in Its Novel.* Austin: University of Texas Press, 1966.

_____. *The Romantic Novel in Mexico.* Columbia, Mo.: University of Missouri Studies, 1954.

BRUSHWOOD, JOHN S., and ROJAS GARCIDUEÑAS, JOSÉ. *Breve historia de la novela mexicana.* Mexico City: Ediciones de Andrea, 1959.

CARBALLO, EMMANUEL. *Diecinueve protagonistas de la literatura mexicana del siglo XX.* Mexico City: Empresas Editoriales, 1965.

_____. *El cuento mexicano del siglo XX.* Mexico City: Empresas Editoriales, 1964.

CARDONA PEÑA, ALFREDO. *Semblanzas mexicanas.* Mexico City: Ediciones Libro-Mex, 1955.

CASTELLANOS, ROSARIO. *Juicios sumarios.* Jalapa: Universidad Veracruzana, 1966.

―――. *La novela mexicana contemporánea y su valor testimonial.* Mexico City: Instituto Nacional de la Juventud Mexicana, no date.

CASTRO LEAL, ANTONIO, ed. *La novela de la Revolución mexicana.* 2 vols. Mexico City: Aguilar, 1960.

COLL, EDNA. *Injerto de temas de las novelistas mexicanas contemporáneas.* San Juan, Puerto Rico: Ediciones Juan Ponce de León, 1964.

CRUZ, SALVADOR DE LA. *La novela iberoamericana actual.* Mexico City: Secretaría de Educación Pública, 1956.

FLASHER, JOHN J. *México contemporáneo en las novelas de Agustín Yáñez.* Mexico City: Editorial Porrúa, 1969.

FUENTES, CARLOS. *La nueva novela hispanoamericana.* Mexico City: Joaquín Mortiz, 1969.

GAMIOCHIPI DE LIGUORI, GLORIA. *Yáñez y la realidad mexicana.* Mexico City: Porrúa, 1970.

GÓMEZ-GIL, ORLANDO. *Historia crítica de la literatura hispanoamericana.* New York: Holt, Rinehart and Winston, 1968.

GONZÁLEZ, MANUEL PEDRO. *Trayectoria de la novela en México.* Mexico City: Ediciones Botas, 1951.

GONZÁLEZ PEÑA, CARLOS. *Historia de la literatura mexicana.* 4th edition. Mexico City: Editorial Porrúa, 1949.

―――. *History of Mexican Literature.* Dallas: Southern Methodist University Press, 1943.

HARSS, LUIS, and DOHMANN, BARBARA. *Into the Mainstream.* New York: Harper and Row, 1967.

JIMÉNEZ RUEDA, JULIO. *Historia de la literatura mexicana.* 6th edition. Mexico City: Ediciones Botas, 1957.

―――. *Letras mexicanas en el siglo XIX.* Mexico City: Fondo de Cultura Económica, 1944.

KOONS, JOHN FREDERICK. *Garbo y donaire de Rubén Romero.* Mexico City: Imprenta Aldina, 1942.

LAFFORGUE, JORGE, ed. *Nueva novela latinoamericana.* Buenos Aires: Paidos, 1969.

LEAL, LUIS. *Mariano Azuela, vida y obra.* Mexico City: Ediciones de Andrea, 1961.

Los narradores ante el público. Mexico City: Joaquín Mortiz, 1st series, 1966; 2nd series, 1967.

Martínez, José Luis. *Literatura mexicana, siglo XX, 1910–1949.* Mexico City: Antigua Librería Robredo, 1st part, 1949; 2nd part, 1950.

Meléndez, Concha. *La novela indianista en Hispanoamérica.* Madrid: Imprenta de la Librería y Casa Editorial Hernando, 1934.

Mexico y la cultura. Mexico City: Secretaría de Educación Pública, 1946.

Miliani, Domingo. *La realidad mexicana en su novela de hoy.* Caracas: Monte Avila Editores, 1968.

Moore, Ernest R. *Bibliografía de novelistas de la Revolución mexicana.* Mexico City, 1941.

Morton, F. Rand. *Los novelistas de la Revolución mexicana.* Mexico City: Editorial Cultura, 1949.

Navarro, Joaquina. *La novela realista mexicana.* Mexico City: Compañía General de Ediciones, 1955.

Ocampo, Aurora Maura. *Literatura mexicana contemporánea.* Mexico City: Universidad Nacional Autónoma de México, 1965.

Ocampo de Gómez, Aurora Maura, and Prado Velázquez, Ernesto, eds. *Diccionario de escritores mexicanos.* Mexico City: Universidad Nacional Autónoma de México, 1967.

Passafari, Clara. *Los cambios en la concepción y estructura de la narrativa mexicana desde 1947.* Rosario, Argentina: Universidad Nacional del Litoral, 1968.

Poniatowska, Elena. *Palabras cruzadas.* Mexico City: Biblioteca Era, 1961.

Rangel Guerra, Alfonso. *Agustín Yáñez: Un mexicano y su obra.* Mexico City: Empresas Editoriales, 1969.

Read, John L. *The Mexican Historical Novel, 1826–1910.* New York: Instituto de las Españas, 1939.

Rodríguez Alcalá, Hugo. *El arte de Juan Rulfo.* Mexico City: Instituto Nacional de Bellas Artes, 1965.

Sánchez, Luis Alberto. *Proceso y contenido de la novela hispanoamericana.* Madrid: Editorial Gredos, 1953.

Schulman, Ivan A., et al. *Coloquio sobre la novela hispanoamericana.* Mexico City: Fondo de Cultura Económica, 1967.

SOMMERS, JOSEPH. *After the Storm.* Albuquerque: University of New Mexico Press, 1968.

SPELL, JEFFERSON REA. *Contemporary Spanish American Fiction.* Chapel Hill: University of North Carolina Press, 1944.

————. *The Life and Works of José Fernández de Lizardi.* Philadelphia: University of Pennsylvania Press, 1931.

SUÁREZ-MURIAS, MARGUERITE C. *La novela romántica en Hispanoamérica.* New York: Hispanic Institute in the U.S., 1963.

TORRES-RÍOSECO, ARTURO. *Grandes novelistas de la América Hispana.* Vol. I. Berkeley: University of California Press, 1941.

————. *Bibliografía de la novela mejicana.* Cambridge: Harvard University Press, 1933.

TORRES-RÍOSECO, ARTURO, ed. *La novela iberoamericana.* Albuquerque: University of New Mexico Press, 1952.

URBINA, LUIS G. *La vida literaria de México* (1917) y *La literatura mexicana durante la guerra de la independencia* (1910). 2nd edition. Mexico City: Editorial Porrúa, 1965.

USLAR PIETRI, ARTURO. *Breve historia de la novela hispanoamericana.* Caracas: Ediciones Edime, 1957.

VALADÉS, EDMUNDO, and LEAL, LUIS. *La Revolución y las letras.* Mexico City: Instituto Nacional de Bellas Artes, 1960.

VAN CONANT, LINDA M. *Agustín Yáñez: Intérprete de la novela mexicana moderna.* Mexico City: Editorial Porrúa, 1969.

WARNER, RALPH E. *Historia de la novela mexicana en el siglo XIX.* Mexico City: Antigua Librería Robredo, 1953.

YÁÑEZ, AGUSTÍN. *El contenido social de la literatura iberoamericana.* Mexico City: Ediciones El Colegio de México, 1944.

ZUM FELDE, ALBERTO. *Indice crítico de la literatura hispanoamericana: La narrativa.* Mexico City: Editorial Guaranía, 1959.

INDEX